Understanding the Department of Homeland Security

The Cabinet Series

Understanding the Department of Homeland Security

DON PHILPOTT

The Cabinet Series

Lanham • Boulder • New York • London

Published by Bernan Press
An imprint of The Rowman & Littlefield Publishing Group, Inc.
4501 Forbes Boulevard, Suite 200, Lanham, Maryland 20706
www.rowman.com
800-865-3457; info@bernan.com

Unit A, Whitacre Mews, 26-34 Stannary Street, London SE11 4AB

Library of Congress Control Number: 2015954417

ISBN: 978-1-59888-741-9
E-ISBN: 978-1-59888-742-6

∞™ The paper used in this publication meets the minimum requirements of
American National Standard for Information Sciences—Permanence of Paper
for Printed Library Materials, ANSI/NISO Z39.48-1992.

Printed in the United States of America

Contents

Introduction

On September 11, 2001, al-Qaeda launched four coordinated terrorist suicide attacks on the United States crashing two hijacked passenger planes into the twin towers of New York's World Trade Center complex while a third hijacked jet was crashed into the Pentagon. A fourth plane, United Airlines Flight 93, was heading for Washington DC when passengers attacked the terrorists and the aircraft crashed into a field near Shanksville, Pennsylvania.

The attacks killed 2,996 people, caused over $10 billion in damage and was the largest terrorist attack on U.S. soil. It was also the deadliest incident for firefighters and law enforcement officers in U.S. history with 343 and 72 killed respectively.

Eleven days after the September 11, 2001, terrorist attacks, Pennsylvania Governor Tom Ridge was appointed as the first Director of the Office of Homeland Security in the White House. The office oversaw and coordinated a comprehensive national strategy to safeguard the country against terrorism and respond to any future attacks.

With the passage of the Homeland Security Act by Congress in November 2002, the Department of Homeland Security formally came into being as a stand-alone, Cabinet-level department to further coordinate and unify national homeland security efforts, opening its doors on March 1, 2003.

The Department of Homeland Security was created as a direct response to these attacks. The Department has the distinction of being both the newest and the largest department within the federal government.

The DHS was formed with the specific aim of securing the nation from the many threats it faced. It was created by integrating all or part of 22 different

Federal Departments and agencies into a single, unified and integrated body. It was the largest reshuffle of federal departments and agencies in U.S. history.

It has more than 240,000 employees in jobs that range from aviation and border security to emergency response, from cybersecurity analyst to chemical facility inspector. Its duties are wide-ranging, but the goal is clear—keeping America safe.

The Rationale Behind the Creation of the DHS

History teaches us that critical security challenges require clear lines of responsibility and the unified effort of the U.S. government. History also teaches us that new challenges require new organizational structures. For example, prior to 1945, America's armed forces were inefficiently structured with separate War and Navy Departments and disconnected intelligence units. There were no formal mechanisms for cooperation. After World War II, the onset of the Cold War required consolidation and reorganization of America's national security apparatus to accomplish the new missions at hand.

America needed a national security establishment designed to prevent another attack like Pearl Harbor, to mobilize national resources for an enduring conflict, and to do so in a way that protected America's values and ideals. In December 1945, only months after America's decisive victory in World War II, President Harry Truman asked Congress to combine the War and Navy Departments into a single Department of Defense. President Truman declared, "It is now time to take stock to discard obsolete organizational forms and to provide for the future the soundest, most effective and most economical kind of structure for our armed forces of which this most powerful Nation is capable. I urge this as the best means of keeping the peace."

President Truman's goals were achieved with the National Security Act of 1947 and subsequent amendments in 1949 and 1958. The legislation consolidated the separate military Departments into the Department of Defense with a civilian secretary solely in charge, established a Central Intelligence Agency to coordinate all foreign intelligence collection and analysis, and created the National Security Council in the White House to coordinate all foreign and defense policy efforts.

This reorganization of America's national security establishment was crucial to overcoming the enormous threat faced in the Cold War and holds important lessons for our approach to the terrorist threat we face today.

The First Nine Months Following the September II Attacks

- Sep II - Department of Defense begins combat air patrols over U.S. cities
    - Department of Transportation grounds all U.S. private aircraft
    - Federal Emergency Management Agency (FEMA) activates Federal Response Plan
    - U.S. Customs goes to Level I alert at all border ports of entry
    - Department of Health and Human Services activates (for the first time ever) the National Disaster Medical System, dispatching more than 300 medical and mortuary personnel to the New York and Washington, D.C. areas, dispatching one of eight 12-hour emergency "push packages" of medical supplies, and putting 80 Disaster Medical Assistance Teams nationwide and 7,000 private sector medical professionals on deployment alert.
    - Nuclear Regulatory Commission advises all nuclear power plants, non-power reactors, nuclear fuel facilities and gaseous diffusion plants go to the highest level of security. All complied.
    - President Bush orders federal disaster funding for New York
    - FEMA deploys National Urban Search and Rescue Response team
    - FEMA deploys U.S. Army Corp of Engineers to assist debris removal
- Sep 12 - FEMA deploys emergency medical and mortuary teams to NY and Washington
    - Federal Aviation Authority (FAA) allows limited reopening of the nation's commercial airspace   system to allow flights that

were diverted on September 11 to continue to their original destinations

- Sep 13 - President orders federal aid for Virginia
    - Departments of Justice and Treasury deploy Marshals, Border Patrol, and Customs officials to provide a larger police presence at airports as they reopen
- Sep 14 - President proclaims a national emergency (Proc. 7463)
    - President orders ready reserves of armed forces to active duty
    - FBI Releases List of Nineteen Suspected Terrorists
- Sep 17 - Attorney General directs the establishment of 94 Anti-Terrorism Task Forces, one for each United States Attorney Office
- Sep 18 - President signs authorization for Use of Military Force bill
    - President authorizes additional disaster funding for New York
- Sep 20 - President addresses Congress, announces creation of the Office of Homeland Security and appointment of Governor Tom Ridge as Director
- Sep 21 - Department of Health and Human Services (DHHS) announces that more than $126 million (part of $5 billion the President released for disaster relief) is being provided immediately to support health services provided in the wake of the attacks.
- Sep 22 - President signs airline transportation legislation, providing tools to assure the safety and immediate stability of our Nation's commercial airline system, and establish a process for compensating victims of the terrorist attacks.
- Sep 25 - The first of approximately 7,200 National Guard troops begin augmenting security at 444 airports
- Sep 27 - The FBI releases photographs of 19 individuals believed to be the 9/11 hijackers
    - Coast Guard immediately mobilized more than 2,000 Reservists in the largest homeland defense and port security operation since World War II.

- Oct 1 - FEMA declares over $344 million committed to New York recovery so far
- Oct 4 - Robert Stevens dies of anthrax in Florida—first known victim of biological terrorism
- Oct 8 - President swears-in Governor Ridge as Assistant to the President for Homeland Security, and issues Executive Order creating Office of Homeland Security (OHS)
- Oct 9 - President swears-in General (Retired) Wayne Downing as Director of the Office of Combating Terrorism (OCT), and issues Executive order creating OCT.
- Oct 10 - President unveils "most wanted" terrorists
- Oct 12 - FAA restores general aviation in 15 major metropolitan areas
- Oct 16 - President issues Executive Order establishing the President's Critical Infrastructure Protection Board to coordinate and have cognizance of Federal efforts and programs that relate to protection of information systems
- Oct 21 - FAA restores general aviation in 12 more major metropolitan areas
- Oct 22 - President issues Executive Order for HHS to exercise certain contracting authority in connection with national defense functions.
- Oct 23 - U.S. Customs Service creates new Office of Anti-Terrorism
- Oct 25 - Department of Treasury launches Operation Greenquest, a new multi-agency financial enforcement initiative bringing the full scope of the government's financial expertise to bear against sources of terrorist funding.
- Oct 26 - President signs the USA Patriot Act
- Oct 29 - President chairs first meeting of the Homeland Security Council. Issues Homeland Security Presidential Directive-1, establishing the organization and operation of the Homeland Security Council (HSC), and Homeland Security Presidential Directive -2(HSPD-2), establishing the Foreign Terrorist Tracking Task Force and increasing immigration vigilance
- Oct 30 - FAA restricts all private aircraft flying over nuclear facilities

- Nov 8 - President announces that the Corporation for National and Community Service (CNCS) will support homeland security, mobilizing more than 20,000 Senior Corps and AmeriCorps participants
- Nov 8 - President Bush creates the Presidential Task Force on Citizen Preparedness in the War Against Terrorism to help prepare Americans in their homes, neighborhoods, schools, workplaces, places of worship and public places from the potential consequences of terrorist attacks.
- Nov 15 - FEMA announces Individual and Family Grant program for disaster assistance
- Nov 19 - Aviation and Transportation Security Act establishes the Transportation Security Administration (TSA)
- Nov 28 - HHS awards contract to produce 155 million doses of smallpox vaccine by the end of 2002 to bring the total of doses in the nation's stockpile to 286 million, enough to protect every United States citizen.
- Nov 29 - Attorney General Ashcroft announces Responsible Cooperators Program, which will provide immigration benefits to non-citizens who furnish information to help apprehend terrorists or to stop terrorist attacks.
- Dec 3 - FBI implements first phase of headquarters reorganization
- Dec 10 - U.S. Customs launches "Operation Shield America" to prevent international terrorist organizations from obtaining sensitive U.S. technology, weapons, and other equipment
- Dec 12 - Governor Ridge and Canadian Foreign Minister John Manley sign a "smart border" declaration and action plan to improve security and efficiency of the Northern border
- Dec 19 - FAA restores general aviation in 30 major metropolitan areas
- Dec 28 - President issues Executive Orders on succession in federal agencies
- Jan 10 - President signs $2.9 billion bioterrorism appropriations bill
- Jan 11 - FAA publishes new standards to protect cockpits from intrusion and small arms fire or fragmentation devices, such as grenades, requiring operators of more than 6,000 airplanes to install reinforced

ing operators of more than 6,000 airplanes to install reinforced doors by April 9, 2003.

- Jan 17 - President issues Executive Order authorizing the Secretary of Transportation to increase the number of Coast Guard service members on active duty.
  - U.S. Customs announces Container Security Initiative
  - U.S. Border Patrol officials and other representatives of the INS meet with Native American leaders and law enforcement officials jointly strengthen security along the Southwest and Northern borders.
  - FBI releases information, photographs, and FBI laboratory photographic retouches on six suspected terrorists
- Jan 18 - Department of Transportation meets mandate to submit plans for training security screeners and flight crews
- Jan 23 - FBI announces new hiring initiative for FBI Special Agents
- Jan 28 - Congress confirms appointment of John W. Magaw as Under Secretary of Transportation for Security
- Jan 30 - President issues Executive Order establishing the USA Freedom Corps, encouraging all Americans to serve their country for the equivalent of at least 2 years (4,000 hours) over their lifetimes.
- Jan 31 - HHS announces state allotments of $1.1 billion to help strengthen their capacity to respond to bioterrorism and other public health emergencies resulting from terrorism.
- Feb 3 - U.S. Secret Service ensures security of Super Bowl XXXVI, a National Special Security Event
- Feb 4 - President submits the President's Budget for FY 2003 to the Congress, directing $37.7 billion to homeland security, up from $19.5 billion in FY 2002.
- Feb 6 - Attorney General Ashcroft announces rule change to Board of Immigration Appeals to eliminate backlog, prevent unwarranted delays and improve the quality of board decision making while ensuring that those in our immigration court system enjoy the full protections of due process.

- Feb 8-24 - United States Secret Service ensures security of the 2002 Winter Olympics, a National Special Security Event
- Feb 25 - Soldiers of the U.S. Army National Guard begin to deploy to augment border security
- Feb 26 - Nuclear Regulatory Commission (NRC) orders all 104 commercial nuclear power plants to implement interim compensatory security measures, formalizing measures taken in response to NRC advisories since September 11, and imposing additional security enhancements as a result of on-going comprehensive security review.
- Mar 1 - U.S. Customs Service announces action plan to ensure international air carrier compliance with regulations requiring passenger and crew information prior to arrival in the U.S. on flights from foreign locations.
- Mar 5 - Attorney General Ashcroft announces National Security Coordination Council (NSCC) to ensure seamless coordination of all functions of the Department of Justice relating to national security, particularly efforts to combat terrorism.
- Mar 8 - To date, the U.S. Coast Guard has conducted over 35,000 port security patrols and 3,500 air patrols; boarded over 10,000 vessels including over 2,000 "high interest vessels;" escorted 6,000 vessels in and out of ports including 2,000 escorted by Sea Marshalls; maintained over 124 security zones; and recalled 2,900 Reservists to active duty.
- Mar 12 - President establishes the Homeland Security Advisory System (HSPD-3)
- Mar 19 - President issues Executive Order establishing the President's Homeland Security Advisory Council
- Mar 22 - Secretary of State Powell and Mexico Interior Minister Santiago Creel sign a "smart border" declaration and action plan to improve security and efficiency of the Southern border
- Mar 25 - U.S. Customs officers begin partnership with Canadian Customs officers to inspect U.S.- bound cargo upon its first arrival in the ports of Montreal, Halifax, and Vancouver

- Mar 25 - Nuclear Regulatory Commission orders Honeywell International, Inc., a uranium conversion facility in Illinois, to immediately implement interim compensatory security measures.
- Mar 29 - HHS announces it will obtain more than 75 million additional doses of smallpox vaccine from Aventis Pasteur Inc., provided the supply, stored in a secure location since 1972, is proven safe and effective.
- Apr 5 - NRC forms Office of Security to streamline security, safeguards and incident response activities
- Apr 8 - INS implements rule changes governing an alien's ability to begin a course of study the period of time visitors are permitted to remain in the United States
- Apr 16 - U.S. Customs launches the Customs-Trade Partnership Against Terrorism
- Apr 22 - FBI Director Mueller announces key management positions in the counterterrorism division
- Apr 30 - Transportation Security Administration announces successful implementation of Federal passenger screeners at Baltimore-Washington airport
- May 14 - President Signs Border Security and Visa Entry Reform Act
- May 19 - TSA issues 180 day progress report to Congress
- May 22 - CIA creates new position of Associate Director of Central Intelligence for Homeland Security, effective May 28.
- May 24 - Nuclear Regulatory Commission orders decommissioning of commercial nuclear power plants with spent fuel stored in water-filled pools and a spent nuclear fuel storage facility using pool storage to implement interim compensatory security measures for the current threat environment.
- May 29 - Attorney General Ashcroft and FBI Director Mueller announce reorganization of the FBI to achieve top priority of counter-terrorism and better coordination with the CIA.

1

About the Department of Homeland Security

The Concept

Terrorists today can strike at any place, at any time, and with virtually any weapon. This is a permanent condition and these new threats required the United States to design a new homeland security structure.

The United States faced an enormous threat during the Cold War and created a national security strategy to deter and defeat the organized military forces of the Soviet bloc. It emerged victorious from this dangerous period in our history because we organized our national security institutions and prepared ourselves to meet the threat arrayed against us. The United States is under attack from a new kind of enemy—one that hopes to employ terror against innocent civilians to undermine their confidence in our institutions and our way of life. Once again we must organize and prepare ourselves to meet a new and dangerous threat.

Careful study of the current structure—coupled with the experience gained since September 11 and new information learned about our enemies while fighting a war led the President to conclude that our nation needed a more robust and unified homeland security structure.

The Department of Homeland Security would make Americans safer because our nation would have:

- One department whose primary mission is to protect the American homeland;
- One department to secure our borders, transportation sector, ports, and critical infrastructure;
- One department to synthesize and analyze homeland security intelligence from multiple sources;
- One department to coordinate communications with state and local governments, private industry, and the American people about threats and preparedness;
- One department to coordinate our efforts to protect the American people against bioterrorism and other weapons of mass destruction;
- One department to help train and equip for first responders;
- One department to manage federal emergency response activities; and
- More security officers in the field working to stop terrorists and fewer resources in Washington managing duplicative and redundant activities that drain critical homeland security resources.

The Department of Homeland Security would have a clear and efficient organizational structure with four divisions:

- Border and Transportation Security
- Emergency Preparedness and Response
- Chemical, Biological, Radiological and Nuclear Countermeasures
- Information Analysis and Infrastructure Protection

Interim Steps

The President—using the maximum legal authority available to him—created the Office of Homeland Security and the Homeland Security Council in the weeks following the attack on America as an immediate step to secure the homeland. Since then, the government has strengthened aviation and border security, stockpiled more medicines to defend against bio-terrorism, information sharing among our intelligence agencies, and deployed more resources and personnel to protect our critical infrastructure.

The White House Office of Homeland Security continued to coordinate the federal government's homeland security efforts and to advise the President on a comprehensive Homeland Security strategy

The Mission

The mission of the Department of Homeland Security is to:

- Prevent terrorist attacks within the United States
- Reduce America's vulnerability to terrorism and
- Minimize the damage and recover from attacks that do occur.

The Department of Homeland Security will mobilize and focus the resources of the federal government, state and local governments, the private sector, and the American people to accomplish its mission.

Organization

The creation of the Department of Homeland Security empowers a single Cabinet official whose primary mission is to protect the American homeland from terrorism. The Department of Homeland Security has a clear, efficient organizational structure with four divisions.

- Border and Transportation Security
- Emergency Preparedness and Response
- Chemical, Biological, Radiological, and Nuclear Countermeasures
- Information Analysis and Infrastructure Protection

Even after its creation, homeland security still requires the efforts of other Cabinet departments. The Department of Justice and the FBI, for example, remain the lead law enforcement agencies for preventing terrorist attacks. The Department of Defense continues to play a crucial support role in the case of a catastrophic terrorist incident. The Department of Transportation continues to be responsible for highway and rail safety, and air traffic control. The CIA continues to gather and analyze overseas intelligence. Homeland security continues to require interagency coordination, and the President still needs a close adviser on homeland security related issues.

Accordingly, the White House Office of Homeland Security and the Homeland Security Council continue to play a strong role in helping to secure the nation.

Border and Transportation Security

Securing our nation's air, land, and sea borders is a difficult yet critical task. The United States has 5,525 miles of border with Canada and 1,989 miles with Mexico. Our maritime border includes 95,000 miles of shoreline, and a 3.4 million square mile exclusive economic zone. Each year, more than 500 million people cross the borders into the United States, some 330 million of whom are non-citizens.

The Department of Homeland Security is responsible for securing our nation's borders and transportation systems, which straddle 350 official ports of entry and connect our homeland to the rest of the world. The tasks of managing our borders and securing our transportation systems are directly related, and at our international airports and seaports they are inseparable.

The Department manages who and what enters our homeland, and works to prevent the entry of terrorists and the instruments of terrorism while simultaneously ensuring the speedy flow of legitimate traffic. It is the single federal Department in charge of all ports of entry, including security and inspection operations, and manages and coordinates port of entry activities of other federal departments and agencies. The Department leads efforts to create a border of the future that provides greater security through better intelligence, coordinated national efforts, and unprecedented international

coordinated national efforts, and unprecedented international cooperation against terrorists, the instruments of terrorism, and other international threats.

At the same time, it helps ensure that this border of the future better serves the needs of legitimate travelers and industry through improved efficiency.

The Department leads work toward a state-of-the-art visa system, one in which visitors are identifiable by biometric information that is gathered during the visa application process. It ensures that information is shared between databases of border management, law enforcement, and intelligence community agencies so that individuals who pose a threat to America are denied entry to the United States. It also leads efforts to deploy an automated entry-exit system that would verify compliance with entry conditions, student status such as work limitations and duration of stay, for all categories of visas.

To carry out its border security mission the Department incorporates the United States Customs Service (formerly part of the Department of Treasury), the Immigration and Naturalization Service and Border Patrol (Department of Justice), the Animal and Plant Health Inspection Service (Department of Agriculture), and the Transportation Security Administration (Department of Transportation). The Department also incorporates the Federal Protective Service (General Services Administration) to perform the additional function of protecting government buildings, a task closely related to the Department's infrastructure protection responsibilities.

The Department secures our nation's transportation systems, which move people from our borders to anywhere in the country within hours. The Transportation Security Administration, which became part of the Department, has statutory responsibility for security of all modes of transportation and directly employs airport security and law enforcement personnel. Tools it uses include intelligence, regulation, enforcement, inspection, and screening and education of carriers, passengers and shippers. It initally focused on aviation security but now addresses the security needs of other transportation modes. The incorporation of TSA into the Department allowed the Department of Transportation to remain focused on its core mandate of ensuring that the nation has a robust and efficient transportation infrastructure that keeps pace with modern technology and the nation's demographic and economic growth.

Guard, which maintains its existing independent identity as a military organization under the leadership of the Commandant of the Coast Guard. Upon declaration of war or when the President so directs, the Coast Guard would operate as an element of the Department of Defense, consistent with existing law.

The U.S. Coast Guard is charged with regulatory, law enforcement, humanitarian, and emergency response duties. It is responsible for the safety and security of America's inland waterways, ports, and harbors; more than 95,000 miles of U.S. coastlines; U.S. territorial seas; 3.4 million square miles of ocean defining our Exclusive Economic Zones; as well as other maritime regions of importance to the United States.

The Coast Guard has command responsibilities for countering potential threats to America's coasts, ports, and inland waterways through numerous port security, harbor defense, and coastal warfare operations and exercises. In the name of port security specifically, the Coast Guard has broad authority in the nation's ports as "Captain of the Port." The Coast Guard has worked to establish near shore and port domain awareness, and to provide an offshore force gathering intelligence and interdicting suspicious vessels prior to reaching U.S. shores.

Immigration and Visa Services.

The Department of Homeland Security includes the Immigration and Naturalization Service (INS) although separates immigration services from immigration law enforcement. The Department was mandated to build an immigration services organization that would assume the legal authority to issue visas to foreign nationals and admit them into the country. The State Department, working through the United States embassies and consulates abroad, continues to administer the visa application and issuance process. The Department also makes certain that America continues to welcome visitors and those who seek opportunity within our shores while excluding terrorists and their supporters.

Emergency Preparedness and Response

We cannot assume that we can prevent all acts of terror and therefore must continuously prepare to minimize the damage and recover from attacks that do occur. As September 11 showed, the consequences of terrorism can be far-reaching and diverse. The Department of Homeland Security is tasked with ensuring the preparedness of our nation's emergency response professionals, provide the federal government's response, and aid America's recovery from terrorist attacks and natural disasters.

To fulfill these missions, the Department of Homeland Security has built upon the Federal Emergency

Management Agency (FEMA) as one of its key components. It continues FEMA's efforts to reduce the loss of life and property and to protect our nation's institutions from all types of hazards through a comprehensive, risk-based, all-hazards emergency management program of preparedness, mitigation, response, and recovery. And it continues to change the emergency management culture from one that reacts to terrorism and other disasters, to one that proactively helps communities and citizens avoid becoming victims.

In terms of preparedness, the Department assumes authority over federal grant programs for local and state first responders such as firefighters, police, and emergency medical personnel. Various offices in the Department of Justice, the Department of Health and Human Services, and the Federal Emergency Management Agency previously managed those programs. In addition, the Department has developed and manages a national training and evaluation system to design curriculums, set standards, evaluate, and reward performance in local, state, and federal training efforts.

The Department continues FEMA's practice of focusing on risk mitigation in advance of emergencies by promoting the concept of disaster-resistant communities. It also continues current federal support for local government efforts that promote structures and communities that have a reduced chance of being impacted by disasters. It brings together private industry, the insurance sector, mortgage lenders, the real estate industry, homebuilding associations, citizens, and others to create model communities in high-risk areas.

Search Teams, Radiological Emergency Response Team, Radiological Assistance Program, Domestic Emergency Support Team, National Pharmaceutical Stockpile, and the National Disaster Medical System, and manages the Metropolitan Medical Response System. The Department would also coordinate the involvement of other federal response assets such as the National Guard in the event of a major incident.

The consequences of a terrorist attack are wide-ranging and can include: loss of life and health, destruction of families, fear and panic, loss of confidence in government, destruction of property, and disruption of commerce and financial markets. The Department leads federal efforts to promote recovery from terrorist attacks and natural disasters. The Department maintains FEMA's procedures for **aiding recovery from natural and terrorist disasters.**

Incident Management

The Department works with federal, state, and local public safety organizations to build a comprehensive national incident management system for response to terrorist incidents and natural disasters. This system clarifies and streamlines federal incident management procedures, eliminating the artificial distinction between "crisis management" and "consequence management." The Department also consolidated existing federal government emergency response plans—namely the Federal Response Plan, the National Contingency Plan, the U.S. government Interagency Domestic Terrorism Concept of Operations Plan, and the Federal Radiological Emergency Response Plan—into one genuinely all-hazard plan. In time of emergency, the Department would manage and coordinate federal entities supporting local and state emergency response efforts.

Interoperable Communications

In the aftermath of any major terrorist attack, emergency response efforts would involve hundreds of offices from across the government and the country. It is crucial for response personnel to have and use equipment and

Department to supply the emergency response community with the technology that it needs for this mission.

Countermeasures

The knowledge, technology, and material needed to build weapons of mass destruction are spreading inexorably. If our enemies acquire these weapons and the means to deliver them, they will use them potentially with consequences far more devastating than those we suffered on September 11.

The Department of Homeland Security leads the federal government's efforts in preparing for and responding to the full range of terrorist threats involving weapons of mass destruction. To do this, the Department sets national policy and establish guidelines for state and local governments. It directs exercises and drills for federal, state, and local chemical, biological, radiological, and nuclear (CBRN) response teams and plans. The result of this effort has been to consolidate and synchronize the disparate efforts of multiple federal agencies scattered across several departments. This has created a single office whose primary mission is the critical task of protecting the United States from catastrophic terrorism.

The Department is also responsible for several distinct capabilities and institutions that focus on specific elements of this mission. The Department has unified much of the federal government's efforts to develop and implement scientific and technological countermeasures to CBRN terrorist threats. The Department also provides direction and establishes priorities for national research and development, for related tests and evaluations, and for the development and procurement of new technology and equipment to counter the CBRN threat. The Department incorporates and focuses the intellectual energy and extensive capacity of several important scientific institutions, including Lawrence Livermore National Laboratory (formerly part of the Department of Energy) and the Plum Island Animal Disease Center (Department of Agriculture).

The Department unifies our defenses against human, animal, and plant diseases that could be used as terrorist weapons. The Department sponsors outside research, development, and testing to invent new vaccines, antidotes, diagnostics, and therapies against biological and chemical warfare agents; recognize, identify, and confirm the occurrence of an attack; and to minimize the morbidity and mortality caused by any biological or chemical agent.

The Department excludes agricultural pests and diseases at the border and has strengthened national research programs and surveillance systems to shield agriculture from natural or deliberately induced pests or disease. Working with the Department of Agriculture and the Department of Health and Human Services, it ensures that rigorous inspection and quality assurance programs protect the food supply from farm to fork.

Science & Technology Agenda

In the war against terrorism, America's vast science and technology base provides us with a key advantage. The Department presses this advantage with a national research and development enterprise for homeland security comparable in emphasis and scope to that which has supported the national security community for more than fifty years. This is appropriate, given the scale of the mission and the catastrophic potential of the threat. Many of the needed systems are potentially continental in scope, and thus the technologies has had to be scaled appropriately, in terms of complexity, operation, and sustainability.

This research and development is driven by a constant examination of the nation's vulnerabilities, constant testing of our security systems, and a constant evaluation of the threat and its weaknesses. The emphasis within this enterprise is on catastrophic terrorism—threats to the security of our homeland that would result in large-scale loss of life and major economic impact. It is aimed at both evolutionary improvements to current capabilities as well as the development of revolutionary new capabilities.

The following are examples of the types of research and development projects that the Department is pursuing with its scientific assets.

- Preventing importation of nuclear weapons and material. The Department of Homeland Security has made defeating this threat a top priority of its research and development efforts. This nuclear denial develops and deploys new technologies and systems for safeguarding nuclear material stockpiles and for detecting the movement of those materials. In particular, it focuses on better detection of illicit nuclear material transport on the open seas, at U.S. ports of entry, and throughout the national transportation system.

- Detecting bioterrorist attacks. The anthrax attacks of October 2001 proved that quick recognition of biological terrorism is crucial to saving lives. The Department of Homeland Security leads efforts to develop, deploy, manage, and maintain a national system for detecting the use of biological agents within the United States. This system consists of a national public health data surveillance system to monitor public and private databases for indications that a bioterrorist attack has occurred, as well as a sensor network to detect and report the release of bioterrorist pathogens in densely populated areas.

The technologies developed not only make us safer, but also make our daily lives better. While protecting against the rare event, they also enhance the commonplace. Thus, the technologies developed for homeland security fit well within our physical and economic infrastructure, and our national habits. System performance has to balance the risks associated with the threat against the impact of false alarms and impediments to our way of life.

Information Analysis and Infrastructure Protection

The Department of Homeland Security has merged under one roof the capability to identify and assess current and future threats to the homeland, map those threats against our current vulnerabilities, inform the President, issue timely warnings, and immediately take or effect appropriate preventive and protective action.

Threat Analysis and Warning

Actionable intelligence is essential for preventing acts of terrorism. The timely and thorough analysis and dissemination of information about terrorists and their activities improves the government's ability to disrupt and prevent terrorist acts and to provide useful warning to the private sector and our population. Prior to the DHS, the U.S. government had no institution primarily dedicated to analyzing systematically all information and intelligence on potential terrorist threats within the United States, such as the Central Intelligence Agency performs regarding terrorist threats abroad. The Department of Homeland Security, working together with enhanced capabilities in other agencies such as the Federal Bureau of Investigation makes America safer by pulling together information and intelligence from a variety of sources.

The prevention of terrorist acts requires a proactive approach that enhances the capability of policymakers and law enforcement personnel to preempt terrorist plots and warn appropriate sectors. The Department fuses and analyzes legally accessible information from multiple available sources pertaining to terrorist threats to the homeland to provide early warning of potential attacks. This information includes foreign intelligence, law enforcement information, and publicly available information. The Department is a full partner and consumer of all intelligence-generating agencies, such as the Central Intelligence Agency, the National Security Agency, and the FBI. By obtaining and analyzing this information, the Department has the ability to view the dangers facing the homeland comprehensively, ensure that the President is briefed on relevant information, and take necessary protective action.

Following September 11, the Attorney General revised the guidelines governing how the FBI gathers information and conducts investigations. The new guidelines reflected the President's commitment to preventing terrorism by allowing the FBI to intervene and investigate promptly, while also protecting American's constitutional rights, when information suggests the possibility of terrorism. The revised guidelines empowered FBI agents with new investigative authority at the early stage of preliminary inquiries, as well as the ability to search public sources for information on future terrorist

obtained from lawful sources, such as foreign intelligence and commercial data services, with the information derived from FBI investigations.

In addition, the revised guidelines removed a layer of "red tape" by allowing FBI field offices to approve and renew terrorism enterprise investigations rather than having to obtain approval from headquarters.

The Department of Homeland Security complement the FBI's enhanced emphasis on counterterrorism law enforcement by ensuring that information from the FBI is analyzed side-by-side with all other intelligence. The Department and the Bureau has also ensured cooperation by instituting standard operating procedures to ensure the free and secure flow of information and exchanging personnel as appropriate.

The Department's threat analysis and warning functions support the President and, as he directs, other national decision-makers responsible for securing the homeland from terrorism. It coordinates and, as appropriate, consolidates the federal government's lines of communication with state and local public safety agencies and with the private sector, creating a coherent and efficient system for conveying actionable intelligence and other threat information. The Department administers the Homeland Security Advisory System and is responsible for public alerts.

The Department of Homeland Security now translates analysis into action in the shortest possible time—a critical factor in preventing or mitigating terrorist attacks, particularly those involving weapons of mass destruction. Because of the central importance of this mission, the Department has built excellence in its threat analysis and warning function, not only in terms of personnel, but also in terms of technological capabilities.

This fully reflected the President's absolute commitment to safeguard our way of life, including the integrity of our democratic political system and the essential elements of our individual liberty. The Department of Homeland Security is in every sense a domestic intelligence agency.

Critical Infrastructure Protection

The attacks of September 11 highlighted the fact that terrorists are capable of causing enormous damage to our country by attacking our critical structure—those assets, systems, and functions vital to our national security, governance, public health and safety, economy, and national morale.

The Department of Homeland Security coordinates a national effort to secure America's critical infrastructure. Protecting America's critical infrastructure is the shared responsibility of federal, state, and local government, in active partnership with the private sector, which owns approximately 85 percent of our nation's critical infrastructure. The Department of Homeland Security concentrates this partnership in a single government agency responsible for coordinating a comprehensive national plan for protecting our infrastructure. The Department gives state, local, and private entities one primary contact instead of many for coordinating protection activities with the federal government, including vulnerability assessments, strategic planning efforts, and exercises.

The Department builds and maintains a comprehensive assessment of our nation's infrastructure sectors: food, water, agriculture, health systems and emergency services, energy (electrical, nuclear, gas and oil, dams), transportation (air, road, rail, ports, and waterways), information and telecommunications, banking and finance, energy, transportation, chemical, defense industry, postal and shipping, and national monuments and icons. The Department also develops and harnesses the best modeling, simulation, and analytic tools to prioritize effort, taking as its foundation the National Infrastructure Simulation and Analysis Center (formerly part of the Department of Energy). The Department directs or coordinates action to protect significant vulnerabilities, particularly targets with catastrophic potential such as nuclear power plants, chemical facilities, pipelines, and ports, and establishes policy for standardized, tiered protective measures tailored to the target and rapidly adjusted to the threat.

Our nation's information and telecommunications systems are directly connected to many other critical infrastructure sectors, including banking and finance, energy, and transportation. The consequences of an attack on our cyber infrastructure can cascade across many sectors, causing widespread disruption of essential services, damaging our economy, and imperiling public safety. The speed, virulence, and maliciousness of cyber-attacks have increased dramatically in recent years. Accordingly, the Department of Homeland Security places an especially high priority on protecting our cyber structure from terrorist attack by unifying and focusing the key cyber security activities performed by the Critical Infrastructure Assurance Office (formerly part of the Department of Commerce) and the National Infrastructure Protection Center (FBI). The Department augments those capabilities with the response functions of the Federal Computer Incident Response Center (formerly with the General Services Administration).

Because the information and telecommunications sectors are increasingly interconnected, the Department also assumes the functions and assets of the National Communications System (formerly Department of Defense), which coordinates emergency preparedness for the telecommunications sector.

State, Local, and Private Sector Coordination

The nature of American society and the structure of American governance make it impossible to achieve the goal of a secure homeland through federal Executive Branch action alone. The Administration's approach to homeland security is based on the principles of shared responsibility and partnership with the Congress, state and local governments, the private sector, and the American people.

The Department of Homeland Security coordinates, simplifies, and where appropriate consolidates government relations on its issues for America's state and local agencies. It also coordinates federal homeland security programs and information with state and local officials.

The Department gives state and local officials one primary contact instead of many, and gives these officials one contact when it comes to matters related to training, equipment, planning, exercises and other critical homeland security needs. It manages federal grant programs for enhancing the preparedness of firefighters, police, and emergency medical personnel and sets standards for state and local preparedness activities and equipment to ensure that these funds are spent according to good statewide and regional plans. To fulfill these preparedness missions, the Department of Homeland Security incorporates the Department of Justice's Office of Domestic Preparedness, the Federal Bureau of Investigation's National Domestic Preparedness Office, and the Federal Emergency Management Agency's Office of National

United States Secret Service

The primary mission of the United States Secret Service is to protect the President, Vice President, and other national leaders. The Service also contributes its specialized protective expertise to planning for events of national significance (National Special Security Events). In addition, the Service combats counterfeiting, cyber-crime, identity fraud, and access device fraud, all closely tied to the terrorist threat.

Under the presidential directive, the Secret Service now report directly to the Secretary of Homeland Security. While the Service remains intact and is not merged with any other Department function, the Service's unique and highly specialized expertise complements the core mission of the DHS.

Non-Homeland Security Functions

The Department of Homeland Security has a number of functions that are not directly related to securing the homeland against terrorism. By incorporating the emergency management mission of FEMA, it is also responsible for natural disasters. Through the Coast Guard, it is responsible for search and rescue and other maritime functions. By incorporating the INS, it is responsible for immigration and naturalization services. Through the Secret Service, it is responsible for fighting counterfeiters. And by incorporating the Customs Service it is responsible for stopping drug smuggling.

The aim in setting up DHS was to improve efficiency without growing government. DHS has to be an agile, fast-paced, and responsive organization that takes advantage of 21st-century technology and management techniques to meet a 21st-century threat.

Funding and Increased Efficiency

The DHS did not require additional funding. From the outset it was funded by monies already budgeted for the existing components that were merged to

analysis unit and the state, local, and private sector coordination functions), as well as department-wide management and administration units, were funded from savings achieved by eliminating redundancies inherent in the former structure.

Since then, increased resources have been required to meet emerging challenges, but by minimizing duplication of effort and lack of coordination any growth has been limited to what is absolutely required. By combining and integrating functions that were currently fragmented, the Department of Homeland Security was able to:

- Enhance operational efficiencies in field units with overlapping missions. For example, the deployment of a cross-trained work force provided more cost efficient inspection activities at the ports of entry whereas before this was done by three separate units. Integration has allowed for a more productive workforce at the agent level and elimination of parallel overhead structures in the field, as well as at headquarters.

- Reduce redundant information technology spending. Development of a single enterprise architecture for the department resulted in elimination of the sub-optimized, duplicative, and poorly coordinated systems that were then prevalent in government. It also led to a rational prioritization of projects necessary to fund homeland security missions based on an overall assessment of requirements rather than a tendency to fund all good ideas beneficial to a separate unit's individual needs even if similar systems are already in place elsewhere.

- Effective management of research and development spending was facilitated by central control of research and development funding based, again, on overall homeland security priorities.

- Better asset utilization has been gained through consolidation and joint, comprehensive capital planning, procurement, and maintenance. This pertains to boats, vehicles, and planes, as well as property management.

- Consolidated, streamlined grant making has promoted targeted, effective programs at the state and local level, stretching the federal further than is possible in the environment of multiple funding sources with sometimes overlapping missions. In order to respond to rapidly changing conditions, the Secretary has the great latitude in redeploying resources, both human and financial. The Secretary also has broad reorganizational authority in order to enhance operational effectiveness, as needed. Moreover, the Department has significant flexibility in hiring processes, compensation systems and practices, and performance management to recruit, retain, and develop a motivated, high-performance and accountable workforce. When a job needs to be done the Department is able to fill it promptly, at a fair compensation level, and with the right person. Likewise, employees receive recognition for their achievements, but in cases where performance falls short, they are held accountable. Finally, the new Department has flexible procurement policies to encourage innovation and rapid development and operation of critical technologies vital to securing the homeland.

Subsequent Changes

The following directorates, created by the Homeland Security Act of 2002 were abolished by a July 2005 reorganization and their responsibilities transferred to other departmental components:

- Border and Transportation Security
- Emergency Preparedness and Response
- Information Analysis and Infrastructure Protection

Modifications

Secretary Michael Chertoff took office on February 15, 2005, and initiated a Second Stage Review (2SR) to evaluate the department's operations, policies,

ners at the federal, state, local, tribal, and international levels. On July 13, 2005, Secretary Chertoff announced a six-point agenda, based upon the findings, which included a significant reorganization of the department.

Department Six-point Agenda

A six-point agenda for the Department of Homeland Security was developed and announced in July 2005, by Secretary Chertoff to ensure that the Department's policies, operations, and structures are aligned in the best way to address the potential threats—both present and future—that face our nation. The six-point agenda is structured to guide the department in the near term and result in changes that will:

- Increase overall preparedness, particularly for catastrophic events
- Create better transportation security systems to move people and cargo more securely and efficiently
- Strengthen border security and interior enforcement and reform immigration processes;
- Enhance information sharing with our partners
- Improve DHS financial management, human resource development, procurement and information technology
- Realign the DHS organization to maximize mission performance.

Organizational Initiatives: Structural Adjustments

Supporting the agenda, the department proposed to realign the Department of Homeland Security to increase its ability to prepare, prevent, and respond to terrorist attacks and other emergencies. These changes are to better integrate the Department and give department employees better tools to accomplish their mission.

Centralize and Improve Policy Development and Coordination

A new Directorate of Policy was created to:

- be the primary Department-wide coordinator for policies, regulations, and other initiatives
- ensure consistency of policy and regulatory development across the department
- perform long-range strategic policy planning
- assume the policy coordination functions previously performed by the Border and Transportation Security (BTS) Directorate
- include Office of International Affairs, Office of Private Sector Liaison, Homeland Security Advisory Council, Office of Immigration Statistics, and the Senior Asylum Officer.

Strengthen Intelligence Functions and Information Sharing

A new Office of Intelligence and Analysis was developed ensure that information is:

- gathered from all relevant field operations and other parts of the intelligence community
- analyzed with a mission-oriented focus
- informative to senior decision-makers
- disseminated to the appropriate federal, state, local, and private sector partners
- led by a Chief Intelligence Officer reporting directly to the Secretary, this office will be comprised of analysts within the former Information Analysis directorate and draw on expertise of other department components with intelligence collection and analysis operations.
- Improve Coordination and Efficiency of Operations.
  A new Director of Operations Coordination to:

- conduct joint operations across all organizational elements
- coordinate incident management activities
- use all resources within the Department to translate intelligence and policy into immediate action
- The Homeland Security Operations Center, which serves as the nation's nerve center for information sharing and domestic incident management on a 24/7/365 basis, will be a critical part of this new office.

Enhance Coordination and Deployment of Preparedness Assets

The Directorate for Preparedness was created to:

- consolidate preparedness assets from across the Department
- facilitate grants and oversee nationwide preparedness efforts supporting first responder training, citizen awareness, public health, infrastructure and cyber security and ensure proper steps are taken to protect high-risk targets
- focus on cyber security and telecommunications
- include a new Chief Medical Officer, responsible for carrying out the Department's responsibilities to coordinate the response to biological attacks
- Managed by an Under Secretary this Directorate will include infrastructure protection, assets of the Office of State and Local Government Coordination and Preparedness responsible for grants, training and exercises, the U.S. Fire Administration, and the Office of National Capitol Region Coordination.

Other Department Realignments

Improve National Response and Recovery Efforts by Focusing FEMA on Its Core Functions

FEMA reports directly to the Secretary of Homeland Security. In order to strengthen and enhance our Nation's ability to respond to and recover from manmade or natural disasters, FEMA will focus on its historic and vital mission of response and recovery.

Integrate Federal Air Marshal Service (FAMS) into Broader Aviation Security Efforts

The Federal Air Marshal Service was moved from the Immigration and Customs Enforcement (ICE) bureau to the Transportation Security Administration to increase operational coordination and strengthen efforts to meet this common goal of aviation security.

Merge Legislative and Intergovernmental Affairs

This new Office of Legislative and Intergovernmental Affairs merged certain functions among the Office of Legislative Affairs and the Office of State and Local Government Coordination in order to streamline intergovernmental relations efforts and better share homeland security information with members of Congress as well as state and local officials.

Assign Office of Security to Management Directorate

The Office of Security was moved to return oversight of that office to the Under Secretary for Management in order to better manage information systems, contractual activities, security accreditation, training and resources.

Results from the Second Stage Review, July 2005

On October 13, 2006, Congress passed the Security Accountability for Every Port Act, or SAFE Port Act of 2006 (Public Law 109-347). The act authorized the Domestic Nuclear Detection Office (DNDO) and completed the reorganization of FEMA, transferring the Radiological Preparedness Program and the Chemical Stockpile Emergency Preparedness Program to FEMA.

The Implementing Recommendations of the 9/11 Commission Act of 2007 (Public Law 110-53) was enacted on August 7, 2007. The Act built on the Post-Katrina Emergency Management Reform Act of 2006, focusing on the reorganization of the grant process as administered by FEMA. The Act also reorganized intelligence operations at the Department, elevating the Assistant Secretary for Intelligence and Analysis to the Under Secretary level, requiring Senate confirmation. Additionally, many of the features of the new homeland security architecture align with recommendations contained in the 9/11 Commission Report.

The President's fiscal year 2010 budget requested the transfer of the Federal Protective Service (FPS) from U.S. Immigration and Customs Enforcement (ICE) to the National Protection and Programs Directorate (NPPD)— streamlining decision-making and aligning the protection of federal buildings with DHS' broader critical infrastructure protection mission and the provision was included in the DHS appropriations bill President Obama signed into law on Oct. 28, 2009. It also elevated the Office of Intergovernment Programs from NPPD to a direct report to the Secretary and renamed it to the Office of Intergovernmental Affairs.

In 2010, Secretary Janet Napolitano led the completion of the first-ever Quadrennial Homeland Security Review (QHSR), which established a unified, strategic framework for homeland security missions and goals. Subsequently, DHS conducted a Bottom-Up Review (BUR) to align our programmatic activities and organizational structure to better serve those missions and goals. The QHSR reflects the most comprehensive assessment and analysis of homeland security to date. DHS worked closely with the White House, National Security Staff, other Federal departments and agencies, and our state, local, tribal and territorial partners to represent the whole-of-government approach to national security envisioned by the Administration.

Bottom-Up Review (BUR), July 2010, provided the results of an unprecedented Department-wide assessment of the Department of Homeland Security, begun in November 2009, to align the Department's programmatic activities and organizational structure with the mission sets and goals identified in the QHSR. The BUR report focused on the following questions:

- How can we strengthen the Department's performance in each of the five mission areas?
- How should we improve Departmental operations and management?
- How can we increase accountability for the resources entrusted to the Department?

The BUR serves as a road map for these questions. First and foremost, it provides direction for reinforcing the cornerstone of homeland security: preventing terrorism. The BUR also focused on combating cybersecurity threats, ensuring resilience to all hazards, and the critical need to reform the immigration system. It also provided new emphasis on the importance of enhancing the security and resilience of the global systems that are responsible for the movement of people and goods across our borders. Finally, the review lays a foundation for improving Departmental operations and management and increasing accountability for the resources entrusted to the Department.

Examples of How DHS Makes America Safer

Removing barriers to efficient border security

Previously, when a ship entered a U.S. port, Customs, INS, the Coast Guard, the U.S. Department of Agriculture, and others had overlapping jurisdictions over pieces of the arriving ship. Customs had jurisdiction over the goods aboard the ship. INS had jurisdiction over the people on the ship. The Coast Guard had jurisdiction over the ship while it is at sea. Even the Department of

does have the authority to act as an agent for these other organizations and assert jurisdiction over the entire vessel, in practice the system had not worked as well as it could to prevent the illegal entry of potential terrorists and instruments of terror.

Consider this scenario: if the Coast Guard stopped a ship at sea for inspection and found there were illegal immigrants on the ship, the Coast Guard relied on the INS to enforce U.S. immigration law and prevent their entry. If the Coast Guard found potentially dangerous cargo, it relied on Customs to seize the dangerous cargo. Unfortunately, these organizations did not always share information with each other as rapidly as necessary.

So, instead of arresting potential terrorists and seizing dangerous cargo at sea, the former structure could have allowed these terrorists to enter our ports and potentially sneak into our society. The system might also have allowed the dangerous cargo to actually enter our ports and threaten American lives.

Under the new DHS arrangement, the ship, the potentially dangerous people, and the dangerous cargo can be seized at sea by one Department that has no question about either its mission or its authority to prevent them from reaching our shores.

Protecting our nation's critical infrastructure

Nearly five million Americans live within a five mile radius of the most hazardous chemical facilities in the nation. Before the DHS there was no single agency in the government whose core mission was to protect against and respond to an attack on one of these major facilities.

Consider the pre-2001 homeland security apparatus facing a non-citizen that intended to enter our nation and attack one of our chemical facilities. At our border, INS, Customs, Border Patrol, the Coast Guard, and others shared jurisdiction over preventing this person's entry. These government organizations often did not share information, which made it possible that this potential terrorist might have slipped through the cracks. There were at least twelve different government entities overseeing the protection of our critical infrastructure. Again, many of these government entities did not always share all information, and state and local governments had to work with twelve

information, and state and local governments had to work with twelve separate contacts just to help protect their local infrastructure.

Today, the same Department that analyzes intelligence data on the potential terrorist who wants to attack the chemical plant is also the same Department that can simultaneously alert our border security operatives, alert all of our hazardous materials facilities to ensure that they are prepared to meet this specific new threat from this specific terrorist, and alert all of the affected communities.

Communicating to the American People

Before 2001, if a chemical or biological attack were to occur, Americans could receive warnings and health care information from a long list of government organizations, including HHS, FEMA, EPA, GSA, FBI, DOJ, OSHA, OPM, USPS, DOD, USAMRIID, and the Surgeon General—not to mention a cacophony of state and local agencies. There was no single organization with operational responsibility that could communicate with the American people in a clear, concise, and consistent voice.

Consider another example. Information was provided to local law enforcement entities by multiple U.S. government organizations about potential threats to the Brooklyn Bridge, apartment complexes, shopping malls, the Statue of Liberty, subways and public transit systems, our oil and gas infrastructure, and our financial system. Not all these entities shared all their information and many of these entities did not know how the others were responding to it.

Today, a single government Department communicates with the American people about a chemical or biological attack. The Department is also the organization that coordinates provision of specific threat information to local law enforcement and sets the national threat level. It ensures that local law enforcement entities—and the public—receive clear and concise information from their national government. Citizens also have one Department telling them what actions—if any—they must take for their safety and security.

Intelligence Sharing and Comprehensive Threat Analysis

Multiple intelligence agencies used to analyze their individual data, but no single government entity existed to conduct a comprehensive analysis of all incoming intelligence information and other key data regarding terrorism in the United States. There was no central clearinghouse to collect and analyze the data and look for potential trends.

Today, DHS contains a unit whose sole mission is to assemble, fuse, and analyze relevant intelligence data from government sources, including CIA, NSA, FBI, INS, DEA, DOE, Customs, and DOT, and data gleaned from other organizations and public sources.

With this big-picture view, the Department is more likely to spot trends and be able to direct resources at a moment's notice to help thwart a terrorist attack.

Distribution of Key Pharmaceuticals

Potassium Iodide (KI) is a drug that helps prevent thyroid cancer in the event of exposure to radiation. The drug must be taken within hours of exposure for maximum effectiveness. Pre-2001, if you lived within a ten-mile radius of a nuclear power facility, the distribution of Potassium Iodide was regulated by the Nuclear Regulatory Commission (NRC). The NRC was responsible for getting people this crucial drug, even though the NRC's actual mission is to license nuclear facilities, not provide emergency supplies to the greater population. Outside the ten-mile radius of the nuclear facility, the Federal Emergency Management Agency (FEMA) was responsible for regulating the distribution of Potassium Iodide. The Department of Health and Human Services controlled the national pharmaceutical stockpiles that are sent rapidly into emergencies. And other government agencies control evacuation of the emergency zone. To make matters even more confusing, if you happened to live within a ten-mile radius of a nuclear weapons facility, the Department of Energy controlled the distribution of the Potassium Iodide.

In the event of radiation exposure, states had to work with three separate government organizations to distribute critical pharmaceuticals, organizations whose jurisdictions were divided by an invisible ten-mile border. Consider this possible pre-2001 scenario: the NRC and the state decide to distribute Potassium Iodide to everyone within the ten-mile radius. FEMA, however, disagrees with the state and decides against distributing the drug outside the ten-mile radius. In the middle of the NRC, FEMA and state decision process, the state and local governments decide to begin an evacuation. In the ensuing chaos, many exposed individuals might not receive the critical drugs they need.

Today, one Department is responsible for distributing Potassium Iodide to citizens exposed—no matter where they live. There is no longer an artificial ten-mile barrier to treatment. This same single Department is also responsible for coordination with state and local officials on immediate evacuation from the emergency zone.

Secretaries of DHS

Thomas J. Ridge, Homeland Security Secretary 2003—2005

Following the tragic events of September 11, 2001, Thomas (Tom) Ridge became the first Director of the Office of Homeland Security. On January 24, 2003, Ridge became the first Secretary of the U.S. Department of Homeland Security.

During his tenure, Ridge worked with more than 180,000 employees from a combined 22 components to come together as one agency

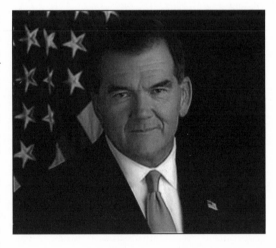

of science and technology to counter weapons of mass destruction, and to create a comprehensive response and recovery division. Ridge served the nation's first Secretary of Homeland Security until February 1, 2005.

Ridge was twice elected Governor of Pennsylvania, serving from 1995 to 2001. He kept his promise to make Pennsylvania "a leader among states and a competitor among nations." Governor Ridge's aggressive technology strategy helped fuel the state's advances in the priority areas of economic development, education, health and the environment.

Born Aug. 26, 1945, in Pittsburgh's Steel Valley, Governor Ridge was raised in a working class family in veterans' public housing in Erie. He earned a scholarship to Harvard, graduating with honors in 1967. After his first year at The Dickinson School of Law, he was drafted into the U.S. Army, where he served as an infantry staff sergeant in Vietnam, earning the Bronze Star for Valor. After returning to Pennsylvania, he earned his law degree and was in private practice before becoming assistant district attorney in Erie County. He was elected to Congress in 1982. He was the first Congressman to have served as an enlisted man in the Vietnam War, and was overwhelmingly re-elected five times.

Michael Chertoff, DHS Secretary, February 2005-January, 2009

On February 15, 2005, Michael Chertoff became the second Secretary of the U.S. Department of Homeland Security. During his tenure, Chertoff worked to strengthen our borders, provide intelligence analysis and infrastructure protection, increased the Department's focus on preparedness ahead of disasters, and implemented enhanced security at airports and borders. Following Hurricane Katrina, Chertoff transformed FEMA into an effective organization. Chertoff served as the nation's Secretary of Homeland Security until January 21, 2009.

Prior to his nomination by President George W. Bush, Chertoff served as a federal judge on the U.S. Court of Appeals for the Third Circuit. Earlier, during more than a decade as a federal prosecutor, he investigated and prosecuted cases of political corruption, organized crime, corporate fraud and terrorism—including the investigation of the 9/11 terrorist attacks. Mr. Chertoff also served as United States Attorney for the District of New Jersey from 1990-1994 and as a clerk to Supreme Court Justice Williams Brennan, Jr. from 1979-1980.

Chertoff was born in Elizabeth, New Jersey on November 28, 1953. He graduated magna cum laude from Harvard College in 1975 and magna cum laude from Harvard Law School in 1978. He is currently the Chairman and Co-Founder of The Chertoff Group, focusing on risk identification, analysis, and mitigation, crisis management, and providing strategic counsel on global security solutions. In addition, Chertoff is senior counsel at Covington & Burling LLP, and a member of the firm's White Collar Defense and Investigations practice group.

Chertoff's official portrait was unveiled at DHS Headquarters in Washington, D.C. on March 27, 2014.

Janet Napolitano, DHS Secretary January 2009- September 2013

Janet Napolitano served as Secretary of the Department of Homeland Security from January 21, 2009 to September 6, 2013. Prior to joining the Obama Administration, Napolitano was mid-way through her second term as Governor of the State of Arizona. While Governor, Napolitano became the first woman to chair the National Governors Association, where she was instrumental in creating the Public Safety Task Force and the Homeland Security Advisors Council. She also chaired the Western Governors Association. Napolitano previously served as the Attorney General of Arizona and the U.S. Attorney for the District of Arizona.

Napolitano's homeland security background is extensive. As U.S. Attorney, she helped lead the domestic terrorism investigation into the Oklahoma City Bombing. As Arizona Attorney General, she helped write the law to break up human smuggling rings. As Governor, she implemented one of the first state homeland security strategies in the nation, opened the first state counter-terrorism center and spearheaded efforts to transform immigration enforcement. She's also been a pioneer in coordinating federal, state, local and bi-national homeland security efforts, and presided over large scale disaster relief efforts and readiness exercises to ensure well-crafted and functional emergency plans.

Napolitano graduated from Santa Clara University in 1979, where she won a Truman Scholarship, and received her Juris Doctor (J.D.) in 1983 from the University of Virginia School of Law. After law school she served as a law clerk for Judge Mary M. Schroeder of the U.S. Court of Appeals for the Ninth Circuit before joining the law firm of Lewis and Roca.

Jeh Johnson, DHS Secretary December 13, 2013—

Jeh Charles Johnson was sworn in on December 23, 2013 as the fourth Secretary of Homeland Security. Prior to joining DHS, Secretary Johnson served as General Counsel for the Department of Defense, where he was part of the senior management team and led the more than 10,000 military and civilian lawyers across the Department. As General Counsel of the Defense Department, Secretary Johnson oversaw the development of the legal aspects of many of our nation's counterterrorism policies, spearheaded reforms to the military commissions system at Guantanamo Bay in 2009, and co-authored the 250-page report that paved the way for the repeal of "Don't Ask, Don't Tell" in 2010.

Secretary Johnson's career has included extensive service in national security, law enforcement, and as an attorney in private corporate law practice. Secretary Johnson was General Counsel of the Department of the Air Force from 1998 to 2001, and he served as an Assistant U.S. Attorney for the Southern District of New York from 1989 to 1991.

In private law practice, Secretary Johnson was a partner with the New York City-based law firm of Paul, Weiss, Rifkind, Wharton & Garrison LLP. In 2004, Secretary Johnson was elected a Fellow in the prestigious American College of Trial Lawyers, and he is a member of the Council on Foreign Relations.

Secretary Johnson graduated from Morehouse College in 1979 and received his law degree from Columbia Law School in 1982.

2

The Federal Emergency Managment Agency

About the Federal Emergency Management Agency (FEMA)

Mission

FEMA's mission is to support our citizens and first responders to ensure that as a nation we work together to build, sustain and improve our capability to prepare for, protect against, respond to, recover from and mitigate all hazards.

Role

The Federal Emergency Management Agency coordinates the federal government's role in preparing for, preventing, mitigating the effects of, responding to, and recovering from all domestic disasters, whether natural or man-made, including acts of terror.

History

For 36 years, FEMA's mission remains: to lead America to prepare for, prevent, respond to and recover from disasters with a vision of "A Nation Prepared."

On April 1, 1979, President Jimmy Carter signed the executive order that created the Federal Emergency Management Agency (FEMA). From day one, FEMA has remained committed to protecting and serving the American people. That commitment to the people and the belief in our survivor centric mission will n President Carter's 1979 executive order merged many of the separate disaster-related responsibilities into the Federal Emergency Management Agency (FEMA).

Among other agencies, FEMA absorbed:

• The Federal Insurance Administration
• The National Fire Prevention and Control Administration
• The National Weather Service Community Preparedness Program
• The Federal Preparedness Agency of the General Services Administration
• The Federal Disaster Assistance Administration activities from HUD
• Civil defense responsibilities were also transferred to the new agency from the Defense Department's Defense Civil Preparedness Agency

FEMA has 14,844 employees across the country—at headquarters, the ten regional offices, the National Emergency Training Center, Center for Domestic Preparedness/Noble Training Center and other locations.

However, FEMA can trace its beginnings to the Congressional Act of 1803. This act, generally considered the first piece of disaster legislation, provided assistance to a New Hampshire town following an extensive fire. In the century that followed, ad hoc legislation was passed more than 100 times in response to hurricanes, earthquakes, floods and other natural disasters.

By the 1930s, when the federal approach to disaster-related events became popular, the Reconstruction Finance Corporation was given authority to make disaster loans for repair and reconstruction of certain public facilities following an earthquake, and later, other types of disasters.

In 1934, the Bureau of Public Roads was given authority to provide funding for highways and bridges damaged by natural disasters. The Flood Control Act of 1965, which gave the U.S. Army Corps of Engineers greater authority to implement flood control projects, was also passed. This piecemeal approach to disaster assistance was problematic. Accordingly, it prompted legislation to require greater cooperation between federal agencies and authorized the President to coordinate these activities.

The 1960s and early 1970s brought massive disasters requiring major federal response and recovery operations by the Federal Disaster Assistance Administration, established within the Department of Housing and Urban Development (HUD). These events served to focus attention on the issue of natural disasters and brought about increased legislation.

In 1968, the National Flood Insurance Act created the Federal Insurance Administration and made flood insurance available for the first time to homeowners. The Flood Disaster Protection Act of 1973 made the purchase of flood insurance mandatory for the protection of property located in Special Flood Hazard Areas.

In the year following, President Nixon passed into law the Disaster Relief Act of 1974, firmly establishing the process of Presidential disaster declarations. However, emergency and disaster activities were still fragmented. When hazards associated with nuclear power plants and the transportation of hazardous substances were added to natural disasters, more than 100 federal agencies were involved in some aspect of disasters, hazards and emergencies.

Many parallel programs and policies existed at the state and local level, adding to the complexity of federal disaster relief efforts.

The National Governor's Association sought to decrease the many agencies with which state and local governments were forced work. They asked President Carter to centralize federal emergency functions.

Statutory Authority

The Robert T. Stafford Disaster Relief and Emergency Assistance Act, Public Law 100-707, signed into law November 23, 1988, amended the Disaster Relief Act of 1974, Public Law 93-288. It created the system in place today by which a presidential disaster declaration of an emergency triggers financial and physical assistance through the Federal Emergency Management Agency (FEMA). The Act gives FEMA the responsibility for coordinating government-wide relief efforts.

It is designed to bring an orderly and systemic means of federal natural disaster assistance for state and local governments in carrying out their responsibilities to aid citizens. Congress' intention was to encourage states and localities to develop comprehensive disaster preparedness plans, prepare for better intergovernmental coordination in the face of a disaster, encourage the use of insurance coverage, and provide federal assistance programs for losses due to a disaster. This Act constitutes the statutory authority for most federal disaster response activities especially as they pertain to FEMA and FEMA programs.

Homeland Security Act of 2002

As part of The Homeland Security Act, FEMA became part of the Department of Homeland Security. Specifically, the Act stated:

SEC. 507. ROLE OF FEDERAL EMERGENCY MANAGEMENT AGENCY. (a) IN GENERAL.—The functions of the Federal Emergency Management Agency include the following: (1) All functions and authorities prescribed by the Robert T. Stafford Disaster Relief and Emergency Assistance Act (42 U.S.C. 5121 et seq.). (2) Carrying out its mission to reduce the loss of life and property and protect the Nation from all hazards by leading and supporting the Nation in a comprehensive, risk-based emergency management program— (A) of mitigation, by taking sustained actions to reduce or eliminate long-term risk to people and property from hazards and their effects; (B) of planning for building the emergency management profession to prepare effectively for, mitigate against, respond to, and recover from any hazard; (C) of response, by conducting emergency operations to save lives and property through positioning emergency equipment and supplies, through evacuating potential victims, through providing food, water, shelter, and medical care to those in need, and through restoring critical public services; (D) of recovery, by rebuilding communities so individuals, businesses, and governments can function on their own, return to normal life, and protect against future hazards; and (E) of increased efficiencies, by coordinating efforts relating to mitigation, planning, response, and recovery. (b) FEDERAL RESPONSE PLAN.— (1) ROLE OF FEMA.—Notwithstanding any other provision of this Act, the Federal Emergency Management Agency shall

Federal Response Plan established under Executive Order No. 12148 (44 Fed. Reg. 43239) and Executive Order No. 12656 (53 Fed. Reg. 47491).

On March 1, 2003, the Federal Emergency Management Agency (FEMA) became part of the U.S. Department of Homeland Security (DHS). The agency coordinated its activities with the newly formed Office of Homeland Security, and FEMA's Office of National Preparedness was given responsibility for helping to ensure that the nation's first responders were trained and equipped to deal with weapons of mass destruction. The new department, headed by Secretary Tom Ridge, brought a coordinated approach to national security from emergencies and disasters—both natural and man-made.

Within months, the terrorist attacks of Sept.11th focused the agency on issues of national preparedness and homeland security, and tested the agency in unprecedented ways.

Billions of dollars of new funding were directed to FEMA to help communities face the threat of terrorism. Just a few years past its 20th anniversary, FEMA was actively directing its "all-hazards" approach to disasters toward homeland security issues.

On October 4, 2006, President George W. Bush signed into law the Post-Katrina Emergency Reform Act. The act significantly reorganized FEMA, provided it substantial new authority to remedy gaps that became apparent in the response to Hurricane Katrina in August 2005, the most devastating natural disaster in U.S. history, and included a more robust preparedness mission for FEMA.

Post Katrina Emergency Management Reform Act

This act amended the Homeland Security Act of 2002 (the Act) following the Katrina disaster to make extensive revisions to emergency response provisions while keeping the Federal Emergency Management Agency (FEMA) within the Department of Homeland Security (DHS).

- Sets forth provisions regarding FEMA's mission, which shall include: (1) leading the nation's efforts to prepare for, respond to, recover from, and mitigate the risks of, any natural and man-made disaster, including catastrophic incidents; (2) implementing a risk-based, all hazards plus strategy for preparedness; and (3) promoting and planning for the protection, security, resiliency, and post-disaster restoration of critical infrastructure and key resources, including cyber and communications assets.

- Sets forth provisions regarding the role, qualifications, authority, and responsibilities of the Administrator of FEMA, who shall: (1) have not less than five years of executive leadership and management experience, significant experience in crisis management or another relevant field, and a demonstrated ability to manage a substantial staff and budget; (2) report to the Secretary of Homeland Security (the Secretary) without being required to report through any other DHS official; (3) be the principal emergency preparedness and response advisor to the President, the Homeland Security Council, and the Secretary; (4) provide federal leadership necessary to mitigate, prepare for, respond to, and recover from a disaster; (5) develop a national emergency management system capable of responding to catastrophic incidents; and (6) develop and submit to Congress annually an estimate of the resources needed for developing the capabilities of federal, state, and local governments necessary to respond to a catastrophic incident.
- Directs the Comptroller General to report to Congress on the amount of increase in the fixed costs or expenses of FEMA during the period of January 1, 2000, through this Act's enactment.
- Transfers to FEMA all functions of the Under Secretary for Federal Emergency Management and of the Directorate of Preparedness. Requires FEMA to be maintained as a distinct entity within DHS.
- Establishes within FEMA a Director for Preparedness and a Director for Response and Recovery.
- Requires: (1) the Administrator to establish 10 regional offices and area offices for the Pacific, for the Caribbean, and in Alaska; (2) each Regional Administrator to establish multi-agency strike teams to respond to disasters, including catastrophic incidents; and (3) the Secretary to establish a National Advisory Council on Preparedness and

- Establishes within FEMA a National Incident Management System Integration Center, a Chief Medical Officer, a National Search and Rescue Response System, and an Office of Emergency Communications. Continues the Metropolitan Medical Response System and the National Infrastructure Simulation and Analysis Center. Establishes within DHS a National Operations Center, a System Assessment and Validation for Emergency Responders Program, an Office for the Prevention of Terrorism, and an Assistant Secretary for Cybersecurity and Telecommunications.
- Authorizes grants for administering and improving the Emergency Management Assistance Compact. Provides for the credentialing of DHS personnel and assets likely to be used to respond to major disasters.
- Directs the Administrator to: (1) provide technical assistance to states and local governments that experience severe weather events, including the preparation of hurricane evacuation studies and plans assessing storm surge estimates, evacuation zones, evacuation clearance times, transportation capacity, and shelter capacity; and (2) ensure state, regional, and local emergency preparedness by establishing minimum performance requirements for public and community preparedness.
- Requires the Administrator, acting through the Director for Emergency Communications, to: (1) develop a National Emergency Communications Strategy to achieve national emergency communications capabilities and interoperable emergency communications; (2) conduct a baseline operability and interoperability assessment; (3) evaluate the feasibility and desirability of DHS developing a mobile communications capability to support emergency communications at the site of a disaster; and (4) review federal emergency communications grants and standards programs.
- Directs: (1) the Secretary to establish a comprehensive research and development program to promote communications capabilities and interoperability among emergency response providers; (2) the

tor to establish at least two pilot projects to develop and evaluate strategies and technologies for such capabilities in a disaster in which there is significant damage to critical infrastructure; and (3) the Administrator, through the Office of Grants and Training, to make grants to states and eligible regions for initiatives to improve emergency communications and interoperability.

- Establishes an International Border Community Interoperable Communications Demonstration Project.
- Title II: Stafford Act Amendments - (Sec. 201) Amends the Robert T. Stafford Disaster Relief and Emergency Assistance Act (Stafford Act) to authorize the President, in a major disaster, to: (1) authorize precautionary evacuations; and (2) provide accelerated federal support in the absence of a specific request and expanded assistance to state and local governments in recovery.
- Directs the President to promulgate guidelines to assist governors in requesting the declaration of a major disaster in advance of a disaster.
- (Sec. 202) Directs the Administrator to develop a National Disaster Recovery Strategy, which shall promote the use of the most appropriate and cost-effective building materials in any area affected by a major disaster, aimed at encouraging the construction of disaster-resistant buildings.
- (Sec. 203) Requires state mitigation plans to identify the natural hazards, risks, and vulnerabilities of areas which substantially increase the risk of damage, hardship, loss, or suffering in the event of an emergency or major disaster.
- (Sec. 204) Directs the Administrator to develop a National Disaster Housing Strategy.
- (Sec. 205) Authorizes the President, in an emergency or major disaster, to use federal equipment, personnel, and other non-monetary resources to assist an essential service provider, in exchange for reasonable compensation. Requires the President to establish a mechanism to set reasonable compensation.

- (Sec. 206) Increases the authorized percentage of federal contributions for a major disaster under the hazard mitigation grant program.
- (Sec. 207) Directs the President to seek the consent of each individual or household before providing a direct housing assistance option. Authorizes making semi-permanent housing units a part of Stafford Act assistance. Allows temporary housing units purchased by the President to house disaster victims to be made available to a state or other governmental entity or voluntary organization for providing temporary housing to disaster victims.
- (Sec. 208) Repeals maximum amounts authorized for repair of owner-occupied private residences, utilities, and residential infrastructure, and for replacement of owner-occupied private residences, damaged by a major disaster.
- (Sec. 209) Requires federal coordinating officers, within areas affected by a major disaster or emergency, to serve as a primary point of contact for, and provide situational awareness to, the Secretary. Authorizes the President, where the affected area includes parts of more than one state, to appoint: (1) a single federal coordinating officer for the entire affected area; and (2) deputy federal coordinating officers.
- (Sec. 210) Modifies the definition of "major disaster" under the Stafford Act to include acts of terrorism, outbreaks of infectious disease, and chemical releases that cause damage. Expands the scope of "private nonprofit facility" to include museums, zoos, libraries, performing arts facilities, senior citizen centers, and homeless shelters.
- (Sec. 211) Sets forth provisions governing catastrophic damage assistance. Authorizes the President, following a declaration of a major disaster in which an assessment indicates that damages qualify as catastrophic, to provide or alter assistance as specified.
- Directs the President to promulgate regulations establishing a threshold for a catastrophic determination that greatly exceeds the threshold for the declaration of a major disaster and which includes consideration of: (1) the dollar amount per capita of damage to the state, its political

divisions, or a region; (2) the impact on the areas ability to perform response and recovery activities and to provide basic services; (3) the estimated impact of revenue loss; (4) the number of displaced individuals and households; (5) the severity of loss of housing stock, utility services, and alternative living accommodations and of the impact on employment rates; and (6) the anticipated length and difficulty of the recovery process.

- Authorizes the President, in the event of a catastrophic damages determination, to: (1) provide to an individual or household assistance authorized in a major disaster; (2) increase the maximum amount of such assistance to not more than twice the maximum authorized for a major disaster; and and (3) increase the federal share of the costs to not more than 100% for assistance provided during the three-month period beginning on the date the President declared the major disaster and not more than 90% for the next nine months.
- Authorizes the President to provide specified: (1) mortgage and rental assistance; and (2) unemployment assistance (limited to 39 weeks after the date on which the President declared the major disaster causing catastrophic damages).
- Authorizes the President to provide to a local government in an area that the President has determined has suffered catastrophic damages specified loan assistance, which may not exceed 50% of the annual operating budget of that local government, to be used for employee salaries.
- Authorizes the President to: (1) reimburse a community for each purchase of supplies distributed to survivors; and (2) establish and operate long-term recovery offices.
- Directs the Administrator to develop guidelines for accommodating individuals with disabilities, including for: (1) accessibility and communications in shelters; and (2) devices used in connection with disaster operations, including first aid stations, mass feeding areas, portable pay-phone stations, portable toilets, and temporary housing.

- Requires the President to issue regulations that prohibit discrimination based on disability in disaster assistance.
- Includes durable medical equipment among essential assistance that federal agencies may distribute, at the President's direction. Authorizes the provision of rescue, care, shelter, and essential needs to individuals with household pets and service animals and to such animals.
- Requires the President's estimate of the eligible cost of repairing, restoring, reconstructing, or replacing a public or nonprofit facility to be made in conformity with applicable disability accessibility requirements.
- Authorizes the President to provide assistance to individuals with disabilities who are displaced or whose predisaster primary residences are rendered inaccessible as a result of a major disaster. Directs: (1) the President to ensure that temporary public transportation services are provided to individuals with disabilities and others with special needs; and (2) the Administrator to include individuals with disabilities in preparedness and planning activities.
- (Sec. 213) Amends the Stafford Act to direct the Administrator to appoint a Disability Coordinator to ensure that the needs of individuals with disabilities are being properly addressed in emergency preparedness and disaster relief.
- (Sec. 214) Modifies requirements regarding temporary housing assistance to require that not less than: (1) 7% of the housing units provided for a major disaster be made accessible for persons with mobility impairments; (2) an additional 2% of such units be made accessible for persons with hearing or vision impairments; and (3) 1% of such units be made accessible for persons with mobility and hearing or vision impairments. Permits any federal, state, or local agency to request an increase in such percentage based upon need or data on the location of persons with disabilities.

- (Sec. 215) Directs the Comptroller General to study and report to Congress on the extent to which emergency shelters for use in response to a major disaster are accessible to individuals with disabilities.
- (Sec. 216) Requires the Administrator, in coordination with the Attorney General, to establish within the National Center for Missing and Exploited Children the National Emergency Child Locator Center (NECLC) to facilitate the expeditious identification and reunification of children with their families. Includes among NECLC responsibilities to: (1) establish a toll-free telephone number to receive reports of displaced children and information about displaced adults; (2) create a website to provide information about displaced children; (3) refer reports of displaced adults to an entity designated by the Attorney General and to the National Emergency Family Registry and Locator System (NEFRLS); (4) enter into cooperative agreements to implement its mission; and (5) develop an emergency response plan to prepare for its activation.
- (Sec. 217) Directs the Administrator to establish NEFRLS to help reunify families separated after an emergency or major disaster. Requires such system to: (1) allow a displaced adult to voluntarily register; (2) include a means of providing information submitted to individuals named by a displaced individual and to law enforcement officials; (3) be accessible through the Internet and through a toll-free number to receive reports of displaced individuals; and (4) include a means of referring displaced children to the NECLC.
- (Sec. 218) Amends the Stafford Act to prohibit the President from denying housing assistance to a displaced individual or household because a member of the predisaster household has already received assistance if such individual or household: (1) has evacuated the predisaster residence and resides in a different location than such member of the predisaster household; (2) is a victim of domestic violence and resides in a different residence than such member of the predisaster household; or (3) has other good cause for maintaining a separate household.

taken into consideration in determining the amount of assistance. Directs the President to provide assistance in an amount up to 120% of fair market rent plus specified costs if the President determines that, as a result of rental market changes caused by the major disaster and its consequences, the fair market rent does not accurately reflect the reasonable cost of rental units available. Permits the President to provide assistance over that percentage in extraordinary circumstances.

- Directs the President to issue public guidance in simple terms explaining the types of housing assistance available under the Stafford Act to individuals and households affected by a major disaster, eligibility requirements, application procedures, relevant local conditions, and modifications of previous policies or procedures.
- (Sec. 219) Amends the Stafford Act to expand the authorization for professional counseling services to victims of major disasters to include substance abuse and mental health counseling. Requires federal agencies providing mental health or substance abuse services, in coordination with state and local officials, to: (1) survey mental health or substance abuse services available to individuals affected by, and emergency responders to, major disasters; and (2) develop a strategy for the adequate provision of such services.
- (Sec. 220) Requires the President, with respect to people with limited English proficiency or individuals with disabilities, to: (1) ensure that all federal entities that provide assistance under the Stafford Act maintain the capability to administer competent interpretation and translation services; and (2) maintain an informational clearinghouse of model language assistance programs and best practices for state and local governments in providing disaster and emergency related services. Requires the President's technical assistance to states in developing comprehensive plans and practicable programs for preparation against disasters to include assistance to individuals with and without English proficiency, disabilities, or other special needs.

- (Sec. 221) Directs the Administrator: (1) in approving standards for state and local emergency preparedness plans, to ensure that such plans take into account the needs of individuals with special needs and individuals with pets; (2) to ensure that each state, in its Homeland Security Strategy or other homeland security plan, provides comprehensive predisaster and postdisaster plans for individuals with special needs and their care givers and that such plans address the evacuation planning needs of those unable to evacuate themselves; and (3) to ensure that state and local emergency preparedness, evacuation, and sheltering plans take into account the needs of individuals with household pets prior to, during, and following a major disaster or emergency.
- Authorizes the Administrator to provide financial and technical support to states and local governments to develop and implement plans for individuals with special needs and requirements, including procuring facilities, medical equipment, and supplies for the care of such individuals. Requires training programs for the instruction of emergency preparedness and response officials in the organization, operation, and techniques of emergency preparedness and response, including planning for and responding to individuals with special needs.
- (Sec. 222) Authorizes the President to provide: (1) transportation assistance to relocate displaced individuals to and from alternative locations for short or long-term accommodation or to return an individual or household to their predisaster primary residence or alternative location; and (2) case management services to state or local government agencies or qualified private organizations to address unmet needs of victims of major disasters.
- (Sec. 223) Authorizes the President to accept and use gifts from foreign organizations and governments in coordination with the Secretaries of Defense and State with respect to the identification of emergency requirements for which such gifts are appropriate.

- (Sec. 225) Provides that in any case in which a state or local government determines that the public welfare would not best be served by repairing, restoring, reconstructing, or replacing any public facility because soil instability or another condition in the disaster area makes such action unfeasible, the state or local government may elect to receive a contribution equal to 90% of the federal share of the estimated cost of such action and management expenses.
- (Sec. 226) Authorizes the President to make contributions to state or local governments for expenses associated with housing volunteers who are assisting the response and recovery efforts in an area affected by a major disaster.
- (Sec. 227) Amends the Stafford Act to include within the provision of temporary housing units authorization to use repaired existing rental units. Authorizes providing funds to state and local governments to contract with owners of private rental housing to provide temporary housing to eligible individuals and households for up to 18 months at a specified rent.
- (Sec. 228) Directs the Administrator to: (1) review all regulations and procedures related to contracting for debris removal; (2) provide additional incentives to recycle debris cleared from a disaster area; and (3) identify any obstacles to increasing the amount of debris recycled following a major disaster.
- (Sec. 229) Directs the Administrator, upon request on behalf of an individual displaced by Hurricanes Katrina or Rita, to place a FEMA manufactured home in a floodway or coastal high hazard area; or in a flood plain without elevating such home up to the base flood level or without complying with specified decision-making process and mitigation requirements. Prohibits the Administrator from making such a placement without having received an evacuation plan for the placement area. Shields the Administrator from liability for damages related to the flooding of such a manufactured home. Requires the Administrator to provide written notice of the potential risks associated

provide written notice of the potential risks associated with such placement and such limitations on liability.

- Title III: Staffing Improvements - (Sec. 301) Directs the Administrator to submit to Congress a strategic human capital plan to shape and improve FEMA's workforce, including: (1) a workforce gap analysis; (2) an action plan to address gaps in critical skills and competencies; and (3) a discussion of the number, qualifications, and training of DHS employees and individuals not employed by FEMA serving in the Surge Capacity Force that states where the Force is able to adequately prepare for, respond to, and recover from a disaster and that describes any additional authorities or resources necessary to address any deficiencies in the Force.
- (Sec. 302) Directs the Administrator to: (1) identify and publish appropriate career paths for personnel, including the education, training, experience, and assignments necessary for career progression within FEMA; (2) provide personnel the opportunity to qualify for promotion; and (3) establish a position assignment policy that balances the need to serve in career enhancing positions and the need for a sufficient period of service to provide the stability, responsibility, and accountability necessary.
- (Sec. 303) Directs the Secretary to establish the National Homeland Security Academy, which shall include a National Homeland Security Education and Strategy Center, to provide strategic education and training to carry out DHS missions. Requires: (1) the Academy's Executive Director to appoint a Director of Admissions and a National Homeland Security Education Network; and (2) the Secretary to establish a Board of Visitors and appoint a State and Local Education and Training Coordinator.
- (Sec. 304) Directs the Administrator to establish a Surge Capacity Force for deployment of individuals to disasters, including catastrophic incidents. Sets forth provisions regarding capabilities and training of the Force. Requires the Administrator to establish and maintain a database regarding Force members, including the skills, qualifications,

- (Sec. 305) Directs the Secretary to establish the Homeland Security Rotation Program for DHS employees, with goals to: (1) expand the knowledge base of DHS; and (2) invigorate the workforce with exciting and professionally rewarding opportunities. Includes among the responsibilities of the Chief Human Capital Officer (who shall administer the Program) establishing a framework that promotes cross-disciplinary rotational opportunities.
- (Sec. 306) Requires: (1) the Administrator to report to Congress on FEMA vacancies; and (2) the Inspector General of DHS to report to Congress evaluating the implications of converting some portion of FEMA's temporary workforce into permanent full-time positions.
- Title IV: Planning, Preparedness, and Training - (Sec. 402) Directs the Secretary, acting through the Administrator, to employ the National Incident Management System (NIMS) and the National Response Plan (NRP) as the framework for emergency response and domestic incident management. Provides that: (1) the NRP shall be the governing plan for any federal involvement or assistance in a disaster or other Incident of National Significance declared by the Secretary under the NRP; and (2) NIMS shall be the incident management system for any federal involvement or assistance in a disaster or other Incident of National Significance declared by the Secretary under the NRP.
- (Sec. 403) Requires the Secretary, by May 1, 2007, acting through the Administrator in conjunction with the federal agencies and nongovernmental organizations that are signatories to the NRP and with the National Advisory Council, to: (1) conduct a comprehensive review of the adequacy of the NRP, incorporating lessons learned from Hurricane Katrina; and (2) update the NRP to incorporate findings.
- Requires that review and update to ensure that the position of Principal Federal Official under the NRP is eliminated. Requires the NRP to provide for a clear chain of command to lead and coordinate the federal response to any disaster. Authorizes the President or the Secretary to designate a federal coordinating officer for Incidents of National

nificance or other domestic incidents not considered an emergency or major disaster.

- Requires the NRP to: (1) include measures to reunify families separated after a major disaster or catastrophic event; (2) address the public health and medical needs of evacuees, special needs populations, and the general population affected and to assign the responsibility for mortuary activities; (3) address the full range of search and rescue requirements and environments for disasters and designate coordinating, primary, and supporting agencies; and (4) clearly describe the roles and responsibilities of the Senior Federal Law Enforcement Officer.

- Requires: (1) the need for an additional emergency support function annex within the NRP focused on the identification, protection, resiliency, and restoration of critical infrastructure and key resources to be considered; and (2) the NRP to assign a single federal agency to coordinate maritime-salvage needs; (3) the Secretary and the Administrator to consult with state and local government officials in reviewing and revising the NRP; and (4) the Secretary (acting through the Administrator) to ensure that the NRP is written in a manner that provides clear, unambiguous, and accessible guidance and information in revising or updating the NRP.

- (Sec. 404) Directs the Secretary, acting through the Administrator, to develop a unified system of strategic and operational plans to respond effectively to disasters, in support of the NRP, which shall include: (1) plans for specific geographic regions and for specific types of high-risk events; and (2) such elements as concepts of operation for appropriate disasters, critical tasks and department and agency responsibilities, and provision for special needs populations in all planning.

- Requires the Administrator to: (1) develop comprehensive operational plans to respond to catastrophic incidents; and (2) provide clear standardization, guidance, and assistance to ensure a common terminology, approach, and framework for all strategic and operational planning and consideration of natural and man-made threats.

- Sets forth required elements of planning, including: (1) preparedness and deployment of health and medical resources; (2) operational plans for the expeditious location of missing children and family reunification; (3) development of a National Search and Rescue Plan; (4) plans to support mass evacuations; (5) plans for military support of civilian authorities under the NRP; (6) incorporation of the use of the Department of Defense (DOD), the National Air and Space Administration (NASA), the National Oceanic and Atmospheric Administration (NOAA), and commercial aircraft and satellite remotely sensed imagery to ensure timely situational awareness; (7) incorporation of coordination with and integration of support from the private sector and nongovernmental organizations during response efforts; (8) plans to allow salvage to proceed in a timely manner during a disaster; and (9) coordination and delineation of primary and supporting responsibilities by the Environmental Protection Agency (EPA) and other agencies under the NRP's Public Works and Engineering Emergency Support Function Annex provisions for the safe handling and sorting of debris.
- Directs the Secretary, acting through the Administrator, to ensure: (1) the development of an inventory of federal resources available for deployment and employment in response to disasters; (2) the development of pre-scripted mission assignments in conjunction with the appropriate federal agencies and departments with coordinating, primary, and supporting responsibilities under the NRP; and (3) the determination of appropriate representatives of DHS to the U.S. Northern Command and the U.S. Pacific Command and the integration of such representatives into national planning, training, exercising, and responses to a disaster to promote better coordination.
- Directs the Secretary and the Secretary of the Department of Health and Human Services (HHS), by March 1, 2007, to: (1) establish a memorandum of understanding defining their roles and responsibilities in providing for public health and medical care under the NRP or in a

event, including deployment, operational control, and resupply of National Disaster Medical System and Metropolitan Medical Response System assets; and (2) create a pilot project for establishing special needs registries for use by emergency and evacuation personnel and transportation providers in an emergency to best meet the needs of special needs individuals and seniors in the community.

- Directs the Secretary, acting through the Administrator, by May 1, 2007 and annually thereafter until May 1, 2017, to report to Congress on all federal planning and preparedness efforts relating to the NRP, including an evaluation of the status of national disaster planning, particularly for catastrophic incidents.
- (Sec. 405) Requires the Administrator, in conjunction with other federal agencies with NRP functions, the National Homeland Security Academy, and the National Incident Management System Integration Center, to ensure that planning and preparedness requirements are effectively trained and exercised to provide for a fully coordinated national response to disasters.
- (Sec. 406) Requires each NRP primary or support agency for any emergency support function to provide the coordinating organization with a detailed description of its plan to fulfill its NRP responsibilities for the current year and the succeeding year, including: (1) a certification that it is capable and prepared to fulfill its responsibilities; or (2) a remedial plan.
- Requires: (1) each NRP coordinating agency to evaluate plans submitted by the primary and support agencies; and (2) each NRP coordinating organization for an emergency support function to provide the Administrator with a detailed description of its coordinated plan for the relevant emergency support function for the current year and the succeeding year, including a certification that it is capable and prepared to fulfill its responsibilities or a remedial plan.
- Requires the Administrator to ensure that each NRP coordinating, primary, or support agency is capable and prepared to carry out its responsibilities and to report annually to Congress.

- Title V: Prevention of Fraud, Waste, and Abuse - (Sec. 501) Directs the Administrator for Federal Procurement Policy to prescribe regulations prohibiting excessive pass-through charges on executive agency contracts, subcontracts, or task or delivery orders that are in excess of the simplified acquisition threshold. Makes such regulations inapplicable to any firm, fixed-price contract, subcontract, or task or delivery order that is: (1) awarded on the basis of adequate price competition; or (2) for the acquisition of a commercial item.
- (Sec. 502) Directs the Comptroller General to report to Congress with an analysis of fraud prevention programs used by DHS in connection with assistance programs, including: (1) an assessment of the effectiveness of, and adherence to, the fraud prevention controls for registration and payment processes; and (2) recommendations for additional fraud prevention controls, including requiring that data provided by registrants be validated against other federal government or third-party sources to determine the accuracy of identification and residence information.
- Directs the Secretary to conduct training on fraud awareness for key DHS personnel, including contracting officers and the Surge Capacity Force for the purpose of preventing fraud in DHS assistance programs.
- (Sec. 503) Authorizes the Director of the Office of Management and Budget (OMB) to establish a Contingency Contracting Corps, composed of executive agency contracting officers who are trained and available to perform on a temporary and volunteer basis services necessary to assist agencies with contracting activities during unplanned events.
- Requires an executive agency employee to receive the agency's approval prior to performing services for the Corps that substantially reduce the amount of time such employee is able to perform normal functions. Allows the employee to perform such services for at least 30 days but not more than one year. Prohibits removal from employment of an employee performing such services for the Corps.

entity, using available funds in the Acquisition Workforce Training Fund; and (2) each member of the Corps to be provided all necessary forms and regulations in a portable, electronic format to facilitate compliance with all relevant laws and to be familiar with such forms and regulations.

- (Sec. 504) Directs the Administrator to establish an identity verification process for the Individuals and Households Program registrants applying via the Internet or by telephone to provide reasonable assurance that disaster assistance payments are made only to qualified individuals.

- (Sec. 505) Directs the Secretary to ensure that DHS information technology systems ensure the validity of claims for assistance under the Stafford Act to deter waste, fraud, and abuse.

- (Sec. 506) Directs the Administrator to create a registry of contractors who are capable of performing debris removal, distribution of supplies, reconstruction, and other disaster or emergency relief activities, to be available on FEMA's Internet site.

- (Sec. 507) Authorizes the Administrator to provide for the use by state or local governments of GSA federal supply schedules for procurement of supplies or services to be used to prepare for or respond to a presidentially declared emergency or major disaster.

- (Sec. 508) Amends the Stafford Act to require any expenditure of federal funds for major disaster or emergency assistance activities which may be carried out by a contract or agreement with private organizations, firms, or individuals that is not awarded to an entity residing or doing business primarily in the area affected to be justified in writing. Requires an agency performing response, relief, and reconstruction activities, to the maximum extent feasible, to transition work performed under contracts in effect on the date the President declares the emergency or major disaster to such an entity residing or doing business primarily in the affected area. Provides that nothing herein shall be construed to require any federal agency to breach or renegotiate any contract in effect before the occurrence of a major

- (Sec. 509) Requires the Administrator to report to Congress identifying: (1) recurring disaster response requirements for which FEMA can and cannot contract in advance of disasters in a cost-effective manner; and (2) a contracting strategy that maximizes the use of advance contracts. Directs the Administrator to: (1) enter into such contracts through competitive procedures; and (2) maintain contracts for appropriate levels of goods and services.
- (Sec. 510) Requires the Director of OMB to issue guidelines to assist executive agencies in improving the management of the use of the government-wide commercial purchase card for making micro-purchases. Directs the Administrator of General Services to: (1) continue efforts to improve reporting by financial institutions that issue such cards so GSA has the data needed to identify opportunities for achieving savings; and (2) actively pursue point-of-sale discounts with major vendors accepting the card. Requires: (1) the senior procurement executive for each agency to report to the Director on actions taken under the guidelines; (2) the Director to report to Congress summarizing progress made; (3) GSA to develop procedures to subject purchase card payments to federal contractors to the Federal Payment Levy Program; and (4) the Administrator to report annually on first class and business class travel by executive agency employees.
- (Sec. 511) Requires the head of each executive agency that uses purchase cards and convenience checks to implement safeguards and internal controls.
- (Sec. 512) Directs the Comptroller General to report to Congress on: (1) DHS compliance with the Single Audit Act of 1984; (2) DHS's ability to comply with the Improper Payments Information Act of 2002 regarding disasters similar to Hurricane Katrina; and (3) the number of contracts and subcontracts entered into during the previous two years to carry out the Stafford Act or relating to Hurricane Katrina between DHS and small businesses and small businesses owned and controlled by socially

and economically disadvantaged individuals, by women, and by service-disabled veterans.

- (Sec. 515) Directs the President, in the event of a catastrophic incident or when the President has elected to establish and operate long-term recovery offices for any other emergency, to: (1) establish an Office of Catastrophic Incident or Long-term Recovery in the Executive Office of the President; and (2) appoint a Chief Financial Officer to head the Office and to be responsible for the efficient and effective use of federal funds in all activities relating to the recovery from a catastrophic incident or other emergency.

- Title VI: Miscellaneous Provisions - Authorizes appropriations for FY2007-FY2010, including for Administrative and Regional Operations, for Readiness, Mitigation, Response, and Recovery, and for the Office for Emergency Communications.

- Sandy Recovery Improvement Act of 2013 (SRIA)

- The Sandy Recovery Improvement Act of 2013—(Sec. 2) further amended the Robert T. Stafford Disaster Relief and Emergency Assistance Act to authorize the President, acting through the Administrator of the Federal Emergency Management Agency (FEMA), to approve public assistance projects for major disasters or emergencies under alternative procedures with the goal of: (1) reducing the costs to the federal government of providing such assistance; (2) increasing flexibility in the administration of assistance; (3) expediting the provision of assistance to a state, tribal or local government, or owner or operator of a private nonprofit facility; and (4) providing financial incentives and disincentives for the timely and cost-effective completion of projects.

- Requires such alternative procedures, with respect to grants for facility repair, restoration, or replacement, to allow: (1) such grants to be made on the basis of fixed estimates if the state, tribal, or local government or the owner or operator of the private nonprofit facility agrees to be responsible for any actual costs that exceed the estimate; (2) a grantee to elect to receive an in-lieu contribution, without reduction, on the basis

and management expenses; (3) consolidating state, local, or tribal facilities as a single project; and (4) the Administrator to permit a grantee, when completed project costs are less than the estimated costs, to use excess funds for activities that reduce the risk of future damage, hardship, or suffering from a major disaster and for other activities to improve future public assistance operations or planning.

- Requires such alternative procedures, with respect to grants for debris removal, to allow: (1) such grants to be made on the basis of fixed estimates to provide financial incentives and disincentives for the timely or cost-effective completion if the grantee agrees to be responsible for any actual costs that exceed the estimate; (2) use of a sliding scale for determining the federal share for removal of debris and wreckage based on the time it takes to complete; (3) use of program income from recycled debris without offset to the grant amount; (4) reimbursement of wages for grantee employees and extra hires performing or administering debris and wreckage removal; (5) incentives to a state, local, or tribal government to have a debris management plan approved by the Administrator and to have pre-qualified contractors before the date of declaration of the major disaster; and (6) the Administrator to permit a grantee, when actual project costs are less than estimated costs, to use the excess funds for debris management planning, acquisition of debris management equipment for current or future use, and other activities to improve future debris removal operations.
- (Sec. 3) Authorizes the President to enter into lease agreements for, and make repairs or improvements to, multifamily rental property located in areas covered by a major disaster declaration when the President determines it would be a cost-effective alternative to other temporary housing options.
- (Sec. 4) Directs the President, for purposes of hazard mitigation assistance, to ensure that: (1) environmental reviews and historic preservation reviews are completed on an expeditious basis; and (2) the shortest existing applicable process under the National Environmental

Act of 1969 and the National Historic Preservation Act is utilized. Authorizes the President to provide not more than 25% of the amount of the estimated cost of hazard mitigation measures to a state grantee before eligible costs are incurred.

- (Sec. 5) Directs the Administrator to establish procedures under which an applicant, through December 31, 2015, may request the use of alternative dispute resolution, including arbitration by an independent review panel to resolve disputes relating to eligible assistance.
- (Sec. 6) Directs the President to establish a unified interagency review process to ensure compliance with environmental and historic requirements relating to disaster recovery projects in order to expedite the recovery process.
- (Sec. 7) Requires the President: (1) within one year, to complete an analysis to determine whether an increase in the threshold for eligibility for the provision of federal disaster or emergency assistance on the basis of the amount of the federal estimate of assistance necessary is appropriate; and (2) if so, to establish such threshold, adjust it annually for inflation, and review it every three years.
- (Sec. 8) Authorizes the President: (1) to provide child care assistance to an individual or household adversely affected by a major disaster; and (2) after declaring a major disaster or emergency for an area within the jurisdiction of a state, tribal, or local government, to reimburse such government for costs relating to basic pay and benefits and overtime and hazardous duty compensation for permanent employees of such government conducting emergency protective measures.
- (Sec. 9) Requires the Administrator to review, update, and revise factors relating to trauma to measure the severity, magnitude, and impact of a disaster.
- (Sec. 10) Authorizes Indian tribal governments to submit requests for major disaster or emergency declarations directly to the President.
- (Sec. 11) Directs the Administrator to submit recommendations for the development of a national strategy for reducing future costs, loss of life,

and injuries associated with extreme disaster events in vulnerable areas of the United States.

On Thursday, February 1, 2012 FEMA Deputy Administrator Richard Serino introduced a vision of a FEMA, aimed at transforming the total FEMA workforce into a more professional and deployable organization. Under the theme, "every employee is an emergency manager," the organization aims to harness the dedication and expertise of every employee.

Deputy Administrator Serino said: "FEMA's fundamental goal, and the inspiration and motivation for many FEMA employees, is to serve the Nation by helping its people and first responders, especially when they are most in need."

FEMA has devoted significant resources and emphasis on developing and implementing a number of key initiatives to improve and enhance the work experience of the total disaster workforce. Whether a part-time, full-time, permanent or temporary employee, this disaster workforce transformation will benefit the agency in many significant ways.

FEMA Corps

An Innovative Cost-Saving Partnership to Strengthen Disaster Response and Expand Opportunities for Young People. On March 13, 2012, the White House announced an innovative partnership between the Department of Homeland Security's Federal Emergency Management Agency (FEMA) and the Corporation for National and Community Service (CNCS) to establish a FEMA-devoted unit of 1,600 service corps members within AmeriCorps National Civilian Community Corps (NCCC) solely devoted to disaster preparedness, response, and recovery.

This partnership builds on the historic collaboration between the two agencies and enhances the federal government's disaster capabilities, increases the reliability and diversity of the disaster workforce, promotes an ethic of service, expands education and economic opportunity for young people, and achieves significant cost savings for the American taxpayer. When the program is at full operational capability, and in an average disaster year, FEMA expects to see a savings of approximately $60 million in a year.

2011-2014 STRATEGIC PLAN

The FEMA FY 2011-2014 Strategic Plan built on and expanded existing efforts to create a stronger organization, which will contribute to a more capable emergency management community. It provided the foundation for how the Agency will foster community engagement, establish priorities to stabilize an event, build upon the understanding of risk, and learn from the things FEMA does with the emergency management team. The Strategic Plan described FEMA's way forward and builds on the 2010 "Administrator's Intent", which linked FEMA's strategic focus to the broader principles of the President's National Security Strategy, Presidential Policy Directive 8, and the Secretary's Quadrennial Homeland Security Review. All of these documents recognize the importance of working as a team to strengthen the Nation's resilience.

FEMA Administrators

John Macy

John Macy was named as FEMA's first director in 1981. Macy emphasized the similarities between natural hazards preparedness and the civil defense activities.   FEMA began development of an Integrated Emergency Management System with an all-hazards approach. This approach encompassed "direction, control and warning systems which are common to the full range of emergencies from small isolated events to the ultimate emergency—war." The new agency was faced with many unusual challenges in its first few years that emphasized how complex emergency management can be. Early disasters and emergencies included the contamination of Love Canal, the Cuban refugee crisis and the accident at the Three Mile Island nuclear power plant. Later, the Loma Prieta Earthquake in 1989 and Hurricane Andrew in 1992 focused major national attention on FEMA.

James L. Witt

In 1993, President Clinton nominated James L. Witt as the new FEMA director, becoming the first agency director with experience as a state emergency manager. He initiated sweeping reforms that streamlined disaster relief and recovery operations, insisted on a new emphasis regarding preparedness and mitigation, and focused agency employees on customer service. The end of the Cold War also allowed Witt to redirect more of FEMA's limited resources from civil defense into disaster relief, recovery and mitigation programs.

Joe M. Allbaugh

In February 2001, President George W. Bush appointed Joe M. Allbaugh as the director of FEMA. He served until FEMA's transfer into the newly created Department of Homeland Security, after which he resigned in March 2003.

Michael Brown

Michael Brown was appointed in January 2003 also by President George W. Bush and resigned soon after Hurricane Katrina, the deadliest and most destructive Atlantic tropical cyclone of the 2005 Atlantic hurricane season.

Robert David Paulison

Robert David Paulison was appointed by President George W. Bush on September 12, 2005.   At the 2009 National Hurricane Conference, he announced he would resign January 21, 2009.

W. Craig Fugate

Craig Fugate was appointed as the FEMA Administrator in May 2009 by President Barack Obama and remains as the current Administrator (April,

FEMA's Role

To serve disaster victims and communities more quickly and effectively, FEMA builds on experience, applies lessons learned and best practices from field operations, gathers feedback from many sources, and constantly strives to improve upon its operational core competencies:

Service to Disaster Victims—Responsive and compassionate care for disaster victims is FEMA's top priority. FEMA provides rapid, ready, clear and consistent access to disaster assistance to all eligible individuals and communities. The agency also is able to assist individuals with multilingual or special needs requirements.

Integrated Preparedness—FEMA works closely with federal, tribal, state and local governments, voluntary agencies, private sector partners, and the American public to ensure the nation is secured and prepared to respond to and recover from terror attacks, major disasters and other emergencies.

Operational Planning and Preparedness –Working closely with federal, tribal, state and local partners, FEMA's Operational Planners assist jurisdictions to develop planning capabilities and write area- and incident-specific operational plans that will guide local response activities.

Incident Management—With a forward leaning posture, FEMA can respond more swiftly and decisively to all hazards with around-the-clock support. The agency continues to professionalize its workforce by training and certifying staff in emergency management skills and techniques. FEMA also works closely with external partners to improve and update standards, and support the enduring efforts of America's first responders.

Disaster Logistics –FEMA implements 21st century logistics and procurement systems to help efficiently and effectively plan, identify, track and distribute supplies needed by disaster victims, emergency responders and other users on the ground. Working with an array of public and private strategic partners, donors and pre-arranged contractors, a businesslike FEMA provides improved logistics integration and customer support.

Hazard Mitigation –FEMA works proactively to reduce the physical and financial impact of future disasters through improved risk analysis and hazard mitigation planning, risk reduction and flood insurance. FEMA helps implement effective hazard mitigation practices in order to create safer

ties, promote rapid recovery from floods and other disasters, and reduce the financial impact at the federal, tribal, state and local levels.

Emergency communications—FEMA is a leader in emergency communications by working with federal, tribal, state and local partners to establish and facilitate consistent disaster emergency communications standards, plans and capabilities. As part of this leadership role, FEMA works to forge an integrated operational link before, during and immediately after an event and is an advocate for disaster emergency communications at the national level on behalf of first responders.

Public Disaster communications –FEMA coordinates all hazards messaging before, during and after national emergencies using three strategies: public risk communications, partnership management and employee communications. By successfully managing these elements, FEMA supports operational efforts and ensures clear, consistent and effective information for disaster victims and emergency management partners and stakeholders.

Continuity Programs –FEMA supports upgrades to and implementation of the Integrated Public Alert and Warning System. It is the lead agent for the Nation's programs in ensuring the continuity of government operations and essential functions and the endurance of our constitutional form of government in a catastrophic event.

FEMA Offices and Agencies

National Advisory Council

The National Advisory Council (NAC) was established by the enactment of the Post-Katrina Emergency Management Reform Act of 2006 to ensure effective and ongoing coordination of Federal preparedness, protection, response, recovery, and mitigation for natural disasters, acts of terrorism, and other manmade disasters. The NAC advises the FEMA Administrator on all aspects of emergency management. The NAC incorporates state, local, and tribal governments; nonprofit, and private sector input in the development and of the National Preparedness Goal, the National Preparedness System, the National Incident Management System, and other related plans and strategies.

The NAC consists of up to 35 members appointed by and serving at the pleasure of the Administrator. Members are designated as Representatives, Special Government Employees (SGEs), or *Ex Officio*. SGEs are defined in section 202(a) of Title 18 United States Code. To the extent practicable, the members are geographically diverse and represent a substantive cross-section of officials, emergency managers, and emergency response providers from state, local, and tribal governments, the private sector, and nongovernmental organizations.

Office of Disability Integration and Coordination

The Office of Disability Integration and Coordination leads FEMA's commitment to achieving whole community emergency management, inclusive of individuals with disabilities and others with access and functional needs, by providing guidance, tools, methods and strategies to establish equal physical, program and effective communication access.

Office of Equal Rights

The Office of Equal Rights serves the Agency and the Nation by promoting affirmative employment, a discrimination-free work place, and equal access to FEMA programs and benefits. It perform its mission by providing expert guidance and proactive support. Its customers are the employees and managers of FEMA, State and local government officials, and the American people.

Its goals are to bring the fullest human value to the work of the Agency and to fulfill its responsibilities under the Constitution.

Equal Employment Opportunity Program

Federal discrimination laws cover all FEMA personnel, including DAES and applicants for employment. Title VII of the Civil Rights Act of 1964 provides protection from discrimination on the basis of race, color, national

Civil Rights Program

Any person eligible to receive disaster aid or other services from FEMA is entitled to those benefits without discrimination. Title VI of the Civil Rights Act of 1964 protects individuals from discrimination on the basis of their race, color, or national origin in programs that receive Federal financial assistance.

Office of External Affairs (OEA)

The Office of External Affairs was created in 2007, bringing together several independent offices and adding two new divisions to enhance a coordinated communications program for the agency. The Office's purpose is to maintain visibility regarding public and internal communications; coordinate routine and special communications; ensure accurate, useful, timely, synchronized, targeted communication; and provide continuous messaging to meet the needs of the situation. The Office also serves as an advisor to FEMA program and support offices on decision making, development, and maintenance of policies and programs to ensure that activities are responsive to stakeholder, media, congressional and other audiences

Its mission is to engage, inform and educate all FEMA stakeholders in support of the Agency's programs and initiatives to achieve its mission.

Congressional Affairs

The Congressional Affairs Division (CAD) is the Federal Emergency Management Agency's primary liaison with the United States Congress. The division maintains communications with Congress in both official and informal capacities. CAD's mission is to proactively engage and communicate with Members of Congress and their staff to build strong working relationships that will advance the Agency's legislative and emergency management priorities.

national significance or incidents requiring a coordinated federal response. The Director of Disaster Operations also serves as the senior External Affairs official on all incident response activations and operations.

Intergovernmental Affairs

The Intergovernmental Affairs Division (IGA) provides direct communication and outreach to state, local, tribal, and territorial (SLTT) officials, including governors and state officials, state legislators, tribal governments, small states and rural constituencies, territorial governments, county/parish officials, mayors and city managers, and city councils. In addition, IGA fosters and maintains relationships with national associations who represent SLTT governments, emergency managers, and homeland security officials. IGA also continues to build relationships with key constituency groups that have been traditionally underserved by the Federal government.

Private Sector

FEMA established a Private Sector Division within the Office of External Affairs in October 2007. The Division's mission is to communicate, cultivate and advocate for collaboration between the U.S. private sector and FEMA, to support FEMA's capabilities and to enhance national preparedness, protection, response, recovery, and mitigation of all hazards. Additionally, the division's vision is to establish and maintain a national reputation for effective support to our private sector stakeholders through credible, reliable and meaningful two-way communication.

Public Affairs

The Public Affairs Division provides information to the American public that helps them prepare for, prevent, respond to, and recover from disasters by establishing and maintaining effective, ongoing relationships with the media to promote the Agency's programs, goals and core values; servicing our internal and external customers by developing communication strategies that

rate information, and managing communications to demonstrate an effective federal response to disasters.

Strategic Communications

FEMA established a Strategic Communications Division within the Office of External Affairs to establish proactive planning and coordination for agency offices and programs. The division, through its strategic communications advisors, will coordinate internally with agency offices to prioritize, organize, and implement communication strategies, produce materials for stakeholder audiences, and support program policies and initiatives. The division will foster a whole community approach to its planning efforts, including the recognition and integration of specialized communications tactics that consider needs related to language barriers, cultural diversity, and disability.

Coordination and Business Operations

The Coordination and Business Operations Division provides consolidated management and administrative support for External Affairs. The mission of the division is to ensure External Affairs staff has the resources, training, and processes necessary to meet the External Affairs mission, and that these resources are managed effectively on behalf of the Agency and the U.S. citizens.

Ready Campaign

Launched in February 2003, Ready is a national public service advertising campaign designed to educate and empower Americans to prepare for and respond to emergencies including natural and man-made disasters. The goal of the campaign is to get the public involved and ultimately to increase the level of basic preparedness across the nation.

Office of National Capitol Region Coordination

The Homeland Security Act of 2002 established the Office of National Capital Region Coordination (NCRC) to address challenges related to emergency management planning and incident response coordination unique to the National Capital Region (NCR) due to the large number of federal departments and agencies, numerous state and local jurisdictions within our Nation's Capital. The NCRC enhances preparedness and promotes resiliency by enabling better communication and planning between and among federal, state, local, regional, nonprofit and private sector stakeholders in the NCR.

The NCRC oversees and coordinates federal programs for and assists with developing relationships among—state, local, and regional authorities in the NCR. In addition, the NCRC serves as a liaison between federal and state, local, regional authorities, and the private sector within the NCR to facilitate and integrate homeland security efforts. The NCRC engages the "whole community" within the NCR to effectively prepare for, protect against, respond to, recover from, and mitigate against any disaster, and helps develop collective, mutually supportive regional capabilities.

An example of an NCRC program is the The Full-Spectrum Risk Knowledge Base, which is a secure, web-based resource that aids diverse stakeholders in building all-hazards risk knowledge and enhancing risk-informed decision making.

Office of Policy & Program Analysis

On behalf of, and in support of the FEMA Administrator, the Office of Policy and Program Analysis (OPPA) fosters strategic coherence; ensures availability of critical resources; leads Agency policy, strategy, and innovation; provides objective analysis; drives strategy, budget, execution, performance integration and accountability.

In 2014, OPPA refined its core functions and re-aligned its strategic priorities to FEMA's strategic priorities. OPPA will continue to promote efficiency and effectiveness across the Agency while strengthening the linkages among strategy, budget, execution, and performance.

OPPA has three core functions and five priorities. The core functions are what OPPA must do well and the priorities are what OPPA must accomplish to drive FEMA forward and deliver on senior leadership expectations.

- Ensure FEMA's strategic direction
- Inform sound decisions with independent analysis
- Facilitate cross-agency interactions

Strategic Priorities

- Strategic Integration: Fully integrate the strategy-program-budget-performance processes within FEMA and institutionalize them.
- Strategic Direction: Design, develop, and facilitate execution of FEMA's vision and strategy.
- Business Intelligence: Build a high-impact, real-time, decision analysis capability within OPPA and across FEMA.
- Policy Formulation: Establish consistent and interconnected policy FEMA-wide.
- 21st Century Collaboration: Reshape the way we work—within OPPA, across FEMA, the inter-agency and internationally—to take advantage of inter-disciplinary expertise and deliver better services.

OPPA Divisions

The Policy Division integrates and oversees policy coordination across the Agency, and works collaboratively with both internal and external stakeholders to shape overall Agency policy.

The Enterprise Analytics Division effectively drives FEMA forward by building a high-impact, real-time, decision analysis and business intelligence capability within OPPA and across FEMA. The division includes FEMASTAT, Field Operations, Resource Intelligence, and Capability Building for the data analytics community of practices.

The Strategic Planning and Analysis Division facilitates integrated strategic thinking and planning to ensure a common direction and coordinated outcomes across FEMA.

The Defense Production Act (DPA) Program Division provides coordination and guidance for the DPA plans and programs of Federal departments and agencies and supports use of DPA authorities by FEMA and other DHS components.

The International Affairs Division engages and partners with the international emergency management community to enhance Agency learning and continuous improvement.

The Audit Liaison Division is responsible for the internal management of all audits by external entities. The Division provides oversight, monitoring, and coordination of the Agency's responses to audits, inspections, and reviews, which are primarily conducted by the DHS OIG and GAO. The Division also facilitates transparency of the Agency to the Department of Homeland Security and the U.S. Congress.

Office of Regional Operations

FEMA Regional Operations serves as the Agency's Office through which all policy, managerial, resource and administrative actions that affect or impact the Regions receive effective coordination between headquarters and the Regional Offices. The Office of Regional Operations also ensures that FEMA policies, programs, administrative and management guidance are implemented in the Regions in a manner consistent with the Agency's overall goals.

- The principal functions of the Office of Regional Operations are:
- Liaison between the Regional Administrators and Headquarters leadership
- Advising the headquarters leadership on matters affecting or impacting the Regions
- Providing guidance to Regional Administrators on policy, programs, operations, and administrative matters

Office of Response and Recovery

The Office of Response and Recovery (ORR) provides leadership to build, sustain, and improve the coordination and delivery of support to citizens and State, local, tribal and territorial governments to save lives, reduce suffering, protect property and recover from all hazards.

The Office of Response and Recovery (ORR) is comprised of the following offices and components:

- Office of the Associate Administrator, ORR
- Executive Oversight
- Strategic Integration Group
- Executive Communication and Coordination Group
- Disaster Declarations Unit
- Office of Readiness and Assessment

Response Directorate

The Response Directorate provides the core, coordinated Federal operational response capability needed to save and sustain lives, minimize suffering, and protect property in a timely and effective manner in communities that become overwhelmed by natural disasters, acts of terrorism, or other emergencies.   Response program activities encompass the coordination of all Federal emergency management response operations, response planning and integration of Federal, state, tribal and local disaster programs.   This coordination ensures efficient and effective delivery of immediate emergency assistance to individuals and communities impacted and overwhelmed by these disasters, emergencies, or acts of terrorism.

Disaster Emergency Communications Division

Disaster Emergency Communications is a specialized field within the broader field of emergency communications. Emergency communications covers all technical means and modes for public safety agencies at all levels of government (e.g. law enforcement, fire services, emergency medical services) to perform their routine, daily communications. Disaster emergency communications applies to those technical means and modes required to provide and maintain operable and interoperable communication before, during, and after presidentially declared emergencies, disasters, or planned National Special Security Events.

The Disaster Emergency Communications Division has six geographically dispersed Mobile Emergency Response Support (MERS) detachments and a number of Mobile Communications Office Vehicles (MCOV).

The Disaster Emergency Communications Division establishes, maintains, and coordinates effective disaster emergency communications services and information systems critical to FEMA's role in coordinating the Federal government's response, continuity efforts, and restoration of essential services before, during, and after an incident or planned event. The DEC Division promotes and provides operable and interoperable communications and information systems capabilities across all levels of government to ensure mission–critical information and situational awareness for emergency management decision makers and support elements. This is accomplished through:

- Supporting effective tactical operable and interoperable voice, video, and information systems for federal emergency response teams.
- Identifying and documenting mission-critical disaster emergency communication and information systems capabilities, requirements, solutions, and mitigation strategies.
- Developing effective command and control communications frameworks.
- Supporting the coordination and delivery of secure communications solutions.
- Promoting communications interoperability with Federal, State, tribal, and local emergency response providers.

The DEC Division at FEMA headquarters provides the executive leadership, program support, guidance, planning, and national intra-and interagency coordination required for the effective delivery of FEMA disaster

issues impacting the communications needs of emergency responders, engages across the Federal government to support response to State and local governments and help establish consistent DEC operability and interoperability standards and capabilities, and facilitates a coordinated emergency communications response framework. Specifically, the DEC Division headquarter element performs the following roles:

- Programmatic oversight and support, to include:
- Doctrine, policy, and standards development and maintenance
- Planning
- Logistics and Budget
- Interagency Coordination
- Regional Emergency Communications Coordination Working Groups
- Research, Testing, Development, and Evaluation
- Lifecycle Management
- Integration Management
- Training and Exercises
- Readiness Reporting
- Security
- Administrative Support
- Engineering Review Board
- Change Control Board
- Operations:
- Deployment and support of MERS Detachments
- Spectrum management
- Interagency all-hazards response coordination

Recovery Directorate

Recovery's mission is to support communities in rebuilding so individuals, civic institutions, businesses, and governmental organizations can function on their own, return to normal life, and protect against future hazards.

It includes the Disaster Survivor Assistance Program whose mission is to build and sustain an expeditionary cadre that can address disaster survivor's immediate needs by:

- Establishing a timely presence;
- Providing in-person, tailored information and services;
- Providing referrals to whole community partners as needed;
- Collecting targeted information to support decision-making; and
- Identifying public information needs so critical messaging can be developed and disseminated.

The Disaster Survivor Assistance Program supports Local, State, Tribal, Territorial, and Federal requirements during disaster response and recovery operations. DSA staff have the ability to quickly deploy in anticipation of (or immediately following) a disaster declaration, and can provide operational/situational awareness of conditions, needs, and activity in the affected area. They provide support to disaster survivors at their homes or in their communities, offering options for how to access programs that can help them move forward in their recovery.

Logistics Management Directorate

Logistics Management Directorate (LMD) is a very dynamic Directorate with a business process concept that continues to transform. Our mission is to effectively plan, manage and sustain national logistics response and recovery operations, in support of domestic emergencies and special events, acting as the National Logistics Coordinator (NLC) or Single Logistics Integrator for domestic incident support. As the National Logistics Coordinator we are establishing national procedures, fostering transparency through collaboration and coordination and, we are focused on technology enhancements to expand Region & State level logistics capabilities.

LMD is organized around the following four core competencies:

- Logistics Operations—Manages and executes the national logistics command and coordination, tracking and reporting for all-hazards erations utilizing the National Logistics Coordinator concept. Operates the Logistics Management Center (LMC) serving as the central reporting element for the National Response Coordination Center on all logistics actions and operational activities. Stores, maintains and deploys Temporary Housing Units and Mobile Disaster Recovery Centers.

- Logistics Plans and Exercises—Develops and provides cohesive and synchronized logistics plans and exercises to achieve both short and long term readiness requirements. Ensures deliberate planning efforts result in coordinated ConOps and Plans resulting in repeatable processes supporting optimized national logistics response and recovery operations supporting domestic emergencies and special events.
- Distribution Management—Manages a comprehensive supply chain, warehouse and transportation operation using a Strategic Alliance to effectively and efficiently distribute supplies, equipment and services to support emergencies.
- Property Management—Provides management oversight, internal control and technical reviews in the areas of property accountability, reutilization, and disposal of Disaster Operations equipment. We are in the process of implementing an enterprise-wide property accounting and asset visibility system that is designed and implemented to ensure best value.

Our strategic direction in LMD is focused on four key areas:

- People: Develop a professional logistics workforce, including regional staff, through hiring, training, credentialing and professional development; foster an accountability and results based culture.
- Customers: Develop collaborative relationships with key stakeholders; foster both horizontal and vertical coordination; develop bottom up requirement process.

velop and document key business policy and processes; perform analysis and take systematic approach to task/ issue resolution.

- Systems: Modernize the logistics system network; upgrade and fully integrate our systems to achieve maximum capability effectiveness.

Office of Federal Disaster Coordination

The mission of the Office of Federal Disaster Coordination (OFDC) is to access, train, equip, and manage FEMA's Federal Coordinating Officers (FCO) and Federal Disaster Recovery Coordinators (FDRC) to ensure their availability for rapid deployment in response to any disaster; deliver training to develop and sustain FCO and FDRC professional competencies, and coordinate both FCO and FDRC assignments to meet the on-scene needs of FEMA and its emergency management partners.

OFDC's goals are to:

- Strengthen FEMA's Operational Readiness—participate in key exercises, partner strategically with key organizations, implementation and sustain all-hazards capability, identify and leverage collateral specialties.
- Provide exemplary national leadership at disasters and emergencies—facilitating efficient, effective, compassionate, fair, and consistent response, while ensuring the prudent use of resources; recognized leaders across all FEMA programs, flawless delivery.
- Select and develop the right leader – purposive recruiting and hiring, strong diversity, exemplary training and credentialing, properly equipped and readily available.
- Lead the Federal Disaster Coordination Cadres—program resource management responsibilities, develop field leadership doctrine, coordinate approval of field operations policy, serve as project advisors to major acquisitions/contracts, serve as instructors for field operations and emergency management.

Office of the Senior Law Enforcement Advisor

Its mission is to integrate the law enforcement, security, and emergency management communities by enhancing communication and coordination between FEMA, private security, and state, local, tribal, and territorial law enforcement.

Its principal functions are to:

- Liaise between law enforcement officials and FEMA leadership
- Advise FEMA leadership on matters affecting or impacting the law enforcement community
- Provide guidance to FEMA programmatic areas on policy, programs, operations, and administrative matters

"Law Enforcement" is a term that describes the individuals and agencies responsible for enforcing laws and maintaining public order and public safety. Additionally, law enforcement serve as first responders and answers the call to virtually any situation, including acts of terrorism and other large-scale emergencies that may impact their community. FEMA partners with the law enforcement community in support of its mission to support our citizens and first responders to ensure that as a nation we work together to build, sustain, and improve our capability to prepare for, protect against, respond to, recover from, and mitigate all hazards.

Its role is to enhance communication and coordination between FEMA and these law enforcement communities. As the Agency strengthens the nation's resilience to disasters, it builds unity of effort among the entire emergency management team, including engagement with the law enforcement community. The office strives to develop better emergency management practices and in doing so adheres to FEMA's Core Values of *compassion, fairness, integrity and respect*; and the Guiding Principles of *teamwork, engagement, getting results, preparation, empowerment, flexibility, accountability and stewardship*. The Office of the Senior Law Enforcement Advisor supports these values and principles and works with its partners to meet the needs of survivors, address the most significant risks and improve capabilities.

Protection and Preparedness

Protection and National Preparedness (PNP) is responsible for the coordination of preparedness and protection related activities throughout FEMA, including grants, planning, training, exercises, individual and community preparedness, assessments, lessons learned, continuity of government and national capital region coordination.

Protection and National Preparedness (PNP) is comprised of the following offices and components:

- Office of the Deputy Administrator, PNP
- Office of Counterterrorism and Security Preparedness
- Office of Preparedness Integration and Coordination
- Strategic Resource Management Office

Grant Programs Directorate

The purpose of FEMA's Grant Programs Directorate (GPD) is to strategically and effectively administer and manage FEMA grants to ensure critical and measurable results for customers and stakeholders.

Its mission is to manage federal assistance to measurably improve capability and reduce the risks the Nation faces in times of man-made and natural disasters. The focus of GPD is to:

- Provide exceptional customer service to all grantees, as well as internal and external partners
- Establish and promote consistent outreach and communication with state, local and tribal stakeholders
- Ensure transparency in the grant process
- Enhance the Nation's level of preparedness and the public's ability to prevent, protect and mitigate against, and respond to and recover from all hazards

National Continuity Programs Directorate

FEMA's National Continuity Programs Directorate (NCP) is the Federal Executive Branch Lead Agent for continuity of national essential functions. Its goal is to minimize the disruption of essential operations in order to guarantee an Enduring Constitutional Government in response to a full threat spectrum of emergencies. The scope of its mandate includes development and promulgation of Continuity of Operations (COOP) directives and guidance, education and training, and coordination between the Federal, State, local, territorial, tribal and private sectors. NCP also coordinates and participates in Federal, State and local COOP exercises.

NCP also manages the Integrated Public Alert and Warning System (IPAWS), the Nation's next generation alert and warning capability developed by NCP in partnership with multiple Federal Departments and Agencies. IPAWS meets the requirements of Executive Order 13407, signed by the President in 2006, which called for the development and implementation of an "effective, reliable, integrated, flexible, and comprehensive system to alert and warn the American people... and to ensure under all conditions the President can communicate with the American people."

Its mission is to serve the public by protecting our Nation's constitutional form of government, and its vision is to become the Nation's center of excellence for government continuity planning, guidance, and operations.

Integrated Public Alert and Warning System

Executive Order 13407 states, "It is the policy of the United States to have an effective, reliable, integrated, flexible, and comprehensive system to alert and warn the American people....and to ensure under all conditions the President can communicate with the American people." FEMA is designated within the Department of Homeland Security to implement the policy of the United States for a public alert and warning system and has established the Integrated Public Alert and Warning System (IPAWS). FEMA, as well as numerous public and private industry partners, are working together to transform the national alert and warning system to enable rapid dissemination of authenticated alert information over as many communications pathways as possible.

Its vision is to provide 'Timely Alert and Warning to American People in the preservation of life and property' and its mission is to 'Provide integrated services and capabilities to local, state, and federal authorities that enable them to alert and warn their respective communities via multiple communications methods.'

It has three Strategic Goals:

- Goal 1—Create and maintain an integrated interoperable environment for alert and warning
- Goal 2—Make alert and warning more effective
- Goal 3—Strengthen the Resilience of IPAWS Infrastructure

IPAWS allows alerting authorities to write their own message using open standards. The message is then authenticated by the IPAWS Open Platform for Emergency Networks, or IPAWS-OPEN, to be delivered simultaneously through multiple communications devices reaching as many people as possible to save lives and protect property. IPAWS must ensure the President can reach the American people, but FEMA recognizes that most alerts and warnings are issued at a state and local level.

In addition to the President, alerting authorities include state, local, territorial, and tribal public safety officials who are designated within their level of government as an authority responsible for communicating emergency alerts and warnings to the public. After completing FEMA-sponsored training, alerting authorities become authenticated for access to IPAWS. They can then use Common Alerting Protocol (CAP) compliant emergency and incident management tools to create location-specific alerts that are scaled to cover areas as big as their entire jurisdiction or a much smaller area within their jurisdiction. Once created, the alert can then be sent to IPAWS-OPEN for relay to the Emergency Alert System (EAS), National Oceanic and Atmospheric Administration (NOAA) Weather Radio and other National Weather Service systems, the Commercial Mobile Alert System (CMAS), and other private sector systems. The specific geographic area to which these alerts can then be delivered depends on the capabilities of the dissemination channel used.

the Common Alert Protocol, IPAWS allows for growth and integration with future consumer technologies. While older systems relied on audio and text-only systems, Common Alerting Protocol (CAP) and IPAWS-OPEN make picture and video feeds possible and allows for the seamless incorporation of emerging technologies.

Once the alert is received from the alerting authorities, IPAWS-OPEN authenticates the source and validates that the alert input conforms to the Common Alerting Protocol standard and IPAWS profile. This provides a standard for everyone across all levels of government as well as the private sector.

Emergency alerts will be delivered across multiple pathways to the American people. Alerts will be delivered by the Emergency Alert System, using AM, FM, and satellite radio as well as broadcast, cable, and satellite TV. The Commercial Mobile Alert System (CMAS) will send Wireless Emergency Alerts (WEA) to cell phones and other commercial mobile network devices based on their location, even if cellular networks are overloaded and can no longer support calls, text, and emails. Wireless Emergency Alerts will not track an individual's locations or personal data, as it uses SMS-CB, a broadcast (one-way) technology. This assures that authorities cannot collect any subscriber-related data, including details on who is in the targeted area, who has successfully received the emergency alert, or who may have opted out. State, local, territorial, and tribal alerting systems such as emergency telephone networks, giant voice sirens, and digital road signs may also receive alerts from IPAWS-OPEN and future alerting technologies and systems can be easily integrated into the IPAWS.

When disaster strikes, the IPAWS allows emergency managers and alerting authorities at all levels to send one message to more people over more devices, to save lives and protect property. No matter where you are: at home, at school, at work, or even on vacation, you can get life-saving alerts.

The advent of new media has brought a dramatic shift in the way the public consumes information. IPAWS, as the next generation emergency alert and warning system, capitalizes on multiple electronic media outlets to ensure that the public receives life-saving information during a time of national emergency.

than 40 percent of the populace during the work day. While less than 12 percent of the population is watching TV in the middle of the night, an even smaller number is tuned into the radio, at 5 percent of the populace. Television and radio will continue to be valuable sources of public information, but their reach is decreasing. Further, these information sources can only target a state or regional sized area and do not encompass alerting for people who do not speak English or those with disabilities, including the 29 million suffering from hearing impairment.

Today, the internet, including video and email, and cellular and residential phones are increasingly popular and therefore, valuable, sources of information. One study showed that the Internet has a 62 percent usage rate, averaging at 108 minutes a day. While television remains the most popular source for information, the Internet ranked either first or second at both work and home.

National Preparedness Directorate

The National Preparedness Directorate (NPD) provides the doctrine, programs, and resources to prepare the Nation to prevent, protect, mitigate, respond to and recover from disasters while minimizing the loss of lives, infrastructure, and property.

NPD carries out these responsibilities through the following NPD divisions:

- NPD Front Office
- Individual and Community Preparedness Division (ICPD)
- National Integration Center (NIC)
- National Training & Education (NTE)
- Center for Domestic Preparedness (CDP)
- Emergency Management Institute (EMI)
- National Training and Education Division (NTED)
- National Exercises Division (NED)
- National Preparedness Assessment Division (NPAD)

vestments, activities, and accomplishments as they relate to national preparedness. In addition to this mission, the directorate and division are driven also by legislative mandate, Presidential Policy Directive 8 (PPD-8) and The Post-Katrina Emergency Management Reform Act of 2006 (PKEMRA). NPAD accomplishes this mission through the following objectives:

- Assessing Whole Community preparedness—Qualitative and quantitative assessment of the 31 core capabilities in the National Preparedness Goal for the Whole Community—Federal, State, local, Tribal, and territorial governments, private sector, non-government organizations, faith-based and community-based organizations and the American public.

- Developing preparedness assessment and analytical policy—Analyzing the targets, accomplishments, and gaps within the 31 core capabilities of the National Preparedness Goal.

- Developing standardized methods of preparedness data collection and assessment—Standardizing collection methods include determining necessary data—both existing as well desired—including a list of data sources, a process to continually review and update this list, and the ability to identify gaps in data collection and the means to fill the gap. This process includes collaborating with stakeholders to develop data that is not currently collected. Standardized assessment methodology ensures analytic consistency across the various datasets and the 31 core capabilities.

- Developing and delivering national preparedness assessment-based reporting products—Drafting written and visual products that communicate National Preparedness to stakeholders throughout the Whole Community.

practices and innovative ideas in a secure environment. Sponsored and administered by FEMA's National Preparedness and Assessment Division (NPAD), *LLIS.gov* is designed as a "user-driven," interactive program that relies upon the whole community for generation and sharing of best practices and lessons learned.

Technological Hazards Division (THD)

FEMA established the Radiological Emergency Preparedness Program to:

- Ensure the health and safety of citizens living around commercial nuclear power plants would be adequately protected in the event of a nuclear power plant accident and
- Inform and educate the public about radiological emergency preparedness. REP Program responsibilities encompass only "offsite" activities, that is, state, tribal and local government emergency planning and preparedness activities that take place beyond the nuclear power plant boundaries. Onsite activities continue to be the responsibility of the NRC.
-

The Chemical Stockpile Emergency Preparedness Program (CSEPP) is a partnership between the FEMA and the U.S. Department of the Army that provides emergency preparedness assistance and resources to communities surrounding the Army's chemical warfare agent stockpiles. CSEPP's mission is to "enhance existing local, installation, tribal, state and federal capabilities to protect the health and safety of the public, work force and environment from the effects of a chemical accident or incident involving the U.S. Army chemical stockpile."

Radiological Emergency Preparedness Program (REPP)

On December 7, 1979, following the Three Mile Island nuclear power plant accident in Pennsylvania, President Carter transferred the federal lead role in offsite radiological emergency planning and preparedness activities from the

U.S. Nuclear Regulatory Commission to the Federal Emergency Management Agency (FEMA).

FEMA established the Radiological Emergency Preparedness Program to

Ensure the health and safety of citizens living around commercial nuclear power plants would be adequately protected in the event of a nuclear power plant accident; and

Inform and educate the public about radiological emergency preparedness.

REP Program responsibilities encompass only "offsite" activities, that is, state, tribal and local government emergency planning and preparedness activities that take place beyond the nuclear power plant boundaries. Onsite activities continue to be the responsibility of the NRC.

Chemical Stockpile Emergency Preparedness Program

The Chemical Stockpile Emergency Preparedness Program (CSEPP) is a partnership between the FEMA and the U.S. Department of the Army that provides emergency preparedness assistance and resources to communities surrounding the Army's chemical warfare agent stockpiles.

CSEPP's mission is to *"enhance existing local, installation, tribal, state and federal capabilities to protect the health and safety of the public, work force and environment from the effects of a chemical accident or incident involving the U.S. Army chemical stockpile."*

CSEPP's mission aligns with FEMA and Army goals by protecting people who live and work near the two remaining Army chemical depots in the unlikely event of a chemical accident or incident. The Army is fulfilling its mission to eliminate aging chemical munitions and warfare materials. This objective is in accordance with international treaties and national policy. CSEPP will remain in place until the stockpiles are completely destroyed.

Federal Radiological Preparedness Coordinating Committee

The FRPCC is a national-level forum for the development and coordination of radiological prevention and preparedness policies and procedures. It also provides policy guidance for federal radiological incident management

ties in support of state, tribal and local government radiological emergency planning and preparedness activities. The FRPCC is an interagency body consisting of the coordinating and cooperating agencies discussed in this Nuclear/Radiological Incident Annex (NRIA), chaired by DHS/FEMA.

3

The Transportation Security Administration

The Transportation Security Administration (TSA) protects the nation's transportation systems to ensure freedom of movement for people and commerce.

About TSA

Following September 11, 2001, the Transportation Security Administration (TSA) was created to strengthen the security of the nation's transportation systems and ensure the freedom of movement for people and commerce. Today, TSA secures the nation's airports and screens all commercial airline passengers and baggage. TSA uses a risk-based strategy and works closely with transportation, law enforcement and intelligence communities to set the standard for excellence in transportation security.

Mission, Vision and Core Values

TSA has established guiding principles to maintain the security of the traveling public and continuously set the standard for excellence in transportation security.

Mission

Protect the Nation's transportation systems to ensure freedom of movement for people and commerce.

Vision

Provide the most effective transportation security in the most efficient way as a high performing counterterrorism organization.

Core Values

To enhance mission performance and achieve our shared goals, TSA is committed to promoting a culture founded on these values:

Integrity

- Respect and care for others and protect the information we handle.
- Conduct ourselves in an honest, trustworthy and ethical manner at all times.
- Gain strength from the diversity in our cultures.

Innovation

- Embrace and stand ready for change.
- Courageous and willing to take on new challenges.
- Have an enterprising spirit, striving for innovation and accepting the risk-taking that comes with it.

Team Spirit

- Open, respectful and dedicated to making others better.
- Have a passion for challenge, success and being on a winning team.
- Build teams around our strengths.
- Hard work, professionalism and integrity in everything we do.

TSA—At a Glance

- Responsible for the security of nearly 450 federalized airports
- 50,000 transportation security officers keep people secure
- Nearly 700 aviation transportation security inspectors ensure regulatory compliance
- More than 50 percent of TSA officers have five years or more experience as counterterrorism professionals
- More than 20 percent of TSA employees are veterans or still proudly serving
- TSA screens nearly 2 million passengers daily and 660 million every year
- TSA screens 1.1 million checked bags for explosives and other dangerous items daily
- TSA screens 3 million carry-on bags for explosives and other prohibited items every day.
- Responsible for the security of 25,000 domestic flights per day
- Responsible for the security of 2,500 outbound international flights per day
- There are more than 700 advanced imaging technology machines with privacy protecting software at airports nationwide
- In 2014, officers detected approximately 2,212 firearms at airport checkpoints, averaging six firearms per day
- More than 900 improvised explosive device drills are conducted every day at airport checkpoints

TSA risk-based security is based on the understanding that the vast majority of people traveling pose little to no threat to aviation and applies an intelligence-driven approach focusing on higher-risk and unknown passengers. Through risk-based security:

- Approximately 5 million passengers each week experience expedited screening
- TSA Pre-screening is operating at 125 airports

- There are more than 300 TSA Pre-screening application centers open nationwide.

Layers of Security

TSA uses layers of security to ensure the security of the traveling public and the Nation's transportation system. Because of their visibility to the public, TSA is most associated with the airport checkpoints that Transportation Security Officers operate. These checkpoints, however, constitute only one security layer of the many in place to protect aviation. Others include intelligence gathering and analysis, checking passenger manifests against watch lists, random canine team searches at airports, federal air marshals, federal flight deck officers and more security measures both visible and invisible to the public.

Each one of these layers alone is capable of stopping a terrorist attack. In combination their security value is multiplied, creating a much stronger, formidable system. A terrorist who has to overcome multiple security layers in order to carry out an attack is more likely to be pre-empted, deterred, or to fail during the attempt.

Innovation and Technology

TSA understands that threats to aviation security continue to evolve. They are more sophisticated and more complex than ever before. TSA uses every tool at its disposal to address those threats and develop methods of combating them. The use of new and innovative technology helps TSA stay ahead of those intent on harming our nation.

TSA is constantly moving forward its technology usage, staying ahead of emerging threats. It knows there's no silver bullet technology, no cure all, no end-all-be-all; but when used by TSA's highly trained workforce and combined with the other layers of security, technology helps close down vulnerabilities.

ploy its technology resources at airports, in subways, at ports and on rail. Daily vetting of passengers and airport employees against watch lists allows it to protect the airports. And biometrics helps it prevent unauthorized access at our nations' ports.

The suite of technology has grown considerably in the years since TSA took over airport security. Everyone remembers the walk through metal detector, which still serves an important function at the checkpoint. You may notice some new and unfamiliar machines at your local airports.

Credential Authentication Technology: Automatically authenticates identity documents that are presented to TSA by passengers during the security checkpoint screening process. The Credential Authentication Technology (CAT) automatically authenticates identity documents that are presented to TSA by passengers during the security checkpoint screening process. In late 2013, TSA issued a Request for Information (RFI) to conduct market research to better understand capabilities available in industry for CAT. TSA anticipates that the new technology will enhance security and increase efficiency by automatically verifying passenger identification and obtaining the passenger's vetting status.

Paperless Boarding Pass: TSA and the airlines have expanded the use of paperless boarding passes at airports nationwide. The paperless boarding pass pilot enables passengers to download their boarding pass on their cell phones or personal digital assistants (PDAs). This innovative approach streamlines the customer experience while heightening the ability to detect fraudulent boarding passes. Each paperless boarding pass is displayed as an encrypted two-dimensional bar code along with passenger and flight information. TSA security officers use scanners to validate the authenticity of the boarding pass at the checkpoint. At the checkpoint, a TSA travel document checking officer will instruct the passenger on how to scan their cell phone or PDA so that TSA can verify the authenticity of the boarding pass. Passengers will still be required to show photo identification so officers can validate that the name on the boarding pass matches the name on the ID.

Biometrics: Raising the bar on security through biometric technology. Retinal scans. Fingerprint identification. A few years ago these things seemed like something out of a science fiction movie. Today, they are becoming an important parts of our risk-based approach to security. Biometric

tion allows TSA to verify a person is who they say they are by using their own unique set of identifiers—fingerprints, iris scans or a combination of the two. TSA continues to test this technology at airports and harbors across the country, allowing it to control access to important facilities.

Bottled Liquids Scanners: Flexible technology used to screen accessible property, Bottled liquids scanner (BLS) screening systems are used across the nation by Transportation Security Officers to detect potential liquid or gel threats which may be contained in a passenger's property. The technology differentiates liquid explosives from common, benign liquids and is used primarily to screen medically necessary liquids in quantities larger than 3.4 ounces. BLS units use a variety of technologies including lasers, infrared, and electromagnetic resonance. Current units may be used to screen clear and tinted glass and plastic bottles.

Following the disruption of the UK/US airline bombing plot in August 2006, TSA issued new rules that, with a few exceptions, effectively banned liquids, gels, and aerosols on aircraft. After conducting extensive research, TSA determined small amounts of liquids are not a threat. On September 26, 2006, TSA permitted small amounts of liquids, gels and aerosols in travel size containers, and exempted baby formula/milk/juices, medicines, and other medically-required liquids.

Explosives Detection System: Technology that can be used to screen checked or carryon baggage. Ever wonder what happens to your bag once you check it with your airline? TSA screens every bag placed on an airplane, whether taken as carry-on or checked with an airline. With nearly 2 million people flying each day, it's a Herculean task. TSA is able to meet this requirement by using Explosive Detection System (EDS) machines, which work like the CT machines in a doctor's office. Through a sophisticated analysis of each checked bag, the EDS machines can quickly capture an image of a single bag and determine if a bag contains a potential threat item. If a bag requires additional screening, it may be automatically diverted to a resolution room where security officers will quickly inspect it to ensure it doesn't contain a threat item. Once cleared, the bag is reintroduced to the system, where it continues onto the aircraft. In some cases, the alarm is quickly resolved and in others law enforcement and/or the bomb squad may be called in. When used in conjunction with an airport's automated inline baggage handling system, it

tion with an airport's automated inline baggage handling system, it achieves dramatic improvements in both security and efficiency.

Explosives Trace Detection: This technology tests for traces of explosives. Explosives Trace Detection (ETD) is technology used at security checkpoints around the country to screen baggage and passengers for traces of explosives. Officers may swab a piece of carry-on or checked baggage or a passenger's hands and then place the swab inside the ETD unit to analyze it for the presence of potential explosive residue. In 2010, TSA expanded its use of ETD technology in airports as part of its layered approach to aviation security and to keep passengers safe.

Passengers may experience screening of their hands using an ETD swab at the security checkpoint, in the checkpoint queue, or boarding areas. To ensure the health of travelers, screening swabs are disposed of after each use. Since ETD technology is used on a random basis, passengers should not expect to see the same thing at every airport or each time they travel.

Threat Image Projection: In addition to classroom training, TSA uses on-the-job training to keep its security officers' skills sharp. Through the daily use of Threat Image Projection (TIP) software program, security officers are routinely tested on their ability to detect weapons and explosives by X-ray. Potential threats, including guns and explosives, are projected onto X-ray images of carry-on bags so the security officers remain focused and attentive. These tests allow TSA to evaluate individual performance and shape training programs appropriately. Because X-ray equipment is linked to a vast internal network, every airport and X-ray monitor receives automatic image updates from the technology lab. This link allows TSA to quickly upgrade technology using the latest intelligence on potential and emerging threats and convey it to security officers across the nation.

Imaging Technology: More than 740 Advanced Imaging Technology units deployed at almost 160 airports nationwide. Advanced imaging technology safely screens passengers for metallic and nonmetallic threats, including weapons and explosives, which may be concealed under clothing without physical contact to help TSA keep the traveling public safe.

Office of Global Strategies

The mission of OGS is to develop and promote the implementation of effective global transportation security worldwide while ensuring compliance with international and TSA standards.

Mission areas include:

Outreach/Engagement: OGS conducts extensive outreach and engagement at the global, regional, and bilateral levels to raise awareness about the continued high threat to the aviation sector to advance the implementation of mitigation measures with foreign partners and through international organizations to counter these new and emerging threats as they arise.

Capacity Development: OGS works to effectively address the needs of foreign partner nations to build sustainable aviation security practices through capacity development. An important part of this effort is aviation security training and technical assistance, which TSA provides based on risk analysis and in response to needs identified by a number of entities, among them the Departments of Homeland Security, State, and Transportation, as well as the civil aviation authorities of foreign governments.

Compliance: OGS conducts security assessments of international airports from which foreign airlines fly directly to the United States, those served by U.S. air carriers, those that pose a high risk to international air travel, and others as determined by the Secretary of Homeland Security. OGS International Transportation Security Specialists visit over 300 airports at one-to three-year intervals; frequency is based on risk computations of current threat, documented vulnerabilities, and flight data. Additionally, OGS inspects all U.S. carriers and foreign carriers servicing the United States on an annual basis to ensure compliance with TSA security standards.

OGS Operational Elements:

International Operations: Responsible for reducing risk by conducting outreach and engagement with international government counterparts, with an emphasis on best practices to raise the level of transportation security. Also TSA's focal point for industry outreach and engagement to foreign air carriers and U.S. flag carriers operating outside the United States, and for receiving and coordinating the sharing of aviation security-related requirements, intelligence, and/or threat information affecting passengers, air carriers, and the overall security of the U.S. and global aviation systems.

Global Compliance: Responsible for identifying and documenting vulnerabilities in the global transportation system through foreign airport assessments and air carrier inspections. The Cargo Branch is responsible for developing and promoting a secure and resilient supply chain that facilitates commerce through a risk-based framework.

Integrated Plans and Support: Responsible for analyzing risk to target vulnerabilities in the international transportation network and mitigating these risks by providing capacity development, in the form of aviation security training and technical assistance, as well as through management and expansion of the Preclearance Program. Also supports the OGS mission through the development of incident management protocols, IT enterprise data management, and workforce development.

Law Enforcement

Office of Law Enforcement/Federal Air Marshall Service

The mission of the Office of Law Enforcement/Federal Air Marshal Service is to promote public confidence in the security of our nation's transportation domain.

To achieve this mission, OLE/FAMS deploys federal air marshals on U.S. aircraft world-wide; conducts protection, response, detection and assessment activities in airports and other transportation systems; maintains TSA's state of preparedness and coordinates incident management; trains and manages armed pilots; and trains TSA canine assets.

Federal air marshals serve as the primary law enforcement entity within TSA. We deploy on flights around the world and in the U.S. While our primary mission of protecting air passengers and crew has not changed much over the years, federal air marshals have an ever expanding role in homeland security and work closely with other law enforcement agencies to accomplish their mission. The men and women who make up the Federal Air Marshal

Service are dedicated, well trained law enforcement professionals, each equipped with the knowledge, skills and abilities necessary to keep our aviation system safe and secure.

Programs

Federal Air Marshals. The Federal Air Marshal Service promotes confidence in the nation's civil aviation system through the effective deployment of Federal Air Marshals (FAMs) to detect, deter, and defeat hostile acts targeting U.S. air carriers, airports, passengers, and crews.

Federal Air Marshals must operate independently without backup, and rank among those Federal law enforcement officers that hold the highest standard for handgun accuracy. They blend in with passengers and rely on their training, including investigative techniques, criminal terrorist behavior recognition, firearms proficiency, aircraft specific tactics, and close quarters self-defense measures to protect the flying public.

Federal Air Marshals have an ever expanding role in homeland security and work closely with other law enforcement agencies to accomplish their mission. Federal Air Marshals are assigned as Assistant Federal Security Directors for Law Enforcement at many airports nationwide to provide law enforcement coordination with airport stakeholders and other TSA components. Currently, air marshals are also staff several positions at different organizations such as the National Counterterrorism Center, the National Targeting Center, and on the FBI's Joint Terrorism Task Forces. In addition, they are distributed among other law enforcement and homeland security liaison assignments during times of heightened alert or special national events.

Successful accomplishment of the Federal Air Marshal's mission is critical to civil aviation and homeland security.

Visible Intermodal Prevention and Response (VIPR). VIPR operations promote confidence in and protect the nation's transportation systems through targeted deployment of integrated TSA assets utilizing screening and law enforcement capabilities in coordinated activities to augment security of any mode of transportation. The objective is the deterrence and prevention of terrorism.

Under the *Aviation and Transportation Security Act* (ATSA) and the *Implementing Recommendations of the 9/11 Commission Act of 2007*, TSA has broad responsibility to enhance security in all modes of transportation nationwide. TSA's Visible Intermodal Prevention and Response (VIPR) program is part of a nationwide transportation security program that serves all modes of transportation.

Following the Madrid train bombing in 2004, TSA developed the VIPR program to allow TSA security and law enforcement assets to augment federal, state, and local law enforcement and security agencies in the transportation domain.

TSA's VIPR teams provide a full range of law enforcement and security capability; the exact makeup of VIPR teams is determined jointly with local authorities and can include Federal Air Marshals(FAMs), Transportation Security Officers (TSOs), Behavior Detection Officers (BDOs), TSA certified explosive detection canine teams, Transportation Security Inspectors (TSIs), Transportation Security Specialists—Explosives (TSSEs), explosives operational support, security and explosive screening technology, radiological/nuclear detection, and local law enforcement officers.

TSA VIPR teams can be deployed at random locations and times in cooperation with local authorities to deter and defeat terrorist activity; or teams may be deployed to provide additional law enforcement or security presence at transportation venues during specific alert periods or in support of special events. TSA routinely conducts thousands of VIPR operations each year in transportation systems nationwide.

Experience shows that regional planning and implementation provide the greatest security impact by aligning the frequency of deployments with terrorist risk reduction benefits for specific locations. VIPR teams work with local security and law enforcement officials to augment existing security resources; provide a deterrent presence and detection capabilities; and introduce an element of unpredictability to disrupt potential terrorist planning or operational activities.

Overview

TSA VIPR teams are specifically authorized by the Implementing Recommendations of the 9/11 Commission Act of 2007 to "augment the

any mode of transportation at any location within the United States." In order to fulfill this mission, TSA creates relationships with our various stakeholders and coordinates joint operations, promoting communication and teamwork throughout all levels of government to ensure the safety of the traveling public and the transportation systems.

The VIPR program applies a risk-based approach to work nationwide with transportation and law enforcement stakeholders to plan and conduct VIPR operations. The capabilities of TSA personnel are applied at transportation locations to mitigate vulnerabilities of those locations to terrorist activities.

VIPR teams provide additional detection and response capabilities, and expand the unpredictability of security measures to deter and disrupt potential terrorist activity.

What is important to remember: In the wake of the tragic events of 9/11, federal, state, and local governmental agencies have been committed to developing partnerships and increasing interagency communications to ensure the safety of our Nation's transportation systems. TSA's VIPR program provides the mechanism through which our law enforcement and security stakeholders can establish solid working relationships to protect you today, as well as in the event of a catastrophic event.

Crew Member Self Defense Training Program

Administered by the TSA Office of Law Enforcement / Federal Air Marshal Service (OLE/FAMS), the Crew Member Self Defense Training (CMSDT) program is available to all actively employed or temporarily furloughed U.S. passenger and cargo crew members. The program, which is available at 22 sites nationwide, is delivered at TSA facilities across the nation. Crew members are encouraged to register to attend this 4-hour "hands-on" training developed by the OLE/FAMS to help prepare crew members to face potential threat situations—both on and off the aircraft. CMSDT is provided at no cost to crew members who are welcome to attend the training as often as desired.

Law Enforcement Officers Flying Armed

The Office of Law Enforcement/Federal Air Marshal Service maintains oversight of the Law Enforcement Officers flying armed program under Title

49 Code of Federal Regulation (CFR) § 1544.219 Carriage of Accessible Weapons. To qualify to fly armed, Federal Regulation states that an officer must meet the following basic requirements:

- Be a Federal Law Enforcement Officer (LEO) or a full-time municipal, county, or state LEO who is a direct employee of a government agency.
- Be sworn and commissioned to enforce criminal statutes or immigration statutes.
- Be authorized by the employing agency to have the weapon in connection with assigned duties.
- Have completed the training program, "Law Enforcement Officers Flying Armed."

In addition to the above requirements, the officer must need to have the weapon accessible from the time he or she would otherwise check the weapon until the time it would be claimed after deplaning. The need to have the weapon accessible must be determined by the employing agency, department, or service and be based on one of the following:

- The provision of protective duty, for instance, assigned to a principal or advance team, or on travel required to be prepared to engage in a protective function.
- The conduct of a hazardous surveillance operation.
- On official travel required to report to another location, armed and prepared for duty.
- Employed as a Federal LEO, whether or not on official travel, and armed in accordance with an agency-wide policy governing that type of travel established by the employing agency by directive or policy statement.
- Control of a prisoner, in accordance with Title 49 CFR § 1544.221, or an armed LEO on a round trip ticket returning from escorting, or traveling to pick up a prisoner.
- Examples of positions or travel that have been determined to NOT meet the threshold for carriage of accessible weapons are:
- Retired, Contract, Reserve, Auxiliary or Annuitant LEOs
- LEOs who do not have general arrest authority and are limited expressly to governmental facilities.

- Any LEO who is employed by a department, agency, or service that is not fully taxpayer funded. (e.g. part of all paid by private or public corporation)
- Attendance of non-operational or enforcement related activities (e.g. Police Week, Memorial Services, training, conferences, etc.)

State, Local, Territorial, Tribal, and approved Railroad LEOs flying armed must submit a National Law Enforcement Telecommunications System (NLETS) message prior to travel. The NLETS message replaces the Original Letter of Authority, commonly referred to as the "Chief's Letter." Failure to use the NLETS message will result in denial to the sterile area for failure to comply with the "Letter of Authority." More information on this procedure is contained in the training program.

The Law Enforcement Officers Flying Armed training is a 1.5 to 2 hour block of instruction that is comprised of a structured lesson plan, slide presentation, FAQs, NLETS procedures, and applicable codes of federal regulation. This material is provided to Federal, State, Local, Territorial, Tribal, and approved Railroad Law Enforcement agencies and departments to properly instruct their officers on the subject of flying on board commercial aircraft while armed. The training includes protocols in the handling of prohibited items, prisoner transport, and dealing with an act of criminal violence aboard an aircraft.

IdeaFactory

The TSA IdeaFactory is an innovative tool that has provided a venue for more than 130 ideas to be implemented that have saved money, improved security and training, and enhanced employee morale. Through an open site, employees post ideas related to program-specific categories, participate in agency-wide challenges, and provide feedback on specific topics chosen by senior leadership sponsors. The site now has over 800 official responses from senior leaders and program offices.

The IdeaFactory is a Web-based tool that empowers all TSA employees to:
- Submit ideas.
- Provide comments on how to improve new concepts.

- Rate ideas that should be recommended for implementation.

Ensuring that the workforce is involved in operational decision-making has changed the way TSA does business. The program was launched to address three key requirements:

To engage employees and ensure that every member of its large workforce at more than 450 airports and other locations could communicate with headquarters.

To collect constant, fresh input and perspectives on improvements to keep the agency flexible and effectively mitigate security threats.

To disseminate information about new and existing programs, initiatives and policies to front-line employees and provide a forum for communication between employees.

April 25, 2014 marked the IdeaFactory's 7th anniversary. The IdeaFactory works extremely hard to keep the program relevant to its users and external counterparts across government. Throughout the years the IdeaFactory has shared information with over 50 government agencies that want to mirror its innovative success. IdeaFactory's vision is to support TSA's mission by fostering a community that engages employees and encourages collaboration to initiative innovation. The strategic plan also identified three key goals:

- Support innovation as a TSA core value.
- Continue to improve the efficiency and effectiveness of the innovation process.
- Expand and evolve IdeaFactory outreach, collaboration and communication.

After the initial launch period, the IdeaFactory team enhanced functionality, reengineered the evaluation process and completely redesigned the site to increase community building efforts and make the site more user-friendly. Also, the IdeaFactory team developed a communications strategy to meet the needs of the TSA field employees.

The IdeaFactory Users

Before the launch of TSA's IdeaFactory, and during the course of two years of operation, the IdeaFactory team evaluated and reevaluated the culture of

TSA and the needs of its workforce, including conducting audience assessments, need assessments and adjusting for volume of site usage as a percentage of the entire workforce. The IdeaFactory team conducts regular user surveys and focus groups of core users to analyze IdeaFactory users and obtain further data about usage by geographic location.

The TSA workforce is comprised of about 60,000+ employees at over 450 airports and other locations. Approximately 85 percent of TSA's workforce is stationed at non-headquarters, field locations. These employees:

- Perform their job duties without regular access to a TSA computer and seldom check email.
- Have limited time to access TSA "extras," such as IdeaFactory, the TSA blog and other message vehicles.
- Are oversaturated with messages, which generally aren't targeted to address specific peer groups.

On average, TSA receives 300 ideas each month and each idea receives 10 comments and 25 votes on average.

TSA IdeaFactory gets more than 12,000 unique page views from employees every month, and about 5,000 every week. To date over 10,000 submissions have been posted to the site.

Grants

DHS provides security grants to mass transit and passenger rail systems, intercity bus companies, freight railroad carriers, ferries and the trucking industry to help protect the public and nation's critical transportation infrastructure against acts of terrorism and other large-scale events. The grants support high-impact security projects that have a high efficacy in reducing the most risk to our nation's transportation systems.

Transit Security Grant Program 2015

The Transit Security Grant Program (TSGP) is one of the grant programs that directly support transportation infrastructure security activities. TSGP is one tool in the comprehensive set of measures authorized by Congress and implemented by the Administration to strengthen the Nation's critical infrastructure against risks associated with potential terrorist attacks. TSGP provides funds to owners and operators of transit systems (which include intra-city bus, commuter bus, ferries, and all forms of passenger rail) to protect critical surface transportation infrastructure and the traveling public from acts of terrorism and to increase the resilience of transit infrastructure.

Transportation Worker Identification Credential (TWIC®)

A vital security measure that ensures individuals who pose a threat do not gain unescorted access to secure areas of the nation's maritime transportation system.

Working with Stakeholders

Intermodal Transportation Systems

TSA's Office of Security Policy and Industry Engagement leads the unified national effort to protect and secure our nation's intermodal transportation systems. It ensures the safe movement of passengers and promote the free flow of commerce by building a resilient, robust, and sustainable network with the public and private sector partners.

Transportation Systems Sector-Specific Plan

The Transportation Systems Sector—a sector that comprises all modes of transportation (Aviation, Maritime, Mass Transit, Highway, Freight Rail, and Pipeline)—is a vast, open, interdependent networked system that moves lions of passengers and millions of tons of goods. The transportation network is critical to the Nation's way of life and economic vitality.

Ensuring its security is the mission charged to all sector partners, including government (Federal, State, regional, local, and tribal) and private industry stakeholders. Every day, the transportation network connects cities, manufacturers, and retailers, moving large volumes of goods and individuals through a complex network of approximately 4 million miles of roadways, more than 140,000 miles of active rail, 600,000 bridges and tunnels, more than 350 maritime ports, hundreds of thousands of pipeline, nearly 30 million trips using mass transit and passenger rail, and more than 450 U.S. commercial airports.

The Office of Security Policy and Industry Engagement has developed and is in the process of executing, a strategy to ensure effective, efficient, and standardized operations within and among transportation modes. In short, the strategy calls for:

- Completion of industry threat, vulnerability, and consequence assessment
- Development of baseline security standards
- Assessment of operator security status versus existing standards
- Development of plan to close gaps in security standards
- Enhancement of systems of security

Related Statistics:

- 3.9 million miles of public roads
- 1.2 million trucking companies operating 15.5 million trucks including 42,000 HAZMAT trucks
- 10 million licensed commercial vehicle drivers including 2.7 million HAZMAT drivers
- 2.2 million miles of hazardous liquid and natural gas pipeline
- 120,000 miles of major railroads
- Nearly 15 million daily riders on mass transit and passenger rail systems nationwide
- 25,000 miles of commercial waterways

- 9.0 million containers through 51,000 port calls
- 11.2 million containers via Canada and Mexico
- 19,576 general aviation airports, heliports, and landing strips
- 459 Federalized commercial airports
- 211, 450 general aviation aircraft
- General aviation flights represents approximately 77% of all flights in the US

Aviation Security Advisory Committee

Its mission is to examine areas of civil aviation security with the aim of developing recommendations for the improvement of civil aviation security methods, equipment, and procedures.

Screening Partnership Program

The Aviation Transportation Security Act (ATSA) of 2001 required TSA to conduct a pilot program with up to five airports where screening would be performed by private contractors under federal oversight. At the conclusion of the pilot in 2004, TSA created the Screening Partnership Program (SPP). Currently, 21 airports have been awarded a contract and are participating in the program. Airport directors may submit their application to participate in SPP to TSA at any time. Private contract companies must adhere to TSA's security standards and contract screeners must meet ATSA requirements applicable to federally employed screeners.

Secure Flight Program

Secure Flight is a behind-the-scenes program that enhances the security of domestic and international commercial air travel through the use of improved watch list matching. Collecting additional passenger data improves the travel experience for all airline passengers, including those who have been misidentified in the past. When passengers travel, they are required to provide

tified in the past. When passengers travel, they are required to provide the following Secure Flight Passenger Data (SFPD) to the airline:

- Name (as it appears on government-issued ID the passenger plans to use when traveling)
- Date of Birth
- Gender
- Redress Number (if applicable
- Known Traveler Number (if applicable)

The airline submits this information to Secure Flight, which uses it to perform watch list matching. This serves to prevent individuals on the No Fly List from boarding an aircraft and to identify individuals on the Selectee List for enhanced screening. After matching passenger information against government watch lists, Secure Flight transmits the matching results back to airlines so they can issue passenger boarding passes.

Program Background

Prior to the implementation of Secure Flight, airlines were responsible for matching passenger information against the watch lists. Secure Flight is a program developed by the Department of Homeland Security (DHS) in response to a key 9/11 Commission recommendation: uniform watch list matching by the Transportation Security Administration (TSA). The mission of the Secure Flight program is to strengthen the security of commercial air travel into, out of, within, and over the United States through the use of improved and expanded watch list matching using risk-based security measures.

By transferring these watch list matching responsibilities from the airlines to TSA, Secure Flight:

- Decreases the chance for compromised watch list data by limiting its distribution
- Provides earlier identification of potential matches, allowing for expedited notification of law enforcement and threat management
- Provides a fair, equitable, and consistent matching process across all airlines

- Offers consistent application of an integrated redress process for misidentified individuals through the Department of Homeland Security's Travel Redress Inquiry Program (DHS TRIP)

As of November 2010, Secure Flight conducts uniform prescreening of passenger information against federal government watch lists for all covered U.S. and foreign flights into, out of, and within the United States—fulfilling a key 9/11 Commission recommendation a month ahead of schedule. This also includes point-to-point international flights operated by U.S. airlines. Secure Flight also performs watch list matching for flights that overfly, but do not land in, the continental United States (i.e., lower 48 contiguous states, excluding Alaska and Hawaii).

The program's goals are to:

- Support TSA's Risk-Based Security (RBS) mission by identifying high-risk passengers for appropriate security measures/actions and identifying low-risk passengers for expedited screening
- Prevent individuals on the No Fly List from boarding an aircraft
- Identify individuals on the Selectee List for enhanced screening
- Minimize misidentification of individuals as potential threats to aviation security
- Incorporate additional risk-based security capabilities to streamline processes and accommodate additional aviation populations
- Protect passengers' personal information from unauthorized use and disclosure

How It Works

Under the Secure Flight program, passengers making a reservation are required to provide their full name (as it appears on the government-issued identification they plan to use when traveling), date of birth, and gender.

TSA matches this information against government watch lists.   After matching passenger information against government watch lists, Secure Flight transmits the matching results back to airlines so they may issue passenger boarding passes.

Privacy

Ensuring the privacy of individuals is a cornerstone of Secure Flight. TSA developed a comprehensive privacy plan to incorporate privacy laws and practices into all areas of Secure Flight. The program worked extensively to maximize individual privacy. In addition to assuring compliance and reinforcing its commitment to protecting privacy, Secure Flight created an environment dedicated to guaranteeing its privacy mission that is front and center every day.

The Secure Flight Privacy Program includes:

- Foundational Privacy Principles: Tenets that underpin and guide all Secure Flight behaviors, requirements, systems, and processes
- Privacy Organization: Dedicated Privacy Officer and privacy staff, processes, and procedures responsible for privacy compliance, for assessing Secure Flight privacy risks, and for developing and implementing plans to effectively manage those risks
- Privacy Policy: Secure Flight privacy policies, procedures, standards, and rules of behavior as well as ways to adhere to them
- Systems Development and Security: Administrative, physical, and technical safeguards that manage privacy risks throughout the lifecycle of the Secure Flight system
- Awareness and Training: Programs to make the Secure Flight organization and its stakeholders, including the traveling public and the airlines, aware of Secure Flight's privacy posture and practices
- Monitoring and Compliance: Programs to monitor adherence to statutory and regulatory privacy requirements and Secure Flight's privacy principles, policies, procedures, standards and rules of behavior
- Redress and Response: Systems and processes to respond, if needed, to privacy inquiries, issues, and incidents
- Privacy Risk Management: Tools and techniques to support Secure Flight privacy risk management

Personal Information

TSA collects the minimum amount of personal information necessary to conduct effective watch list matching. Furthermore, personal data is collected, used, distributed, stored, and disposed of according to stringent guidelines and all applicable privacy laws and regulations. Secure Flight published a Privacy Impact Assessment (PIA) in conjunction with the Secure Flight Final Rule and published a System of Records Notice (SORN) in the Federal Register to provide detailed information about the program's privacy approach. TSA does not collect or use commercial data to conduct Secure Flight watch list matching.

Sensitive Security Information (SSI)

TSA is committed to securing America's transportation systems by safely sharing Sensitive Security Information (SSI). SSI is information obtained or developed which, if released publicly, would be detrimental to transportation security. It strives to balance this information sharing by keeping its programs transparent to the American public while protecting information that could be used to endanger lives.

In response to increasing threats against aviation security, including hijackings in the 1960's and 1970's, Congress created the *Air Transportation Act of 1974* which clarified that the airlines and airports would be responsible for aviation security. The Federal Aviation Administration's (FAA) role was to approve the security plans provided by airlines and airports. Congress also mandated that FAA create SSI to protect the information in these security plans as well as other information related to aviation security. In 1976, FAA published the first SSI Federal regulation. Since then, FAA and later TSA, has updated the regulation as the mandates of these agencies have changed over time. The current SSI regulation lists sixteen categories of information that are considered SSI including security plans, specifications for screening equipment, threat information, and details regarding security screening information.

Certain sensitive transportation security information needs to be shared with transportation partners, which are for the most part private companies

cess to sensitive security information to properly perform their transportation security-related tasks.

If certain information was protected as "classified" information, for example, sharing of this information with private stakeholders would be very difficult. For example, "classified" information may only be shared with persons with a security clearance and there are many persons in the transportation industry who do not have a clearance. Thus, a new category of sensitive but unclassified information was created (SSI) so that the information could be both safely shared and protected as appropriate.

Sensitive Security Information (SSI) is a specific category of sensitive but unclassified (SBU) information that is governed by Federal law. SSI is information obtained or developed which, if released publicly, would be detrimental to transportation security. At TSA, the goal is to release as much information as possible publicly without compromising security.

SSI is not classified national security information and is not subject to the handling requirements governing such information, but is subject to the handling procedures required by the SSI Federal Regulation (49 CFR Part 1520). Unauthorized disclosure of SSI may result in civil penalties and other enforcement or corrective actions.

In order for information to be SSI it must be related to transportation security, the release of the information must be detrimental to transportation security, and it must fall under one of the sixteen categories of SSI. If the information does not meet all three criteria, then the information may not be protected as SSI.

The SSI regulation requires that only "covered persons with a need to know" may have access to SSI. Generally, covered persons have a need to know SSI when access to the information is necessary for the performance of their official duties. The SSI Federal regulation provides a list of covered persons.

Unless you are a covered person with a need to know, you will not be granted access to SSI. A covered person may be required to sign a non-disclosure agreement before gaining access to SSI.

SSI is information that would be detrimental to transportation security if publicly known. Therefore, the regulation specifically states that SSI is shared only with covered persons who have a need to know.

The marking of "Sensitive Security Information" at the top of a document indicates that the document contains SSI. The document must also include the SSI footer which states:

WARNING: This record contains Sensitive Security Information that is controlled under 49 CFR parts 15 and 1520. No part of this record may be disclosed to persons without a "need to know," as defined in 49 CFR parts 15 and 1520, except with the written permission of the Administrator of the Transportation Security Administration or the Secretary of Transportation. Unauthorized release may result in civil penalty or other action. For U.S. government agencies, public disclosure is governed by 5 U.S.C. 552 and 49 CFR parts 15 and 1520.

4

United States Citizenship and Immigration Services

The U.S. Citizenship and Immigration Services (USCIS) is the government agency that oversees lawful immigration to the United States. It secures America's promise as a nation of immigrants by providing accurate and useful information to its customers, granting immigration and citizenship benefits, promoting an awareness and understanding of citizenship, and ensuring the integrity of the U.S. immigration system.

USCIS has 19,000 government employees and contractors working at 223 offices across the world. Achieving its goals becomes possible when the different elements of the organization are engaged and acting as partners working toward a common outcome. Its strategic goals include:

• Strengthening the security and integrity of the immigration system.
• Providing effective customer-oriented immigration benefit and information services.
• Supporting immigrants' integration and participation in American civic culture.
• Promoting flexible and sound immigration policies and programs.
• Strengthening the infrastructure supporting the USCIS mission.
• Operating as a high-performance organization that promotes a highly talented workforce and a dynamic work culture.

Core Values

Integrity

We shall always strive for the highest level of integrity in our dealings with our customers, our fellow employees and the citizens of the United States of America. We shall be ever mindful of the importance of the trust the American people have placed in us to administer the nation's immigration system fairly, honestly and correctly.

Respect

We will demonstrate respect in all of our actions. We will ensure that everyone we affect will be treated with dignity and courtesy regardless of the outcome of the decision. We will model this principle in all of our activities, with each other, our customers and the public. Through our actions, this organization will become known as an example of respect, dignity and courtesy.

Ingenuity

As we meet the challenges to come, we will strive to find the most effective means to accomplish our goals. We will use ingenuity, resourcefulness, creativity and sound management principles to strive for world-class results. We will approach every challenge with a balance of enthusiasm and wisdom in our effort to fulfill our vision.

Vigilance

In this era of increased global threats and national security challenges, we will remain mindful of our obligation to provide immigration service in a manner that strengthens and fortifies the nation. We will exercise a holistic approach to Vigilance as we perform our mission. We will carefully administer every aspect of our immigration mission so that new immigrants and citizens can hold in high regard the privileges and advantages of lawful presence in the United States.

History

On March 1, 2003, U.S. Citizenship and Immigration Services (USCIS) officially assumed responsibility for the immigration service functions of the federal government. The Homeland Security Act of 2002 (Pub. L. No. 107–296, 116 Stat. 2135) dismantled the former Immigration and Naturalization Service (INS) and separated the former agency into three components within the Department of Homeland Security (DHS).

USCIS was formed to enhance the security and improve the efficiency of national immigration services by exclusively focusing on the administration of benefit applications. Immigration and Customs Enforcement (ICE) and Customs and Border Protection (CBP), components within DHS, handle immigration enforcement and border security functions.

It benefited from a legacy of more than 100 years of federal immigration and naturalization administration.

- **1891.** Office of Superintendent of Immigration created and placed in the Treasury Department
- **1895.** Office of Superintendent of Immigration upgraded to Bureau of Immigration
- **1903.** Bureau of Immigration transferred to the newly created Department of Commerce and Labor
- **1906.** Naturalization Service created and Bureau of Immigration became the Bureau of Immigration and Naturalization
- **1913.** Bureau of Immigration and Naturalization divided into separate Bureaus—the Bureau of Immigration and the Bureau of Naturalization—and placed in the new Department of Labor
- **1924.** U.S. Border Patrol created within the Bureau of Immigration
- **1933.** The Bureau of Immigration and the Bureau of Naturalization reunited into a single agency, the INS
- **1940.** The INS transferred from the Department of Labor to the Department of Justice

- **2003.** The INS was abolished and its functions placed under three agencies—USCIS, ICE and CBP—within the newly created DHS

USCIS is divided into directorates and program offices. Directorates are director led departments in charge of multiple divisions i.e. the Refugee, Asylum, and International Operations Directorate.

Programs Offices have a specific function and are led by a chief i.e. the Office of Citizenship.

Petitioners and applicants for certain categories of immigration benefits may appeal a negative decision to the AAO. It conducts administrative reviews of those appeals to ensure consistency and accuracy in the interpretation of immigration law and policy. It generally issues "non-precedent" decisions, which apply existing law and policy to the facts of a given case. After review by the Attorney General, AAO may also issue "precedent" decisions to provide clear and uniform guidance to adjudicators and the public on the proper interpretation of law and policy.

Under authority that the Secretary of the Department of Homeland Security (DHS) has delegated to USCIS, it exercises appellate jurisdiction over approximately 50 different immigration case types. Not every type of denied immigration benefit request may be appealed, and some appeals fall under the jurisdiction of the Board of Immigration Appeals (BIA), part of the U.S. Department of Justice. AAO jurisdiction is listed by both subject matter and form number and includes the following categories:

- Most employment-based immigrant and nonimmigrant visa petitions (Forms I-129 and I-140);
- Immigrant petitions by alien entrepreneurs (Form I-526);
- Applications for Temporary Protected Status (TPS) (Form I-821);
- Fiancé(e) petitions (Form I-129F);
- Applications for waiver of ground of inadmissibility (Form I-601);
- Applications for permission to reapply for admission after deportation (Form I-212);
- Certain special immigrant visa petitions (Form I-360 except for Form I-360 widower appeals, which are appealable to the BIA);
- Orphan petitions (Forms I-600 and I-600A);

- T and U visa applications and petitions (Forms I-914 and I-918) and the related adjustment of status applications;
- Applications to preserve residence for naturalization purposes (Form N-470); and
- Immigration and Customs Enforcement (ICE) determinations that a surety bond has been breached.

AAO also have jurisdiction to review decisions by the USCIS Service Centers to revoke certain previously approved petitions.

If denying a benefit, USCIS sends a letter to the petitioner or applicant that explains the reason(s) for the denial and, if applicable, how to file a motion or appeal. Most appeals must be filed on Form I-290B with a fee and within 30 days of the initial denial. Some immigration categories have different appeal requirements.

Initially, the USCIS office that denied the benefit will review the appeal and determine whether to take favorable action and grant the benefit request. If that office does not take favorable action, it will forward the appeal to the AAO for appellate review. The initial field review should be completed within 45 days. The appellate review should be completed within six months of when the AAO receives the appeal.

Non-Precedent Decisions

AAO generally issue non-precedent decisions. These apply existing law and policy to the facts of a given case. A non-precedent decision is binding on the parties involved in the case, but does not create or modify agency guidance or practice. AAO does not announce new constructions of law nor establish agency policy through non-precedent decisions. As a result, non-precedent decisions do not provide a basis for applying new or alternative interpretations of law or policy.

Precedent Decisions

The Secretary of DHS may, with the Attorney General's approval, designate AAO or other DHS decisions to serve as precedents in all future proceedings involving the same issue or issues. These precedent decisions are binding on DHS employees except as modified or overruled by later precedent decisions, statutory changes, or regulatory changes. AAO precedent decisions may announce new legal interpretations or agency policy, or they may reinforce existing law and policy by demonstrating how it applies to a unique set of facts.

History of the AAO

The Immigration and Naturalization Service (INS) established the Administrative Appeals Unit (AAU) in 1983 to centralize the review of administrative appeals. Prior to 1983, responsibility for the adjudication of administrative appeals and the issuance of precedent decisions was shared by the INS commissioner, four regional commissioners and three overseas district directors.

The INS later established the Legalization Appeals Unit to adjudicate appeals of denied Legalization and Special Agricultural Worker applications under the Immigration Reform and Control Act of 1986. In 1994, INS consolidated the two units to create the AAO. The Homeland Security Act of 2002 separated the INS into three components within the new DHS, and on March 1, 2003, the AAO became a part of USCIS.

Customer Service and Public Engagement Directorate

The Customer Service and Public Engagement Directorate's mission is to provide clear, accurate, and timely response to customer concerns and questions, and engage the public through transparent dialogue that promotes participation and feedback.

The Public Engagement Division (PED) coordinates and directs agency-wide dialogue with external stakeholders. PED actively collaborates with, and seeks feedback from, stakeholders to inform USCIS policies, priorities, and organizational performance reviews. PED facilitates open and transparent communication between the Agency, external stakeholders, and the customers they represent by sharing feedback, working with Agency

closely with other USCIS offices to support the implementation of highly visible outreach programs and public education initiatives.

The Public Engagement Division is composed of two divisions: Community Relations and Engagement and Intergovernmental Affairs.

The Community Relations and Engagement Division is responsible for developing and maintaining collaborative relationships with community-based organizations, faith-based and advocacy groups, employer and employee associations, ESL/Civics instructors, international, business, legal, and law enforcement entities, and all other stakeholders who have daily interactions with the Agency and its customers. This includes directing and facilitating stakeholder interaction at the headquarters, regional, and district levels. This division also manages a national network of USCIS Community Relations Officers (CROs) who forge critical local partnerships, inform stakeholders, and relay external feedback to the Agency.

The Intergovernmental Affairs Division advances outreach and communication with state, local, territorial, and tribal partners, including elected officials, associations, and other intergovernmental component offices. This includes maintaining strong relationships with and disseminating USCIS information to state and local partners such as governors, legislatures, mayor's offices, and other elected and appointed officials. This division works closely with DHS intergovernmental affairs programs to align with Department-wide priorities and partners with other federal agencies as appropriate.

The Customer Service Division (CSD) is dedicated to proactively providing information and guidance to USCIS applicants, petitioners and advocates regarding immigration benefits.

Customer Assistance Office

The Customer Assistance Office (CAO) provides customer service and case resolution by responding to individuals who have encountered problems when applying for immigration services and benefits, or those with unusual or sensitive cases. CAO meets the needs of customers by providing accurate, consistent, and timely written and telephonic responses in case management resolution. CAO provides written and telephonic responses to customer case status inquiries and responds to general immigration-related correspondence ceived at USCIS from stakeholders that include the White House, DHS, the CIS Ombudsman, Office of Civil Rights and Civil Liberties, Office of Special Investigations, and the general public.

With nearly 400 inquiries received monthly, CAO responds to complex immigration inquiries from stakeholders that require a thorough knowledge of immigration law and regulations. CAO also responds to telephonic inquiries received by the Office of the USCIS Director and collaborates with the Transportation and Safety Administration to assist with the DHS Travelers Redress Inquiry Program.

Contact Center Enterprise Office

The Contact Center Enterprise Office (CCEO) is the branch responsible for the oversight of the National Customer Service Center (NCSC) for USCIS. Customers call our toll-free number (800-375-5283) to receive nationwide assistance for immigration services and benefits offered by U.S. Citizenship and Immigration Services (USCIS). The NCSC toll-free number receives more than 1 million inquiries a month.

When a customer calls the NCSC, the call goes directly to an Integrated Voice Response (IVR) system, which is available in English and Spanish. If the customer cannot receive a resolution to their inquiry through the IVR, the customer can request to speak to a Customer Service Representative (CSR). If the customer requires additional support or has a unique or complex issue, the CSR will escalate the call to an Immigration Services Officer (ISO).

Field Operations Directorate

To ensure the integrity of the immigration system and lend assistance to applicants, petitioners, and beneficiaries through the field offices and National Benefits Center, the Field Operations Directorate performs the following functions:

- Provides management and oversight to the diverse operations of the National Benefits Center, and the domestic regional, district, field, and field support offices

- Adjudicates applications and petitions for immigration benefits
- Interviews applicants for immigration benefits
- Conducts naturalization ceremonies nationwide
- Completes required security and background security checks for pending applications and petitions
- Provides immigration information and outreach

The Field Operations Directorate includes:
- Eighty-seven field offices and field support offices that deliver immigration benefit services directly to applicants and petitioners in communities across the United States and its territories
- The National Benefits Center (NBC) which performs centralized front-end processing of applications and petitions that require field office interviews (primarily, family-based I-485s and N-400s). In addition, the NBC adjudicates some form types to completion including I-765s, I-131s, immigration benefits associated with the LIFE Act, legalization-related applications and international adoption cases
- A headquarters office, four regional offices and 26 district offices that provide oversight, direction and support to the field offices, field support offices and NBC

Fraud Detection and National Security Directorate (FDNS)

U.S. Citizenship and Immigration Services (USCIS) created FDNS in 2004 in order to strengthen USCIS's efforts to ensure immigration benefits are not granted to individuals who pose a threat to national security or public safety, or who seek to defraud our immigration system. In 2010, FDNS was promoted to a Directorate which elevated the profile of this work within USCIS, brought about operational improvements, and enhanced the integration of the FDNS mission in all facets of the agency's work. Today FDNS continues to lead the USCIS effort to ensure the integrity of the nation's immigration benefits processes.

FDNS's primary mission is to determine whether individuals or organizations filing for immigration benefits pose a threat to national security, public safety, or the integrity of the nation's legal immigration system. FDNS officers are located in every USCIS Center, District, Field, and Asylum Office. FDNS officers are also located in other government agencies.

Supporting the USCIS mission, FDNS's objective is to enhance USCIS's effectiveness and efficiency in detecting and removing known and suspected fraud from the application process, thus promoting the efficient processing of legitimate applications and petitions.

FDNS officers resolve background check information and other concerns that surface during the processing of immigration benefit applications and petitions. Resolution often requires communication with law enforcement or intelligence agencies to make sure that the information is relevant to the applicant or petitioner at hand and, if so, whether the information would have an impact on eligibility for the benefit.

FDNS officers also perform checks of USCIS databases and public information, as well as other administrative inquiries, to verify information provided on, and in support of, applications and petitions. Administrative inquiries may include:

- Performance of fraud assessments—FDNS officers engage in fraud assessments (including Benefit Fraud and Compliance Assessments) to determine the types and volumes of fraud in certain immigration benefits programs;
- Compliance Reviews—Systematic reviews of certain types of applications or petitions to ensure the integrity of the immigration benefits system, and
- Targeted site visits—Inquiries conducted in cases where fraud is suspected.

FDNS uses the Fraud Detection and National Security Data System (FDNS-DS) to identify fraud and track potential patterns.

USCIS has formed a partnership with Immigration and Customs Enforcement (ICE), in which FDNS pursues administrative inquiries into most application and petition fraud, while ICE conducts criminal investigations into major fraud conspiracies.

Additional FDNS Functions

FDNS also conducts Benefit Fraud and Compliance Assessments to identify the types and volumes of fraud and develop mitigation strategies to deter and disrupt fraud.

In July 2009, FDNS implemented the Administrative Site Visit and Verification Program (ASVVP) to conduct unannounced site inspections to verify information contained in certain visa petitions.   USCIS provides petitioners and their representatives of record (if any) an opportunity to review and address the information before denying or revoking an approved petition based on information obtained during a site inspection. To find out more about ASVVP, please see the link on the right of this page.

Office of Intake and Document Production

The Office of Intake and Document Production performs the following functions:

- Deliver effective, efficient and innovative customer-focused intake and secure document production services.
- Design, print and distribute USCIS forms.
- Manage the paper (USCIS Lockbox facilities) and legacy e-Filing intake systems.
- Troubleshoot intake issues, adjudicate fee waivers and resolve problems with applications.
- Produce and deliver secure benefit documents and cards, such as Permanent Resident Cards.

The office comprises over 100 federal employees located nationwide. The USCIS Lockbox facilities located in Chicago, Illinois; Phoenix, Arizona; and Lewisville, Texas, are operated by a Department of Treasury designated financial agent.

Office of Citizenship

The Office of Citizenship seeks to engage and support partners to welcome immigrants, promote English language learning and education on the rights and responsibilities of citizenship, and encourage U.S. citizenship. It also does the following:

- Develops and enhances educational products and resources that
- Welcomes immigrants
- Promotes English language learning and education on the rights and responsibilities of citizenship
- Prepares immigrants for naturalization and active civic participation
- Leads initiatives to promote citizenship awareness and demystify the naturalization process for aspiring citizens
- Supports national and community-based organizations that prepare immigrants for citizenship by providing grants, educational materials, and technical assistance
- Builds collaborative partnerships with state and local governments and non-governmental organizations to expand integration and citizenship resources in communities
- Conducts training workshops and enhances professional development and classroom resources for educators and organizations preparing immigrants for citizenship
- Promotes integration policy dialogue among different sectors of society and coordinates with stakeholders at all levels to foster integration and community cohesion

The Office of Citizenship is divided into 3 divisions:
- Citizenship Education and Training
- Publications and Outreach
- Grants

Office of Communications

The Office of Communications handles the following duties:

- Oversees and coordinates official USCIS communications to both internal and external audiences.
- Manages communications and messaging to our external audiences.
- Empowers our employees with the information needed to perform their jobs.
- Facilitates consistent messaging and imaging for USCIS.
- Informs the public regarding the immigration services and benefits we provide.
- The Office of Communications consists of the following divisions:
- Strategic Communication:
- Formulates strategic description of each initiative along with approach and overall message.
- Ensures information is clearly defined and targeted to meet each audience's needs.
- Considers communications tactics mapped against messages and audience.
- Determines timelines for each initiative and ensures that specific goals are met.

Media Relations:

- Proactively promotes USCIS events, achievements and policies to maintain and increase public awareness, understanding, and support for USCIS.
- Provides timely responses to requests about USCIS and the immigration process using English and non-English print, television, radio, and social media outlets.

- Establishes and maintains professional relationships with members of the media across the country and around the world.
- Writes communication products to inform the public about current USCIS activities, policies, and priorities through interaction with the media.
- Closely coordinates with public affairs counterparts throughout the Department of Homeland Security as well as media relations representatives in other federal, state, and local agencies, private businesses, and community based organizations.

e-Communications:

- Leads the development, review, publication and maintenance of Web content to provide information to USCIS external and internal audiences.
- Creates and manages USCIS social media content, including:
- The Beacon—USCIS's official blog
- USCIS Twitter and USCIS Twitter Español
- USCIS Facebook
- USCIS YouTube
- Recommends and implements Web-based information policy, standards, guidance, and tools for USCIS.
- Assesses the content and usability of all proposed websites to ensure they are consistent with USCIS policies and goals.

Multimedia Division

- Provides a full-suite of multimedia production services including:
- Streaming Video
- Videoconferencing
- Video Production Studio
- Press Conference and Live Event Support

- DHS and USCIS Town Hall Meetings
- Training Videos

Plain Language and Content

- Ensures quality, consistency and clarity in all Office of Communications products.
- Writes, edits and reviews communication products.
- Reviews documents related to major projects from other USCIS offices.
- Provides training in plain language and writing for the Web to the entire agency including:
- Half-day trainings
- Workshops
- Videos

Agile Communications Division

The Agile Communications Division includes a complete range of resources to support the introduction of the new electronic immigration system while also serving as a special agency communications project team. It handles the following:

- Social and Digital Media (Tweets, BLOGs, etc.)
- Audio podcasting (scripting and talent)
- Internal and external Web content development, layout &design
- Graphic design and photographic support
- Marketing and demographic research
- Spanish language scripting and translation

Office of Legislative Affairs (OLA)

OLA supports USCIS by maintaining effective relationships with Congress through:

- Prompt responses to constituent concerns,
- Proactive outreach on issues of interest, and
- Ongoing educational activities for Members and staff.

These initiatives enhance the integrity of the immigration process and promote the development of sound immigration legislation, policy and practices.

Organization

OLA is divided into three branches: Legislative, National Coordination, and Operations.

The Legislative Branch

Informs Congress of USCIS mission, priorities, and policies

Provides information to Congress when legislation is being debated, particularly the implications of proposed legislation on agency operations

Coordinates USCIS comments on proposed legislation, facilitates Congressional hearings and meetings for USCIS, and tracks legislation for USCIS leadership

The National Coordination Branch

Works to strengthen OLA operations throughout the national USCIS Legislative Affairs Program so that the agency can best represent its efforts to Congress at the local level

The Operations Branch

Assists Members of Congress and staff in identifying, explaining, and resolving constituent inquiries regarding individual cases, institutional problems, or policy issues affecting USCIS customers

Responds to all Congressional casework inquiries

Office of Privacy

The Office of Privacy seeks to preserve and enhance privacy protections for individuals and to promote transparency of USCIS operations.

Vision

USCIS's culture of privacy results from how well executive leadership, managers and employees understand, implement and enforce federal privacy laws and regulations. Privacy stewardship leads to proper handling of our customers' Personally Identifiable Information (PII).

The Office of Privacy:

- Evaluates USCIS legislative and regulatory proposals involving collection, use, and disclosure of PII
- Provides privacy policy and programmatic oversight, and support implementation across USCIS
- Evaluates USCIS programs, systems and operations to identify privacy sensitivities; recommends mitigation strategies to reduce potential privacy impacts; and provides guidance and global assistance to USCIS program offices and directorates in meeting such requirements
- Operates a USCIS-wide Privacy Incident Response Program to ensure that incidents involving PII are properly reported, investigated and mitigated
- Responds to and addresses complaints of privacy violations
- Provides privacy training, education and outreach
- Provides advice and technical assistance to leadership and management to ensure privacy protections are implemented throughout USCIS programs, systems, processes and operations, and ensure USCIS's adherence to federal, regulatory, statutory, departmental and component privacy requirements, mandates, directives and policy

Office of Transformation Coordination

The Office of Transformation Coordination manages and oversees the development of the USCIS Electronic Immigration System (USCIS ELIS) to move the agency from a paper-based application and adjudication process to an electronic one.

In support of this effort, OTC is orchestrating a comprehensive transformation of people, processes and technologies to enhance national security, promote operational excellence and provide superior customer service to those seeking immigration benefits.

OTC is dedicated to ensuring we deliver the most effective and reliable system for the world's largest immigration system.

OTC is composed of four major operational divisions: Business Integration, Stakeholder Readiness, Program Management, and Release Management.

Business Integration

Reengineers and incorporates all relevant immigration/citizenship business processes into USCIS ELIS in order to ensure the creation of a proven business architecture for USCIS.

Stakeholder Readiness

Engages internal and external stakeholders, conducts outreach, and develops training to facilitate a comprehensive and smooth transformation within USCIS.

Program Management

Manages/evaluates contracts and assesses program risks to assure a high level of quality in the transformation effort.

Release Management

Conducts internal testing and manages technical frameworks and release scheduling to guarantee the successful deployment of all USCIS ELIS releases.

Refugee, Asylum, and International Operations Directorate

The Directorate provides immigration, protection and humanitarian services for people who are:

- Fleeing oppression, persecution or torture;
- Facing urgent humanitarian situations; and,
- Best served in our international offices, such as military members who are serving overseas and permanent residents who need replacement documents to return to the U.S.

It protects national security, combat fraud, and prevent ineligible individuals from immigrating to the U.S. through careful screening, vigilant reviews and sound adjudications.

Its global presence includes:

- Offices in Washington, D.C., including headquarters components and the refugee corps;
- Two domestic offices that adjudicate overseas applications not requiring interviews;
- Twenty-five international offices;
- Eight domestic asylum offices; and,
- An office in Miami that provides resettlement and orientation benefits to Cuban and Haitian parolees.

Its officers travel abroad to assist refugees and domestically to adjudicate asylum benefits.

Organization

RAIO is made up of three divisions:

The Refugee Affairs Division provides resettlement benefits to people who are outside their countries and cannot or are unwilling to return to their homes because they fear serious harm.

Under United States law, a refugee is someone who:

- Is located outside of the United States
- Is of special humanitarian concern to the United States
- Demonstrates that they were persecuted or fear persecution due to race, religion, nationality, political opinion, or membership in a particular social group
- Is not firmly resettled in another country
- Is admissible to the United States

A refugee does not include anyone who ordered, incited, assisted, or otherwise participated in the persecution of any person on account of race, religion, nationality, membership in a particular social group, or political opinion.

The Refugee Process

You must receive a referral to the U.S. Refugee Admissions Program (USRAP) for consideration as a refugee. If you receive a referral, you will receive help filling out your application and then be interviewed abroad by a USCIS officer who will determine whether you are eligible for refugee resettlement.

Your case may include your spouse, child (unmarried and under 21years of age), and in some limited circumstances, other family members You may include a same-sex spouse in your application provided that you and your spouse are legally married. As a general matter, USCIS looks to the law of the place where the marriage took place when determining whether it is valid for immigration law purposes. Same-sex partners who are not married but who are qualified to access the U.S. Refugee Admissions under one of the three designated worldwide processing priorities may have their cases cross-referenced so that they can be interviewed at the same time and, if approved by USCIS, resettled in the same geographic area in the United States. There is no fee to apply for refugee status. The information you provide will not be shared with your home country.

United States. After you arrive, you will be eligible for medical and cash assistance.

If you are a refugee in the United States and want your family members who are abroad to join you, you may file Form I-730, Refugee/Asylee Relative Petition, for your spouse and unmarried children under 21. You must file within two years of your arrival to the United States unless there are humanitarian reasons to excuse this deadline.

You may also be eligible to file an Affidavit of Relationship for your spouse, child (unmarried, under 21), or parents. The Affidavit of Relationship is the form used to reunite refugees and asylees with close relatives who are determined to be refugees but are outside the United States. The Affidavit of Relationship records information about family relationships and must be completed in order to begin the application process for relatives who may be eligible to enter the United States as refugees through the U.S. Refugee Admissions Program.

As a refugee, you may work immediately upon arrival to the United States. When you are admitted to the United States you will receive a Form I-94 containing a refugee admission stamp. Additionally, a Form I-765, Application for Employment Authorization, will be filed for you in order for you to receive an Employment Authorization Document (EAD). While you are waiting for your EAD, you can present your Form I-94, Arrival-Departure Record, to your employer as proof of your permission to work in the United States.

Filing for a Permanent Residency (Green Card)

If you are admitted as a refugee, you must apply for a green card one year after coming to the United States.

The Asylum Division manages the U.S. affirmative asylum process, which allows individuals who are already in the U.S. (or at a port of entry), to remain here because they have been persecuted or fear persecution. The individual must not be in removal proceedings to apply under affirmative asylum procedures.

Every year people come to the United States seeking protection because they have suffered persecution or fear that they will suffer persecution due to:

- Race

- Religion
- Nationality
- Membership in a particular social group
- Political opinion

If you are eligible for asylum you may be permitted to remain in the United States. To apply for Asylum, file a Form I-589, Application for Asylum and for Withholding of Removal, within one year of your arrival to the United States. You may include your spouse and children who are in the United States on your application at the time you file or at any time until a final decision is made on your case. To include your child on your application, the child must be under 21 and unmarried.

The International Operations Division, with offices around the world, is the face of USCIS abroad. These offices reunite families, enable adoptive children to come to join permanent families in the U.S., consider parole requests from individuals outside the U.S. for urgent humanitarian reasons or significant public benefit, and provide information services and travel documents to people around the world.

Operating in a dynamic global environment with constantly changing political, cultural, environmental, and socio-economic context, IO has approximately 240 employees located in the US and in three international districts composed of 25 field offices in 22 countries globally. Our employees are highly diverse and include foreign nationals in addition to US citizens; more than half of the IO staff working abroad, and approximately one-third of all IO employees, are foreign nationals.

IO Headquarters

With offices in, Florida, California, and Washington, DC, IO Headquarters is responsible for providing leadership, guidance, and support for all IO programs. IO Headquarters currently is composed of six branches:

Children's Affairs and Parole Policy Branch

Located in Washington, DC, CAPP has the mandate to focus on intercountry adoption and parole policy. CAPP serves as the Department of State liaison on adoption issues, provides guidance on adoption-related cases to the liaisons to the IO field offices and Humanitarian Affairs Branch (HAB), and partners with HAB to develop parole-related policy. Additionally, CAPP is responsible for policy and guidance on DNA and surrogacy matters within IO.

Humanitarian Affairs Branch

Located in Washington, DC, HAB adjudicates requests for humanitarian or significant public benefit parole for individuals outside of the US who have no other means of entering the US. In addition, HAB administers the Cuban and Haitian Entrant Program (CHEP) located in Miami, awarding multi-million dollar grants to non-governmental organizations that provide orientations and resettlement services to Cuban and Haitian migrants paroled into the US.

International Operations Adjudications Support Branch

Located in Anaheim, California, IASB provides adjudicative and program management assistance to international offices by transferring international caseloads to a domestic environment and deploying additional staff to international offices as needed. By directly addressing workload imbalances, IASB creates a more efficient and customer-centric adjudication process and ensures continuity of operations throughout IO. IASB also manages the Cuban Medical Parole Program (CMPP), and provides operational and policy guidance on Applications for Waiver of Ground of Inadmissibility (Form I-601s) and related applications.

Performance and Resource Management

Located in Washington, DC, PRM provides RAIO's infrastructure support through budgeting, workload and resource analysis, production and performance management, record maintenance, and IT initiatives. In 2011, recognized with the prestigious USCIS Director's Vanguard Award for developing and implementing the Case and Activity Management for International Operations system, or "CAMINO," an innovative, person-centric, web-based case management and report generating system that is transforming the adjudication of international cases.

Programs and Integrity Branch

Located in Washington, DC, PIB develops policy and guidance for qualified non-citizen relatives of US citizens and residents seeking to enter the United States, for refugee/asylee family members following-to-join, and for naturalization of non-citizen members of the US military abroad and their qualified family members. PIB is also developing IO's first ever in-house effort to integrate its security-related efforts, such as overseas verifications, security checks, and fraud and national security oversight. PIB serves as liaison to the Department of State in coordinating immigration-related efficiencies and cost-savings.

Quality Assurance, Training, and Communications Branch

Located in Washington, DC, QATC develops and implements quality management and training programs for all IO staff, ensures that internal and external communication is current and accurate, and participates in meetings with governmental and non-government partners to promote the mission of the agency. In particular, QATC is responsible for ensuring that all officers posted abroad have the tools and knowledge they need to address the full range of complicated adjudication issues they will encounter, their host country's culture and traditions, and any safety issues inherent in their new environment.

RAIO Training Programs and Materials

RAIO's success depends on a well-trained workforce. With this goal in mind, Refugee, Asylum and International Operations (RAIO) has developed comprehensive training programs for its officer staff. The RAIO Directorate level training branch develops training materials and conducts training for all officers new to RAIO on topics that are common to all officers. Most of the lesson plans used at the "RAIO Combined Training" are available to the public.

In addition, each RAIO division has its own training section, responsible for job-specific training for their officers. Most of the Asylum Division's training materials are available to the public.

SAVE Program

History

In 1986, Congress passed the Immigration Reform and Control Act of 1986 (IRCA), which required the creation and implementation of a verification system that confirms immigration statuses of individuals applying for certain federally-funded benefits. This system originally came under the jurisdictional purview of legacy Immigration and Naturalization Service (INS). To successfully accommodate this federal mandate, legacy INS created the Systematic Alien Verification for Entitlements (SAVE) Program in 1987 to develop the verification system. With the creation of the Department of Homeland Security in 2003, jurisdiction is now under the United States Citizenship and Immigration Services (USCIS), Verification Division.

Mission

The SAVE Program will provide timely customer-focused immigration status information to authorized agencies in order to assist them in maintaining the integrity of their programs. SAVE will promote the use of automated systems to enhance efficiency, customer service and interagency collaboration, while protecting sensitive information.

5

United States Customs and Border Protection

United States Customs and Border Protection (CBP) is one of the Department of Homeland Security's largest and most complex components, with a priority mission of keeping terrorists and their weapons out of the U.S. It also has a responsibility for securing and facilitating trade and travel while enforcing hundreds of U.S. regulations, including immigration and drug laws. With more than 60,000 employees, CBP is one of the world's largest law enforcement organizations.

As the world's first full-service border entity, CBP takes a comprehensive approach to border management and control, combining customs, immigration, border security, and agricultural protection into one coordinated and supportive activity. The men and women of CBP are responsible for enforcing hundreds of U.S. laws and regulations. On a typical day, CBP welcomes nearly 1 million visitors, screens more than 67,000 cargo containers, arrests more than 1,100 individuals and seizes nearly 6 tons of illicit drugs.

Mission

- We are the guardians of our nation's borders.
- We are America's frontline.
- We safeguard the American homeland at and beyond our borders.
- We protect the American public against terrorists and the instruments of terror.

- We steadfastly enforce the laws of the United States while fostering our nation's economic security through lawful international trade and travel.
- We serve the American public with vigilance, integrity and professionalism.

Core Values

- Vigilance is how we ensure the safety of all Americans. We are continuously watchful and alert to deter, detect and prevent threats to our nation. We demonstrate courage and valor in the protection of our nation
- Service to Country is embodied in the work we do. We are dedicated to defending and upholding the Constitution of the United States. The American people have entrusted us to protect the homeland and defend liberty
- Integrity is our cornerstone. We are guided by the highest ethical and moral principles. Our actions bring honor to ourselves and our agency.

History

On July 31, 1789, the U.S. Congress passed the third of three acts that provided for administering customs tariffs and collecting duties. Earlier on the nation's birthday, the Tariff Act of July 4, 1789, had been passed by Congress followed by the Duties on Tonnage statute on July 20. And on the last day of the month, Congress established customs districts. Administration of customs laws was placed under the secretary of the Treasury by an act of September 2, 1789.

Fiscal administration of customs laws fell under the comptroller of the Treasury from 1792 until the creation of the position of commissioner of Customs by an act of March 3, 1849. These commissioners served as more as auditors of accounts than administrators. The position of commissioner was abolished on July 31, 1894.

division. Fifty-three years later, the division and the Special Agency Service of the Treasury Department were consolidated to form the Bureau of Customs in 1927. A re-envisioned commissioner of customs position was created as the chief administrator of the bureau.

The Customs Service closed with the dawn of CBP, but its commissioner became the leader of CBP and the majority of its staff and responsibilities came to CBP.

Immigration inspectors, can trace their responsibilities to the establishment of the Office of the Superintendent of Immigration on **March 3, 1891.**

The 1891 Immigration Act created the Office of the Superintendent of Immigration in the Treasury Department. The superintendent oversaw a new corps of immigrant inspectors stationed at the country's principal ports of entry. During its first decade, the Immigration Service formalized basic immigration procedures. The service began collecting arrival manifests (also frequently called passenger lists or immigration arrival records) from each incoming ship, a former duty of customs officials since 1820. Inspectors then questioned arrivals about their admissibility and noted their admission or rejection on the manifest records.

Beginning in 1893, inspectors also served on Boards of Special Inquiry that closely reviewed each exclusion case. A congressional act of March 2, 1895, renamed the Office of Immigration as the Bureau of Immigration and changed the title of superintendent of Immigration to commissioner-general of Immigration. A later congressional act of June 6, 1900, consolidated immigration enforcement by assigning enforcement of both alien contract labor laws and Chinese exclusion laws to the commissioner-general.

In 1903, the Bureau of Immigration moved from the Treasury Department to the newly created Department of Commerce and Labor. A fund created from collection of immigrants' head tax financed the Immigration Service until 1909, when Congress replaced the fund with an annual appropriation.

In 1913, the Bureau of Immigration and Naturalization split into the Bureau of Immigration and the Bureau of Naturalization. The two bureaus coexisted separately within the new U.S. Department of Labor until reunited as the Immigration and Naturalization Service (INS) by executive order on June 10, 1933. In 1940, Presidential Reorganization Plan Number V moved the INS from the Department of Labor to the Department of Justice.

The Homeland Security Act of 2002 disbanded INS on March 1, 2003. Its responsibilities and staff were distributed to three components of the newly formed DHS: CBP, Immigration and Customs Enforcement and U.S. Citizenship and Immigration Services.

Agriculture inspectors, who traced their roles to the passage of the Plant Quarantine Act on **Aug. 20, 1912.** The Act of 1912 authorized the U.S. Department of Agriculture (USDA) to inspect agricultural products, to organize border quarantines and to restrict entry of infested agricultural goods.

In 1953, USDA charged the Agricultural Research Service with administering plant quarantine functions until 1970 when Plant Protection and Quarantine was established.

Agricultural inspection services remained part of Plant Protection and Quarantine until March 1, 2003. On that date, approximately 2,500 employees of the Agriculture Quarantine and Inspection force became part of CBP.

Border Patrol agents have maintained the integrity of the U.S. borders since Congress authorized the hiring of Border Patrol personnel on **May 28, 1924.**

Congress established the Border Patrol as part of the Immigration Bureau in the Department of Labor through the Labor Appropriation Act of 1924.

While initially charged with securing the borders between inspection stations, its patrol areas were expanded in 1925 to include the seacoast along the Gulf of Mexico and Florida. In 1932, supervision of the Border Patrol was divided under two directors: one in charge of the Mexican border, the other in charge of the Canadian border.

The Border Patrol was first permitted to board and search a conveyance for illegal aliens in 1952. Agents also were allowed to patrol all territory within 25 miles of a land border.

The Customs Bureau was renamed the U.S. Customs Service in 1973. U.S. Customs was dissolved in 2003 with the newly created Bureau of Customs and Border Protection assuming many of its former roles and responsibilities.

With the creation of DHS in 2003, the U.S. Customs Service's Air and Marine Interdiction Division transitioned to Immigration and Customs Enforcement (ICE). The following year DHS Undersecretary Asa Hutchinson announced the move of Office of Air and Marine Operations from ICE to CBP.

Border Patrol Chief David Aguilar jointly announced the consolidation of air and marine assets in the Office of Air and Marine, which became CBP's third uniformed division on January 17, 2006.

Border Security

CBP's top priority is to keep terrorists and their weapons from entering the U.S. while welcoming all legitimate travelers and commerce. CBP officers and agents enforce all applicable U.S. laws, including against illegal immigration, narcotics smuggling and illegal importation. CBP deploys highly trained law enforcement personnel who apprehend more than 1,000 individuals each day for suspected violations of U.S. laws.

CBP's border security mission is led at ports of entry by CBP officers from the Office of Field Operations, along U.S. borders by agents from the Office of Border Patrol and from the air and sea by agents from the Office of Air and Marine. Also at ports of entry, agriculture specialists are deployed to protect U.S. agriculture from the introduction of pests or disease from overseas sources.

At Ports of Entry

U.S. Customs and Border Protection has a complex mission at ports of entry with broad law enforcement authorities tied to screening all foreign visitors, returning American citizens and imported cargo. CBP provides security and facilitation operations at 328 ports of entry throughout the country.

Port of entry operations include immigration inspections of people entering the country including visitors, Legal Permanent Residents, and U.S. citizens as well as examination and security of all cargo and agriculture products entering the U.S.

Immigration Inspection Program

Individuals seeking entry into the United States are inspected at Ports of Entry (POEs) by CBP officers who determine their admissibility. The inspection process includes all work performed in connection with the entry of aliens and United States citizens into the United States, including preinspection performed by the Immigration Inspectors outside the United States.

"An officer is responsible for determining the nationality and identity of each applicant for admission and for preventing the entry of ineligible aliens, including criminals, terrorists, and drug traffickers, among others. U.S. citizens are automatically admitted upon verification of citizenship; aliens are questioned and their documents are examined to determine admissibility based on the requirements of the U.S. immigration law."

Under the authority granted by the Immigration and Nationality Act (INA), as amended, a CBP officer may question, under oath, any person coming into the United States to determine his or her admissibility. In addition, an inspector has authority to search without warrant the person and effects of any person seeking admission, when there is reason to believe that grounds of exclusion exist which would be disclosed by such search.

The INA is based on the law of presumption: an applicant for admission is presumed to be an alien until he or she shows evidence of citizenship; an alien is presumed to be an immigrant until he or she proves that he or she fits into one of the nonimmigrant classifications.

The mission of the inspections program is to control and guard the boundaries and borders of the United States against the illegal entry of aliens. In a way that:

- Functions as the initial component of a comprehensive, immigration enforcement system;
- Prevents the entry of terrorists, drug traffickers, criminals, and other persons who may subvert the national interest;
- Deters illegal immigration through the detection of fraudulent documents and entry schemes;
- Initiates prosecutions against individuals who attempt or aid and abet illegal entry;

- Cooperates with international, Federal, state and local law enforcement agencies to achieve mutual objectives;
- Contributes to the development and implementation of foreign policy related to the entry of persons;
- Facilitates the entry of persons engaged in commerce, tourism, and/or other lawful pursuits;
- Respects the rights and dignity of individuals;
- Examines individuals and their related documents in a professional manner;
- Assists the transportation industry to meet its requirements;
- Responds to private sector interests, in conformance with immigration law;
- Continues to employ innovative methods to improve the efficiency and cost effectiveness of the inspections process.

Cargo Security and Examinations

Each year, more than 11 million maritime containers arrive at our seaports. At land borders, another 11 million arrive by truck and 2.7 million by rail. CBP is responsible for knowing what is inside, whether it poses a risk to the American people, and ensuring that all proper revenues are collected. Working with the trade community, programs like the Container Security Initiative and the Customs-Trade Partnership Against Terrorism help to increase security and safeguard the world's trade industry.

CSI: Container Security Initiative

As the single, unified border agency of the United States, U.S. Customs and Border Protection's (CBP) mission is extraordinarily important to the protection of America and the American people. In the aftermath of the terrorist attacks on September 11, 2001, U.S. Customs Service began developing antiterrorism programs to help secure the United States. Within months of these attacks, U.S. Customs Service had created the Container Security

CSI addresses the threat to border security and global trade posed by the potential for terrorist use of a maritime container to deliver a weapon. CSI proposes a security regime to ensure all containers that pose a potential risk for terrorism are identified and inspected at foreign ports before they are placed on vessels destined for the United States. CBP has stationed teams of U.S. CBP Officers in foreign locations to work together with our host foreign government counterparts. Their mission is to target and prescreen containers and to develop additional investigative leads related to the terrorist threat to cargo destined to the United States.

The three core elements of CSI are:

- Identify high-risk containers. CBP uses automated targeting tools to identify containers that pose a potential risk for terrorism, based on advance information and strategic intelligence.
- Prescreen and evaluate containers before they are shipped. Containers are screened as early in the supply chain as possible, generally at the port of departure.
- Use technology to prescreen high-risk containers to ensure that screening can be done rapidly without slowing down the movement of trade. This technology includes large-scale X-ray and gamma ray machines and radiation detection devices.

Through CSI, CBP officers work with host customs administrations to establish security criteria for identifying high-risk containers. Those administrations use non-intrusive inspection (NII) and radiation detection technology to screen high-risk containers before they are shipped to U.S. ports.

Announced in January 2002, CSI has made great strides since its inception. A significant number of customs administrations have committed to joining CSI and operate at various stages of implementation.

CSI is now operational at ports in North America, Europe, Asia, Africa, the Middle East, and Latin and Central America. CBP's 58 operational CSI ports now prescreen over 80 percent of all maritime containerized cargo imported into the United States.

C-TPAT: Customs-Trade Partnership Against Terrorism

C-TPAT seeks to safeguard the world's vibrant trade industry from terrorists, maintaining the economic health of the U.S. and its neighbors. The partnership develops and adopts measures that add security but do not have a chilling effect on trade, a difficult balancing act.

A growing partnership

Begun in November 2001 with just seven major importers as members, as of June 2011, the partnership has grown. Today, more than 10,000 certified partners that span the gamut of the trade community have been accepted into the program. These include U.S. importers, U.S./Canada highway carriers; U.S./Mexico highway carriers; rail and sea carriers; licensed U.S. Customs brokers; U.S. marine port authority/terminal operators; U.S. freight consolidators; ocean transportation intermediaries and non-operating common carriers; Mexican and Canadian manufacturers; and Mexican long-haul carriers. These 10,000-plus companies account for over 50 percent (by value) of what is imported into the United States.

Extending the zone of U.S. border security

By extending the United States' zone of security to the point of origin, the customs-trade partnership allows for better risk assessment and targeting, freeing CBP to allocate inspectional resources to more questionable shipments.

The partnership establishes clear supply chain security criteria for members to meet and in return provides incentives and benefits like expedited processing. A corollary is to extend the partnership anti-terrorism principles globally through cooperation and coordination with the international community. Back in 2005, the World Customs Organization created the Framework of Standards to Secure and Facilitate Global Trade, which complements and globalizes CBP's and the partnership's cargo security efforts.

When they join the anti-terror partnership, companies sign an agreement to work with CBP to protect the supply chain, identify security gaps, and implement specific security measures and best practices. Additionally, partners provide CBP with a security profile outlining the specific security measures the company has in place. Applicants must address a broad range of security topics and present security profiles that list action plans to align

topics and present security profiles that list action plans to align security throughout their supply chain.

C–TPAT members are considered low–risk and are therefore less likely to be examined. This designation is based on a company's past compliance history, security profile, and the validation of a sample international supply chain.

An emerging focus: Mutual Recognition Arrangements

CBP has numerous Mutual Recognition Arrangements with other countries. The goal of these arrangements is to link the various international industry partnership programs so that together they create a unified and sustainable security posture that can assist in securing and facilitating global cargo trade.

The goal of aligning partnership programs is to create a system whereby all participants in an international trade transaction are approved by the customs function as observing specified standards in the secure handling of goods and relevant information. C–TPAT signed its first Mutual Recognition Arrangement with New Zealand in June 2007, and since that time has signed similar arrangements with South Korea, Japan, Jordan, Canada, the EU, Taiwan, Israel, Mexico, and Singapore.

Protecting Agriculture

Millions of pounds of fresh fruits, vegetables, cut flowers, herbs, and other items enter the United States via commercial shipments from other countries every year.

Although these items appear to be harmless, there could be hidden threats in that baggage and in those truckloads, trainloads and containers of fresh items that could seriously threaten U.S. agriculture, our natural resources and our economy.

The CBP agriculture specialist and the CBP officer at U.S. ports of entry and international mail facilities target, detect, intercept, and thereby prevent the entry of these potential threats before they have a chance to do any harm.

Each year, CBP agriculture specialists intercept tens of thousands of "actionable pests"—those identified through scientific risk assessment and study as being dangerous to the health and safety of U.S. agricultural resources.

They check containers and trucks for smuggled agricultural products or packaging materials that might contain invasive species that could harm our agriculture and environment.

They examine wooden pallets that could hide the larvae of wood-boring insects poised to attack native trees or nursery stock.

They make sure that imported fruits and vegetables are pest-free.

The CBP agriculture specialists work with specialized x-ray machines that detect organic materials. They utilize agricultural canines specifically trained to sniff out meat and plant materials in international airport passenger areas.

Agro-Terrorism

Unfortunately, our post 9/11 world includes a new and dangerous threat. This threat is agro-terrorism. Agro-terrorism is terrorism targeting some component of agriculture or the food supply. Examples include the intentional introduction of a plant or animal pest or disease or contamination of food materials with a toxic substance. Agricultural inspections have traditionally focused on unintentional introduction of pests or diseases—those unnoticed in someone's luggage or hitchhiking on the walls of a container. Now we need to also focus on the deliberate introduction of these threats.

With the added danger of agro-terrorism, the role of the CBP Agriculture Specialists at our ports of entry is more crucial than ever.

Global Travel and Trade

One in five food items is now imported. We can now have fresh strawberries when it is 20 degrees below zero. American consumers demand fresh limes and blueberries all year round. In fact, during the winter months in the United States, nearly 80 percent of the fresh fruits and vegetables on our tables come from other countries.

With the ever-increasing amount of trade, new pest pathways are discovered, and the agricultural risks to the United States grow. The threat to crops and livestock is real.

Resource Optimization Strategy

CBP officers are responsible for carrying out the complex and demanding mission of securing and expediting international trade and travel at all ports of entry. Since 2009, trade and passenger volumes have increased in air, land, and sea environments; however, CBP officer staffing levels have remained relatively the same.

CBP has engaged in a series of transformation efforts to modernize our processes and maximize the use of existing resources, but these efforts have not been enough to keep pace with the increases in traffic and our increasingly complex mission.

To support these growing volumes in travel and trade, CBP has adopted a three-pronged strategy that maximizes existing resources, identifies our staffing needs, and explores funding sources to support staffing needs.

It is committed to making the best use of available resources and working with all of its stakeholders to address the challenges of its growing and changing mission.

CBP Takes the Next Step in Public-Private Partnerships

There are more people and goods coming through our ports of entry than ever before. Last fiscal year, CBP inspected more than 360 million travelers at our air, land, and sea ports of entry. Since 2009, it has seen growth in both trade and travel. In Fiscal Year 2013, total passenger volume was 6.4% higher and total import value was nearly 40% higher than in Fiscal Year 2011. These trends are expected to continue.

Travel and trade play a critical role in the nation's economic growth, and CBP recognizes its role in driving that growth through its trade and travel facilitation mission. To support increasing volumes, CBP developed a comprehensive Resource Optimization Strategy that includes Business Transformation Initiatives, a data-driven Workload Staffing Model and

of funding that include public-private partnerships — like the reimbursable service pilots authorized last year under Section 560.

Section 559 of the *Consolidated Appropriations Act, 2014*, is another key component of CBP's alternative sources of funding solution. This authority allows it to support requests for expanded services as well as improvements to infrastructure through both reimbursable service agreements and donation acceptance authority, respectively. Reimbursable services under Section 559 include customs, immigration, and agricultural processing; salaries for additional staff; and overtime expenses at airports. The new donation acceptance authority provides even greater flexibility, allowing CBP and the General Services Administration (GSA), to accept donations of real or personal property or non-personal services to be used for construction, alterations, operation, or maintenance of a new or existing port of entry.

CBP views these authorities as an opportunity to proactively work with stakeholders and communities to identify business solutions for a variety of border management needs. CBP has a team in place to support these efforts and to offer a streamlined application and evaluation process, with analytical support and guidance to meet the needs of our prospective partners.

The opportunities available under Section 559 to expand its partnerships will continue to enhance the set of solutions developed to address the increased demands on CBP's existing resources and improve services to interested stakeholders in all port environments. CBP recognizes that increased economic activity can be driven by additional services and enhanced infrastructure; and this is one more way it can accommodate such change.

For parties interested in CBP's donation acceptance authority: Pursuant to Section 559 of the *Consolidated Appropriations Act, 2014* CBP and GSA are authorized to accept donations of real property, personal property (including monetary donations) and non-personal services from private sector and government entities. CBP will evaluate proposals from private corporations, public entities, municipalities, port authorities, consortiums, and any other private sector or Government entity. Donation proposals will be evaluated based on their individual merit and ability to satisfy the evaluation criteria posted on CBP.gov. Please also note that CBP and GSA will only consider submissions that envision Federal ownership of the proposed donation.

Along U.S. Borders

The United States Border Patrol is the mobile, uniformed law enforcement arm of U.S. Customs and Border Protection within the Department of Homeland Security responsible for securing U.S. borders between ports of entry. The Border Patrol was officially established on May 28, 1924 by an act of Congress passed in response to increasing illegal immigration.

As mandated by this Act, the small border guard in what was then the Bureau of Immigration was reorganized into the Border Patrol. The initial force of 450 officers was given the responsibility of combating illegal entries and the growing business of alien smuggling.

Mission

Since the terrorist attacks of September 11, 2001, the focus of the Border Patrol has changed to detection, apprehension and/or deterrence of terrorists and terrorist weapons. Although the Border Patrol has changed dramatically since its inception in 1924, its overall mission remains unchanged: to detect and prevent the illegal entry of aliens into the United States. Together with other law enforcement officers, the Border Patrol helps maintain borders that work, facilitating the flow of legal immigration and goods while preventing the illegal trafficking of people and contraband.

The Border Patrol is specifically responsible for patrolling the 6,000 miles of Mexican and Canadian international land borders and 2,000 miles of coastal waters surrounding the Florida Peninsula and the island of Puerto Rico. Agents work around the clock on assignments, in all types of terrain and weather conditions. Agents also work in many isolated communities throughout the U.S.

One of the most important activities of a Border Patrol agent is line watch. This involves the detection, prevention and apprehension of terrorists, undocumented aliens and smugglers of aliens at or near the land border by maintaining surveillance from a covert position, following up leads, responding to electronic sensor television systems, aircraft sightings, and interpreting and following tracks, marks and other physical evidence. Some of the major activities are traffic check, traffic observation, city patrol,

activities are traffic check, traffic observation, city patrol, transportation check, administrative, intelligence, and anti-smuggling activities.

As one of the most rigorous and demanding law enforcement training programs in the country, U.S. Border Patrol training has become the envy of the federal law enforcement community. Specific Border Patrol Courses include: Immigration and Nationality Law, Criminal Law and Statutory Authority, Spanish, Border Patrol Operations, Care and Use of Firearms, Physical Training, Operation of Motor Vehicles, and Anti-Terrorism Training.

Federal Law Enforcement Center (FLETC) courses are: Communications, Ethics and Conduct, Report Writing, Introduction to Computers, Fingerprinting, and Constitutional Law. The U.S. Border Patrol Academy is located in Artesia, NM.

Border Construction and Support Facilities

Having U.S. Customs and Border Protection (CBP) secure our Nation across roughly 8,000 miles of land and coastal borders—while simultaneously ensuring a smooth flow of legal trade and travel from the borders through the country's interior—requires a vast network of both state-of-the-art support facilities and other tactical infrastructure.

The planning, design, and acquisition (via construction or leasing)—as well as maintenance, repair, and operation—of these structures are critical to:

- Supporting the facilitation of legitimate trade and travel though the official U.S. Ports of Entry (POE)
- Securing our Nation's borders between the POEs via land, air, and maritime patrols, and
- Training, housing, and supporting frontline and administrative personnel.

Under the guidance of the Office of Administration, the Facilities Management & Engineering Directorate is the official entity within CBP charged with performing these functions.

From the Air and Sea

U.S. Customs and Border Protection's (CBP) Office of Air and Marine (OAM) is the world's largest aviation and maritime law enforcement organization, a critical component of CBP's layered enforcement strategy for border security. With 1,200 federal agents, more than 250 aircraft and over 280 marine vessels operating from 91 locations throughout the United States and Puerto Rico. CBP detects, intercepts, and apprehends criminals in diverse environments at and beyond U.S. borders.

OAM protects the American people and the nation's critical infrastructure through the coordinated use of integrated air and marine forces to detect, interdict and prevent acts of terrorism and the unlawful movement of people, illegal drugs and other contraband toward or across the borders of the United States.

OAM's specialized law enforcement capabilities allow OAM to make significant contributions to Department of Homeland Security (DHS) efforts, as well as to federal, state, local and tribal agencies. OAM is uniquely positioned to provide direct air and marine support to multiple agencies and to ensure the success of border protection and law enforcement operations between ports of entry, within the maritime operating areas and within the nation's interior.

Air-to-Land Enforcement involves the capability to search, detect, identify and track suspect ground targets of interest moving by vehicle or on foot. Interdiction can occur on approach to the land border, at crossing points or after the border has been breached. Air-to-land interdiction is conducted in all geographic conditions and at all borders.

International Initiatives

U.S. Customs and Border Protection coordinates and supports foreign initiatives, programs and activities with our external partners around the world.

CBP focuses on international cooperation and strengthening multi- and bi-lateral relationships to achieve international agreements and joint efforts

U.S. borders from beyond by implementing programs and initiatives that promote anti-terrorism, global border security, non-proliferation, export controls, immigration and capacity building.

CBP promotes expansion of the World Customs Organization Framework of Standards for supply chain security and facilitation by providing targeted countries with training and advisory support through programs such as capacity building and Export Control and Border Security.

CBP operates Attaché Offices in 21 countries around the world. Attachés are posted in U.S. Embassies and Consulates and serve as the Chief of Mission's Customs and Border Protection in-house specialists where they inform and advise the U.S. Ambassador or Consul General on CBP programs and capabilities.

CBP Attachés support and oversee all CBP programs in their area of responsibility. Additionally, they seek to educate stakeholders about CBP's international programs such as: the Container Security Initiative; the Immigration Advisory Program; the Customs-Trade Partnership Against Terrorism, and; various capacity building programs.

Customs Mutual Assistance Agreements (CMAA)

In June 1967, the Customs Cooperation Council (CCC), known since 1994 as the World Customs Organization (WCO), adopted a model bilateral convention on mutual administrative assistance for countries to implement as part of a national customs policy. U.S. Customs and Border Protection has used this model as a basis for negotiating Customs Mutual Assistance Agreements (CMAAs) with other foreign administrations since joining the CCC in 1970. Domestic and foreign courts recognize each agreement as a legal basis for wide ranging cooperation.

Such a legal framework is vital because of explosive growth in the volume and complexity of international trade. Great demands are being placed on customs administrations around the world. With government resources not able to keep pace with this growing trade, customs administrations rely on mutual assistance as a powerful investigative tool.

The agreements allow for the exchange of information, intelligence, and documents that will ultimately assist countries in the prevention and gation of customs offenses. The agreements are particularly helpful for U.S. Attaché offices, as each agreement is tailored to the capacities and national policy of an individual country's customs administration.

International Training and Assistance

U.S. Customs and Border Protection (CBP) provides a wide array of short-term and long-term technical training and assistance to host nations Customs and Border security agencies. Based on CBP's expertise as the front-line border security agency for the United States, these programs are designed to build the capacity of foreign law enforcement agencies to implement more effective customs operations, border policing, and immigration inspections.

On average, CBP coordinates and presents over one hundred training programs to thousands of foreign participants each year. Training and assistance programs target the full range of border control and operations, including: weapons of mass effect (WME) training, anti-narcotics, port security, integrity, and commercial operations. The majority of these programs take place outside of the United States, although CBP hosts a limited number of training events at specific U.S. ports of entry so students can observe the manner in which enforcement techniques, inter-agency coordination, and infrastructure combine to produce positive results.

CBP undertakes most of its technical assistance work with funding from the U.S. State Department, the U.S. Agency for International Development, and the U.S. Department of Defense. In addition to implementing established multi-year initiatives such as the Export Control and related Border Security (EXBS) assistance program, port security advisory projects in several Latin American countries, CBP responds to ad hoc requests for assistance channeled through U.S. Embassies around the world.

Proliferation Security Initiative

The Proliferation Security Initiative (PSI) is a global effort that aims to stop trafficking of weapons of mass destruction, their delivery systems, and related materials to and from state and non-state actors of proliferation concern.

Launched by the President May 31, 2003, U.S. involvement in PSI stems from the U.S. National Strategy to Combat Weapons of Mass Destruction issued in December 2002.

In February 2004, U.S. Customs and Border Protection began its involvement when the PSI was expanded to include law enforcement cooperation. Today, more than 100 countries around the world have endorsed the PSI.

United Nations Security Council Resolution (UNSCR) 1540, adopted unanimously by the Security Council, calls on all states to take cooperative action to prevent trafficking in WMD.

PSI is an innovative and proactive approach to preventing proliferation that relies on voluntary actions by states, consistent with national legal authorities and relevant international law and frameworks, to fulfill the U.S. obligation to UNSCR 1540. PSI participants use existing authorities (national and international) to put an end to WMD-related trafficking and take steps to strengthen those authorities as necessary. Operationally, CBP can regularly take action to interdict WMD-related materials through its existing border search authorities.

CBP has been designated as a lead USG agency for law enforcement-related PSI issues, including coordination with other law enforcement agencies and the global law enforcement and Customs community. Law enforcement engagement provides the PSI with expertise in intelligence and information sharing, industry outreach, targeting and analysis, response and interdiction actions, and the methods to halt proliferation networks through criminal investigations, prosecutions and asset seizures.

Since 2004, CBP has maintained a leadership role among the global PSI law enforcement community, through active participation in PSI exercises, policy and operational experts meetings, industry outreach and capacity building around the world.

CBP PSI activities are designed to employ the full range of CBP enforcement programs, automation tools, technology, industry outreach, and highly trained law enforcement personnel in support of non-proliferation efforts. This includes helping other countries in their WMD interdiction efforts. The program builds upon current CBP non-proliferation efforts such as those designed to improve targeting and extend the border.

World Customs Organization Overview

As the lead U.S. agency engaged with the World Customs Organization (WCO), U.S. Customs and Border Protection (CBP) is responsible for preparing U.S. positions on Customs matters and representing those at the WCO. Part of CBP's continued and regular activities related to the WCO include active involvement in the drafting and approval of best practices, guidelines and standards relating to international customs issues. In addition, CBP provides unparalleled training and technical assistance to the WCO in the development and delivery of its international capacity building programs.

Since 1952, the World Customs Organization (WCO), formally known by international convention as the Customs Co-operation Council (CCC), has provided leadership in expanding the avenues of international trade and security. The WCO's accomplishments are both numerous and varied. The organization's successes include work in areas covering the development of global standards, the simplification and harmonization of Customs procedures, trade supply chain security, the facilitation of international trade, the enhancement of Customs enforcement and compliance activities, anti-counterfeiting and piracy initiatives, public-private partnerships, integrity promotion, and sustainable global Customs capacity building activities. The WCO is the only international body dedicated exclusively to international customs and border control matters.

By following the above principles, the WCO has achieved many triumphs across the entire spectrum of customs-based issues. For example, the WCO created and administers several international agreements that facilitate and secure world trade. The major international conventions created or administered by the WCO include the:

Harmonized System Convention (the basis for the U.S. import and export schedules)

WTO Customs Valuation and Rules of Origin Agreements

Customs Convention on the ATA carnet for the temporary admission of goods (ATA Convention)

The International Convention on the simplification and harmonization of Customs procedures (Revised Kyoto Convention).

In June 2005, the WCO Council unanimously adopted the WCO's SAFE Framework of Standards to Secure and Facilitate Global Trade, a global standard-setting document related to the security and facilitation of the international supply chain which was supported by the United States and to a large degree based on the best practices of U.S. Customs and Border Protection (CBP) and other like-minded WCO Members.

Humanitarian Challenges

U.S. Customs and Border Protection deals with multifaceted humanitarian and security issues such as in 2014 when tens of thousands of unaccompanied migrant children arrived at the Southwest U.S. border.

The most immediate problem was caring for the children. As of mid-June 2014, CBP had apprehended more than 52,000 children at the border. Approximately three-quarters of them originated from El Salvador, Guatemala or Honduras after traveling for weeks through Mexico.

"They're arriving exhausted and scared, in need of food and water," said CBP Commissioner R. Gil Kerlikowske. "Our agency and the Department of Homeland Security have mobilized to address this situation in a way consistent with our laws and our American values."

DHS and the Department of Health and Human Services coordinated with the Department of Defense to house and process the children. The federal partners located additional facilities as needed.

DHS Secretary Jeh Johnson on July 1, 2014 announced the immediate deployment of approximately 150 additional Border Patrol agents to the Rio Grande Valley in Texas, where the largest numbers of unaccompanied minors were arriving. The added personnel helped process the influx of children and upheld CBP's work securing the border.

"I have seen CBP employees respond to these difficulties with professionalism and compassion," said Commissioner Kerlikowske. "They've made heroic efforts with these children; rescuing them and caring for them in the most humane and compassionate way. I am extremely proud of their dedication and of how they have risen to this challenge."

The State Department and the White House worked with senior government officials in Guatemala, El Salvador, Honduras and Mexico. "They hope to address the conditions in Central America that are spurring the

ways that we can together assure faster, secure repatriation of these children and families," said Commissioner Kerlikowske.

In addition, the Department of Justice committed to sending more immigration judges to the border to expedite removal proceedings for the children.

The message from the U.S. government on immigration was clear—if you cross illegally into the U.S.:

you cannot earn a path to citizenship;

you are not eligible for the Deferred Action for Childhood Arrivals, or DACA;

you will not get papers that allow you to stay; and

you are putting yourself, or your child, in danger.

Dangers Awareness Campaign

CBP developed a multimedia public awareness campaign to communicate the dangers to the children and their families considering the journey.

The Dangers Awareness Campaign materials included print, radio and TV ads with the universal message:

The journey is too dangerous;

Children will not get legal papers if they make it.

They are the future—let's protect them.

In addition to placing paid advertising in Central America and Mexico through early September, CBP worked with stakeholders in Central America and in the U.S. to encourage them to continue communicating these messages with their constituencies. The agency also reached out to local governments, faith-based organizations, other non-governmental organizations and the news media to use the Dangers Awareness materials.

the United States government to fight human trafficking. A decade later, human trafficking remains prevalent. According to the most recent figures available (Source: United Nations, International Labor Organization):

There are at least 12.3 million enslaved adults and children around the world "at any given time."

Of these, at least 1.39 million are victims of commercial sexual servitude, both internationally and within national borders. More than half, 56 percent, of all forced labor victims are women and girls.

Although the legal definition of human trafficking is complex, the simple meaning of it is not. It occurs when a person is induced by force, fraud or coercion to:

Work under the total or near-total control of another person or organization (slavery or involuntary servitude)

Forced to pay off a loan by working instead of paying money, for an agreed-upon or unclear period of time (debt bondage) or even without an agreement as to the timeframe (peonage)

Perform a sex act for money or anything of value (if under 18, force, fraud or coercion is not required)

According to U.S. Immigration and Customs Enforcement, although many people think of the sex trade when they think of human trafficking, this crime also occurs in such labor situations as:

Domestic servitude

Labor in a prison-like factory

Migrant agricultural work.

In addition, with respect to labor situations, the initial agreement to travel or to perform work does not mean that the employer is later allowed to restrict a victim's freedom or use force or threats to obtain repayment.

Human trafficking and human smuggling are sometimes, but not always, linked, because not all individuals who are smuggled are trafficked, and movement is not required for trafficking to occur.

"Force, Fraud or Coercion"

These terms include any situation where an individual is forced to do something against their will, or where they are tricked into doing something someone who is lying to them or suppressing the truth. According to U.S. Immigration and Customs Enforcement, *force* can be active and physical or indirect and psychological (including threats). This term includes:

- Coercion
- Compulsion
- Constraint
- Restraint

Coercion refers to behaviors including:

- Threats of harm or physical restraint
- Trying to get a person to believe that if they don't do something, it will result in serious harm or physical restraint of themselves or someone else
- The abuse (or threatened abuse) of law or the legal process

Fraud refers to intentionally distorting the truth in order to get someone else (who relies on that version of the truth) to surrender a legal right or give up something valuable that belongs to them.

Human trafficking entangles victims in a nearly impenetrable web, for a number of reasons:

- The victim may not realize that he or she is imprisoned, because coercion is psychological (it may not be physical)
- Victims are typically impoverished and financially dependent on their captors
- Often the crime takes place in plain view-e.g. in a restaurant, worksite, or private home-and is not immediately apparent to observers
- Victims can be exploited for labor, sex, or both, particularly in private homes.

Signs of Human Trafficking

It is sometimes said that human trafficking is an "invisible crime," because its signs are not always obvious to the untrained eye. However, there are some indicators that may serve as a tip-off, particularly when they appear in combination. Suspect that something is amiss if an individual:

- Lacks identification documents or travel documents
- Lives and works in the same place
- Lacks freedom of movement
- Seems to be restricted from socializing, attending religious services or contacting family
- Seems to have been deprived of basic life necessities, such as food, water, sleep or medical care
- Shows signs of having been abused or physically assaulted. Such signs range from the more obvious, such as broken bones, to the more subtle, such as branding or tattooing
- Seems submissive or fearful in the presence of others
- Seems not to control his or her schedule
- Seems to lack concrete short- or long-term plans
- Seems to lack knowledge about the place where he or she lives
- Appears to date much older, abusive or controlling men.

A Government Partnership

Four executive agencies of the U.S. government, along with state and local law enforcement organizations, work together as well as with nonprofit organizations to combat human trafficking. The primary U.S. executive agencies include:

Department of Homeland Security , of which U.S. Customs and Border Protection , U.S. Immigration and Customs Enforcement , and U.S. Citizenship and Immigration Services are component agencies

State Department

Department of Justice

Department of Health and Human Services

DHS Activities Combating Human Trafficking

The Department of Homeland Security and its component agencies have been raising awareness for the past several years about the issue of human trafficking. Most recently, DHS announced an aggressive effort to protect victims and prosecute traffickers, in line with the TVPA's focus on three key goals:

- Prevention
- Protection
- Prosecution

Currently, the Department is focusing on the first of the three goals above, by sponsoring heavily advertised public awareness campaigns about human trafficking created by CBP and its sister agency, Immigration and Customs Enforcement and making potential victims aware that they are in danger, and that the government offers resources to provide them with asylum and other forms of assistance.

Actions CBP Is Taking To Enforce TVPA

With more than 42,000 frontline CBP officers and Border Patrol agents protecting nearly 7,000 miles of land border and 328 ports of entry—including official crossings by land, air, and sea—CBP is uniquely situated to deter and disrupt human trafficking. Currently, the agency is:

Identifying potential victims as they seek to enter the U.S.

Directing potential victims to U.S. agencies providing legal protection and assistance, through printed materials with educational information and telephone numbers where help can be obtained

Raising awareness among the American public of this often-invisible, yet pervasive crime, through public service announcements

Raising awareness internationally among potential border-crossers before they fall into the hands of traffickers, in countries where this crime is pervasive and where border smuggling frequently involves human trafficking

Helping the public to report suspected cases of human trafficking

Identifying imports produced by forced labor and stopping them from entering the country

Partnering with other law enforcement agencies to identify and support victims, such as by educating legal counsel to detect signs of victimization, to disrupt the crime itself and to prosecute human traffickers

Partnering with non-governmental organizations to provide information about government assistance to potential victims

Participating in the development of best practices for law enforcement efforts within the U.S. and internationally.

Within the agency, CBP has implemented comprehensive training for its frontline personnel with more forthcoming. Through its local field and sector offices, CBP is instructing them to recognize potential instances of human trafficking and to take appropriate actions when encountering human trafficking victims.

Human trafficking is a heinous international crime, and as the State Department notes in its most recent report on the subject, it is unfortunately flourishing due to current global financial issues. With global demand for labor decreasing, impoverished workers find themselves taking greater risks than before in order to survive. The result: "a recipe for greater forced labor of migrant workers and commercial sexual exploitation of women in prostitution."

Laboratories and Scientific Services

Laboratories and Scientific Services is the forensic and scientific arm of U.S. Customs and Border Protection (CBP), providing forensic and scientific testing in the area of Trade Enforcement, Weapons of Mass Destruction, Intellectual Property Rights, and Narcotics Enforcement. Laboratories and Scientific Services coordinates technical and scientific support to all CBP Trade and Border Protection activities.

U.S. Customs and Border Protection (CBP) scientists, engineers, and project managers all play an important role in the commerce and border protection of the United States. Their active participation in the detection of Weapons of Mass Destruction contributes to national security efforts.

Chemists and Textile Analysts ensure that imported and exported merchandise has been properly identified. The information they provide can an impact on duty rates, import quota restrictions, or whether merchandise can even be legally allowed into the country.

Health Physicists and Physical Scientists support CBP field personnel, advising them on radiation incidents.

Forensic scientists, such as **Fingerprint Examiners**, support crime scene investigations in the laboratory and remote areas.

General Engineers and Project Managers are responsible for acquiring and deploying the latest non-intrusive inspection systems available. They provide site surveys, site preparation and installations. Current major project areas are non-intrusive inspections, radiation detection technology, and high-technology enforcement equipment.

Customer Service Standards

Our Vision

To provide rapid, quality scientific and forensic services; and weapons of mass destruction interdiction support to our customers.

Our Mission

To provide scientific/forensic support, including on-site support, to CBP officers and other government agencies with regard to the investigation and interdiction of Weapons of Mass Destruction.

To produce timely and effective laboratory reports and crime scene documentation supporting Customs trade compliance and law enforcement missions.

To provide timely and effective scientific/forensic support to CBP officers and the trade community (i.e., training, targeting, health and safety).

To approve and/or accredit and monitor commercial gaugers and laboratories that perform measurements and analysis for CBP purposes.

To provide scientific/forensic support to other Federal agencies, standards writing organizations, foreign governments and international organizations to promote international trade compliance and more effective international efforts to counter the movement of weapons of mass destruction.

Informed Compliance

We will provide a response to your request for technical advice or assistance in a professional and courteous manner within one working day.

We provide, in conjunction with port personnel, consultation on technical issues involving CBP and the importing and exporting community.

We provide support by means of demonstrations or presentations to trade seminars and other business meetings.

We provide technical seminars of interest to the importing and exporting communities at field laboratories or other locations.

Commercial Gauger Approval and Laboratory

We conduct audits of outside facilities for accreditation to perform work under the Customs Modernization Act in the following areas: Botanical Identification; Building Stone, Ceramics, Glassware and Other Mineral Substances; Dairy and Chocolate Products; Essential Oils and Perfumes; Food and Food Products; Inorganic Materials including Inorganic Compounds and Ores; Leather; Metals and Alloys; Organic Materials including Intermediates and Pharmaceuticals; Paper and Paper Products; Petroleum and Petroleum Products; Rubber, Plastics, Polymers, Pigments, and Paints; Spirituous Beverages; Sugar, Sugar Syrups, and Confectionery; and Textiles and related Products including Footwear and Hats

We perform audits of commercial gaugers for approval to perform measurements for Customs purposes.

We perform the required periodic audits of accredited laboratories and approved gaugers upon arrangement with the laboratory or gauger.

Organization and Operations

Headquarters

Headquarters staff provides operational and administrative management and oversight of the laboratory system.

Science Officers plan, coordinate, and execute support operations in three major areas: trade enforcement, Weapons of Mass Destruction recognition and interdiction, crime scene investigations, and forensics. Science Officers also issue technical opinions, provide advice on World Customs Organization issues, and manage CBP Gauger/Laboratory Accreditation program.

General engineers and project managers acquire and deploy the latest non-intrusive inspection systems available. They also maintain performance schedules and expenditure rates, perform contract acceptance functions, provide site surveys, site preparation, and installations.

Springfield Laboratory

The Springfield Laboratory is a centralized facility that provides scientific support to CBP Headquarters and the Field Laboratories.

The Springfield Laboratory was originally established in 1970 as a research facility. Today, the laboratory provide analytical services to CBP legal and regulatory functions and to other Headquarters Offices which may need scientific support including Quality Assurance for the CBP Drug Screening Program and technical assistance for the Canine Enforcement Program and for international drug training programs. The Springfield Laboratory is an important resource in addressing tariff classification issues for high technology products, in developing statistical data to confirm the country of origin of imported commodities, and in providing a sound technical foundation for Intellectual Property Rights (IPR) enforcement involving copyrights, trademarks and patents. The laboratory also develops new analytical methods and evaluates new instrumentation for application by the Field Laboratories.

ensure analytical uniformity among the Field Laboratories and maintains technical and scientific exchange with other federal enforcement agencies, technological branches of foreign customs agencies and the military.

The laboratory is well equipped to meet its analytical objectives with a staff of scientists and state-of-the art instrumentation including a Fourier-transform infrared spectrophotometer (FTIR), high-resolution inductively coupled plasma mass spectrometer (HR-ICP-MS), scanning electron microscope (SEM), and capillary electrophoresis equipment.

New York Laboratory

The New York CBP Laboratory, is accredited by the American Association for Laboratory Accreditation (A2LA), and services the greater New York City area including the New York Seaport, JFK Airport, the Port of Newark and Perth Amboy.

The New York CBP Laboratory provides quality scientific, forensic, and WMD services to our customers.

In support of our primary mission of homeland security, the NY Laboratory WMD services include radiation detection, chemical WMD detection and identification, participation in LSS national WMD strike team, and membership in the Food Emergency Response Network (FERN).

Forensic services include analysis of controlled substances, latent fingerprint lifting, and forensic photography.

The scientific services include analysis of a full range of commodities imported into the US including inorganic products, organic chemicals and products, food products, petroleum, textiles, footwear, raw sugar, polymers, plastics, and paper.

Additional specialized services of the NY Laboratory include:

The laboratory conducts mobile operations throughout its service area. In support of the primary mission of securing our borders, the laboratory screens for radioactive, chemical and biological WMD materials at the ports, airports and terminals.

Chicago Laboratory

The Chicago Laboratory services Illinois, Indiana, Iowa, Kansas, Michigan, Minnesota, Missouri, Nebraska, Ohio, Wisconsin, Connecticut, Delaware, Maine, Massachusetts, New Hampshire, Rhode Island, Vermont, and New York, except the New York Metro area.

The Chicago Laboratory is a full-service laboratory, providing technical advice and analytical services to CBP officers, U.S. Immigration and Customs Enforcement (ICE) agents, Border Patrol agents, and other government entities on a wide range of issues and imported commodities. These services assist CBP officers in meeting the CBP mission of collecting revenue based on import duties, enforcing CBP laws and regulations, and enforcing other federal government laws and regulations. Services provided to ICE agents and Border Patrol agents pertain primarily to forensic and law enforcement issues.

The staff consists of over 20 employees most of whom are chemists and textile analysts. In addition to providing technical advice and analytical assistance, the laboratory also provides training to CBP officers on interdiction, identification, and determination of weapons of mass destruction (WMD) and contraband. The staff of the Chicago Laboratory actively participates in national and international scientific organizations to improve methods of analysis and promote uniformity.

The Chicago Laboratory has the only tensile tester in the CBP laboratory system capable of determining certain physical characteristics of industrial fasteners, metals, and articles of metal. The laboratory has had a strong involvement in the geological identification of building stones under the Harmonized Tariff Schedule. Because of its northern location, NAFTA issues and Canadian merchandise are prevalent.

In the forensics area, the Chicago Laboratory has the capability to enhance video and audio recordings for its law enforcement customers. This capability includes, but is not limited to, audio/video authenticity/continuity, audio/video recovery, audio/video duplication, audio transcription, and audio synchronization. The laboratory also has the capability of developing standard color and black and white film, generate prints, and making enlargements on a variety of media.

The Chicago Laboratory has the capability of being deployed at service area sites with the necessary equipment for WMD and anti-terrorism operations and specialized operations in support of its customer's missions.

The Chicago Laboratory is accredited to international standard ISO/IEC 17025—General Requirements for the Competence of Testing and Calibration Laboratories—in the chemical and mechanical fields of testing.

Savannah Laboratory

The Savannah Customs Laboratory serves ports from Philadelphia, PA to Key West, FL.

The Savannah Laboratory was established in 1918 for the purpose of analyzing raw sugar imported by the Savannah Sugar Refining Corporation. Once a one room "sugar operation" located in the historic Savannah Customhouse, today the Savannah Laboratory is a 20,000 square foot facility.

The laboratory is a full-service analytical laboratory with capabilities for chemical and physical testing of all types of commodities, narcotics and other controlled substances.

The Savannah Laboratory has a technical staff of nineteen and an administrative support staff of three.

Laboratory specializations include textile and apparel analyses. The laboratory is designated as the CBP testing facility for wool, which includes determining clean content and wool grade.

To address country-of-origin issues, the Savannah Laboratory has developed trace element profiles for many agricultural products including garlic, peanuts, fruit juices and tobacco products. Additionally, the laboratory uses SNIF-NMR technologies and IRMS to supplement trace element profiles for country-of-origin investigations.

Because of its proximity to the CBP training facility at the Federal Law Enforcement Training Center (FLETC) in Glynco, GA, the Savannah Laboratory provides specialized technical training to CBP officers and provides support to the agency's International CBP Training program.

The Savannah Laboratory operates two mobile laboratories to meet the onsite testing needs of Southeastern U.S. Ports. The units are state-of-the art, custom-built vehicles capable of simultaneously housing image analysis instrumentation, mobile metal analyzer, IPR electronic testing equipment, GC/MS instrumentation, UV and IR spectrophotometers, conventional "wet" chemistry apparatus and instruments used for the detection of materials for Weapons of Mass Destruction.

Houston Laboratory (Southwest Regional Science Center)

The Houston Laboratory (Southwest Regional Science Center) provides technical and scientific services to all of the Ports of Entry and Border Patrol Sectors in the following eight states: Alabama, Tennessee, Mississippi, Louisiana, Arkansas, Oklahoma, Texas, New Mexico. This geographic area contains 80 percent of the border between the United States and Mexico.

The U.S. Customs & Border Protection Houston Laboratory (Southwest Regional Science Center) provides technical and scientific services in support of the U.S. Customs & Border Protection mission to manage, secure, and control the nation's border and to prevent terrorists and terrorist weapons from entering the United States.

The services provided by the Houston Laboratory (Southwest Regional Science Center) support forensic crime scene investigation, WMD interdiction, and trade enforcement. Forensic scientists provide support to law enforcement investigations with the analysis of latent prints, controlled substances, pharmaceuticals, digital evidence, accident investigation, and expert witness testimony. All analyses are conducted by American Board of Criminalistics (ABC) certified chemists or International Association for Identification (IAI) certified latent print examiners. Additionally, a broad range of trade enforcement analyses are performed on imported and exported commodities to determine whether the merchandise is properly described by the required documentation or identified as contraband according to its physical and chemical nature. This laboratory is also responsible for providing technical support in areas such as drawback, classification issues, and regulatory audit functions.

Because of the Center's location to the Southwest border, there is an increased emphasis on providing technical and scientific support to manage,

tion of clandestine tunnels, response to case investigations to ensure that physical evidence is identified and collected properly for further forensic examination, and the deployment of weapons of mass destruction detection technologies to the front-line.

Los Angeles Laboratory

The Los Angeles Laboratory services all of Southern California, Southern Nevada, including Las Vegas, Arizona, and the California-Mexico border in these areas.

Within its service area, the Los Angeles CBP Laboratory provides analytical services and technical assistance to CBP officers, ICE agents, Border Patrol agents, and other law enforcement agencies. The staff of chemists, textile analysts and physical scientists is trained to assist in meeting the CBP mission in areas of trade, forensics and WMD.

Some laboratory functions, including Specialization, are:

Technical and analytical assistance on imports for classification and identification for compliance with CBP laws and/or other agency requirements enforced by CBP.

The laboratory has mobile vans to travel to its service areas to provide forensic and trade support. Numerous latent print processing and trace evidence collection operations have been conducted. The laboratory is equipped with field instrumentation to analyze and identify some unknown chemicals, textile construction and applications on textiles, controlled substances, explosives, and WMD chemical agents and radiation. The Los Angeles Laboratory has vehicle-mounted detectors for rapid scan and identification of radiation sources from cargo containers and hand-held NaI (sodium iodide) and HPGe (high purity Germanium) detectors to support the LA/LB Seaport and CBP POEs.

San Francisco Laboratory

The laboratory serves the northern two-thirds of California, as well as the states of Oregon, Washington, North Dakota, South Dakota, Minnesota, Alaska, Hawaii, Colorado, Utah, Nevada, Montana, and Idaho. Major ports located in this service area include San Francisco, Portland, Seattle, Blaine, Anchorage, Honolulu, and Denver.

The San Francisco Laboratory is a full-service, ISO/IEC 17025 accredited laboratory that provides technical advice, forensic, and other scientific services to the CBP officials and other agencies on a wide range of imported and exported commodities. Imported and exported products related to trade and forensic include wearing apparels, footwear, papers, building stones, ceramics, metal products, foods, raw sugar, chemicals, petroleum products, woods, paraffin wax candles (antidumping), and Korean dies for memory modules (antidumping), control substances and pharmaceuticals, film development, Intellectual Property Rights (IPR), ITC Exclusion Orders on One-Time use cameras (LFFP) and certain sildenafil. Expedited services are provided on samples involving intellectual property rights (IPR), textiles that require quota and visa and forensics, fingerprint lifting, and controlled substances. If samples cannot be brought to the laboratory, mobile laboratory equipments are readily available to conduct on-site examinations and supports.

The laboratory also provides tremendous supports in Weapons of Mass Destruction (WMD), explosives, hazardous materials, and crime scene investigation. Several staff members are qualified RIID trainers training, and continuously provide RIID Operation trainings, and provide CBP Radiation Detection Program and Response Protocol at the Pacific Northwest National Laboratory Radiation Academy (RADACAD) in Richland, Washington.

Available to the technical staff are scientific/laboratory instruments such as Inductively Couple Plasma (ICP)/Spark Ablation-Inductively Couple Plasma, Inductively Couple Plasma Mass Spectrometer (ICP-MS), optical spectrophotometers, scanning electron microscope (SEM), gas chromatograph-mass (GC-MS) spectrometers, High Performance Liquid Chromatography (HPLC), Fourier Transformed Infrared Spectroscopy (FTIR), portable FTIR, Isotopic Ratio Mass Spectrometer (IR-MS), Nuclear Magnetic Resonance (NMR), X-ray Diffractometers (XRD), X-ray Fluorescence (XRF), photo development/processing, and audio/visual enhancement.

Because of the laboratory's location on the Pacific Rim, there is an emphasis and greater expertise in that commerce which includes: IPR, includes digital millennium copyright act (DMCA), antidumping duties on DRAMs (Korea), and patent through ITC Exclusion orders on One-Time Use Cameras (LFFP); textiles, including intermediates of the manufacturing process as well as finished wearing apparel; oriental food and beverages.

Due to the very significant value of petroleum importations, the laboratory specializes in petroleum analysis. A special emphasis of this work targets the country of origin of crude oil and some of its finished products such as aviation fuel. The National Petroleum chemist is by defacto, the keeper of all commercial gauger audit reports in his or her designated service area.

The San Francisco Laboratory operates a small mobile laboratory unit, which is utilized throughout its service area in the Northwestern United States to provide on-site examination and analyses of commercial shipments and training for local CBP officers. Mobile equipment coupled with expertise and needs cause the focus to be on textiles and IPR issues during these operations, with training being provided across the entire spectrum of works, include Drug Test Kit, Weights and Scale training.

The laboratory also provides supports on-site Crime Scene Investigation (Fingerprint collection), and examination and analysis on any suspicious illicit radioactive materials entering this country. Available WMD equipments include RIID (GR-135), Detective-Ex, GR-460 Mobile Spectrometer, Vapor Tracer 2, Itemiser 3, Hazmat/Sensor IR, First Defender, NucSafe Backpack, JCAD, Bio-Seeq, Bio Threat Alert, Fingerprint Collection Kit, and portable XRF (MiniPal).

San Juan Laboratory

The San Juan Laboratory serves the ports of Puerto Rico and the United States Virgin Isands.

The San Juan Laboratory is a full-service analytical laboratory equipped with the latest state-of-the-art scientific equipment and with capabilities for chemical and physical testing of all wide variety of importations, and forensic related samples. Technical and scientific support is also provided to CBP cers to prevent terrorists and terrorist weapons from entering the United States territories.

The services provided by the San Juan Laboratory include forensic support, Weapons of Mass Destruction (WMD) interdiction, and trade enforcement. Forensic support to CBP Officers, and Border Patrol and ICE Agents includes latent print lifting, crime scene investigation and evidence collection, analysis of unknowns and suspected controlled substances, photography, audio and video duplication, data extraction from media and cellular phones, and expert witness testimony, among others. WMD support includes programmed visits to seaports, airports, and Radiation Monitoring Portals (RPM) during their daily radiation to provide scientific and technical advice. Trade enforcement support includes testing commodities for HTSUS classification, country of origin and marking violations, hazards, quotas, visas and other requirements established by the trade community.

In addition, the San Juan Laboratory provides vital training in areas related to national security and law enforcement such as WMD, Radiation Isotope Identification Detector (RIID) certification, Crime Scene Management, and Narcotics Field Test Identification.

Each San Juan laboratory analyst is capable of working a wide range of commodities. Great expertise has been developed through the years in the identification of unknowns, controlled substances, and trace evidence.

The San Juan Laboratory mobile operations encompass an active participation in CBP's WMD related activities, forensic and trace evidence collection, and crime scene management through all ports of Puerto Rico and the U.S. Virgin Islands.

The San Juan Laboratory is accredited to the international standard ISO/IEC 17025, "General Requirements for the Competence of Testing and Calibration Laboratories". All forensic scientists are licensed by the Puerto Rico Chemistry Board, and/or the American Board of Criminalistics (ABC).

Teleforensic Center

The Teleforensic Center provides scientific reachback support to field personnel on matters related to safeguarding of the nation's borders.

The function of the Teleforensic Center (TC) operation is to provide field personnel with reachback access to scientific and technological resources. These resources help facilitate resolutions for field personnel in the performance of their duties. One of the field personnel's primary duties is detection, isolation and control of potential threats that may result from the presence of chemical, biological, radiological or nuclear (CBRN) materials. TC scientists provide technical support to resolve threat issues related to the execution of this duty. The TC is staffed 24 hours per day, 7 days per-week.

TC scientists' expertise originates from a broad-spectrum of scientific disciplines including chemical, biological, explosives, radiological, and nuclear. TC scientists act in the capacity of technical experts, advisers, and researchers.

Coordinate technical activities with other government agencies including National Laboratories and furnish scientific and technical advisory services.

Initiate, organize, organize and manage a comprehensive program to find solutions to novel and complex issues that result from the interdiction and/or confiscation of seized radioactive material.

Develop conjunctive partnerships and outreach efforts with National Laboratories, the Domestic Nuclear Detection Office (DNDO), and other agencies in preparation of special operations, including international venues, for the interdiction of radioactive material.

Provide scientific and technical advisory services to CBP executives and port officials regarding plans and recommendations for new equipment and interdiction methods for CBP and other agencies using the TC for reachback support.

Interdiction Technology Branch

The Interdiction Technology Branch is a centralized facility that provides system acquisition and technical support to CBP Headquarters and field personnel.

The LSS Interdiction Technology Branch (ITB) consists of general engineers, physical scientists, and project managers to provide CBP with an internal technical capability to ensure that field personnel have the best and

ment of Homeland Security and other organizations are conducting multiple research and development projects for next generation equipment, ITB assists CBP in assessing the "readiness" of equipment proposed for field validation and/or deployment. ITB also acquires and deploys current "off the shelf" equipment for both domestic and international operations. To that end ITB is the technical administrator of all NII procurements and system acquisitions fielded by CBP. To retain "lessons learned" and provide future strategic information for CBP managers, ITB is developing the capability to conduct advanced analysis, "what if" studies, and modeling and simulations to help proactively guide the acquisition, fielding and life cycle support for the high-technology enforcement equipment program. ITB advises CBP executive management on high-technology enforcement and inspection technology and technically represents CBP on these issues with other domestic and foreign agencies, Congress, the media, industry, and academia.

Environmental and Cultural Stewardship

U.S. Customs and Border Protection (CBP) is committed to environmental and cultural stewardship while performing its core missions of border security and the facilitation of legitimate trade and travel. CBP works hand-in-hand with other Federal, Tribal, state, and local agencies, as well as non-governmental organizations (NGOs), to fulfill environmental compliance regulations and to ensure protection of the Nation's natural and cultural resources. Additionally, CBP works diligently to integrate responsible environmental practices—including incorporating sustainable practices—into all aspects of our decision making and operations.

Environmental Management System Policy Statement

U.S. Customs and Border Protection (CBP) is one of the Department of Homeland Security's (DHS) largest and most complex components, with a priority mission of keeping terrorists and their weapons out of the United States. CBP also has a responsibility for securing the border and facilitating lawful international trade and travel while enforcing hundreds of U.S. laws and regulations, including immigration and drug laws. CBP executes its mission while complying with environmental laws and regulations as well as executive direction for conserving valued national resources.

National Environmental Policy Act (NEPA)

U.S. Customs and Border Protection (CBP) integrates environmental stewardship practices into its decision making to avoid and minimize environmental impacts associated with its activities. This includes the evaluation of all prospective projects to ensure compliance with the National Environmental Policy Act (NEPA) of 1969, the Council on Environmental Quality (CEQ) Regulations for Implementing the Procedural Provisions of NEPA, and other associated laws and regulations including the Endangered Species Act, National Historic Preservation Act, Clean Water Act, Clean Air Act, etc.

NEPA requires that Federal agencies assess the potential environmental effects of proposed actions prior to making any decisions. As part of the NEPA review process, CBP requires a comprehensive review of potential environmental impacts; thorough consultation with stakeholders, and; the identification of opportunities to avoid, minimize, and, where appropriate, mitigate for impacts to sensitive resources. CBP prepares the appropriate environmental decision documents and, when required, provides them to the public for a review period.

CBP Environmental Documents

The Department of Homeland Security (DHS) and U.S. Customs and Border Protection (CBP) have prepared documented processes to identify, assess, and sometimes measure the potential environmental impacts associated with proposed actions. In most instances, these documents have been prepared pursuant to the National Environmental Policy Act of 1969, 42 U.S.C. 4321 et seq., (NEPA); the Clean Air Act of 1970, as amended; the Clean Water Act of 1977, as amended; the National Historic Preservation Act of 1966; the Archaeological Resource Protection Act of 1979; various Executive Orders

Additionally, some of the documents on the site have been prepared in response to waivers issued by the DHS Secretary. These Environmental Stewardship Plans (ESPs)—and corresponding Environmental Stewardship Summary Reports (ESSRs)—are very similar in approach and content to traditional NEPA documents and were created to fulfill the DHS Secretary's commitment to responsible environmental stewardship.

Preserving Cultural Resources

U.S. Customs and Border Protection (CBP) is committed to playing a pivotal role in preserving cultural resources for future generations by taking historic preservation into account when planning and executing our operations. CBP follows the rule and spirit of Federal laws, regulations, and Executive Orders— including the National Historic Preservation Act of 1966 and its implementing regulations at 36 CFR § 800, as well as through DHS Directives System Directive 017-01: *Historic Preservation in Asset Management and Operations* (Directive 017-01) and DHS Directives System Instruction 017-01-001: *Guide on the Historic Preservation in Asset Management and Operations* (Instruction 017-01-001)—to preserve and enhance historic properties and sacred sites for future generations by taking historic preservation into account in planning and executing facility and operational activities.

To safeguard traditional and cultural resources and their respectful treatment, CBP promotes communication and partnerships with Tribal groups, the private sector, and relevant government entities. Effective communication about CBP's programs is paramount to reducing conflicts with the public and promoting CBP's commitments to the American public.

Sustainability and Natural Resource Conservation

U.S. Customs and Border Protection (CBP) embraces the concept of promoting conservation of the earth's natural resources and managing energy and water use. CBP aims to implement its national security mission while moving toward a more sustainable future by both leading and supporting an

toward a more sustainable future by both leading and supporting an array of initiatives, including:

Greenhouse Gas Emission Inventory and Reduction: CBP is inventorying greenhouse gas (GHG) emissions and developing a GHG reduction strategy for emission sources such as buildings and vehicles.

High Performance Sustainable Buildings: CBP is building high performance sustainable buildings that use less energy and water and include renewable materials and energy sources.

Sustainable Acquisition: CBP promotes sustainable acquisition by purchasing products and services that meet present needs without compromising the needs of future generations.

Electronic Stewardship: CBP purchases computers, laptops, and cell phones that are manufactured in an environmentally and socially responsible way, use low levels of energy, and can be recycled at the end of their useful life.

Recycling: CBP promotes recycling at all facilities when possible in order to reduce waste of resources, our use of landfills, and greenhouse gas.

These initiatives coincide with the requirements in Executive Order 13423 and Executive Order 13514, as well as demonstrate compliance with Federal laws such as the Energy Policy Act of 2005, the Energy Independence and Security Act of 2007, the Resource Conservation and Recovery Act, and the Clean Air Act. CBP's progress toward meeting these targets is reported in the Department of Homeland Security (DHS) Strategic Sustainability Performance Plan (SSPP) which is publicly available on the following web page: http://sustainability.performance.gov/

Travel

Almost a million times each day, CBP officers welcome international travelers into the U.S. In screening both foreign visitors and returning U.S. citizens, CBP uses a variety of techniques to assure that global tourism remains safe and strong.

NEXUS

The NEXUS alternative inspection program has been completely harmonized and integrated into a single program. NEXUS members now have crossing privileges at air, land, and marine ports of entry. Under the Western Hemisphere Travel Initiative, the NEXUS card has been approved as an alternative to the passport for air, land, and sea travel into the United States for US and Canadian citizens.

The NEXUS program allows pre-screened travelers expedited processing by United States and Canadian officials at dedicated processing lanes at designated northern border ports of entry, at NEXUS (CA Entry) and Global Entry (US Entry) kiosks at Canadian Preclearance airports, and at marine reporting locations. Approved applicants are issued a photo-identification, proximity Radio Frequency Identification (RFID) card. Participants use the three modes of passage where they will either present their NEXUS card, have their iris scanned, or present a WHTI compliant document and make a declaration.

Individuals approved to participate in NEXUS receive an identification card that allows them to:

Receive expedited passage at NEXUS-dedicated lanes, airport kiosks, and by calling a marine telephone reporting center to report their arrival into the United States and Canada; and

Cross the border with a minimum of customs and immigration questioning

NEXUS applicants only need to submit one application and one fee. Applicants may apply on-line via the CBP Global On-Line Enrollment System (GOES) website. Qualified applicants are required to travel to a NEXUS Enrollment Center for an interview. If they are approved for the program at that time, a photo identification card will be mailed to them in 7-10 business days. NEXUS allows United States and Canadian border agencies to concentrate their efforts on potentially higher-risk travelers and goods, which helps to ensure the security and integrity of our borders.

Secure Electronic Network for Travelers Rapid Inspection

SENTRI provides expedited CBP processing for pre-approved, low-risk travelers. Applicants must voluntarily undergo a thorough biographical background check against criminal, law enforcement, customs, immigration, and terrorist indices; a 10-fingerprint law enforcement check; and a personal interview with a CBP Officer.

Applicants may not qualify for participation in the SENTRI program if they:

Provide false or incomplete information on the application;

Have been convicted of any criminal offense or have pending criminal charges to include outstanding warrants;

Have been found in violation of any customs, immigration, or agriculture regulations or laws in any country;

Are subjects of an ongoing investigation by any federal, state, or local law enforcement agency;

Are inadmissible to the United States under immigration regulation, including applicants with approved waivers of inadmissibility or parole documentation;

Cannot satisfy CBP of their low risk status or meet other program requirements.

Once an applicant is approved they are issued a Radio Frequency Identification Document (RFID) that will identify their record and status in the CBP database upon arrival at the U.S. port of entry.

SENTRI users have access to specific, dedicated primary lanes into the United States.

SENTRI was first implemented at the Otay Mesa, California port of entry on November 1, 1995. SENTRI Dedicated Commuter Lanes also exist in El Paso, TX; San Ysidro, CA; Calexico, CA; Nogales, AZ; Hidalgo, TX; Brownsville, TX; Anzalduas, TX; Laredo, TX; and San Luis, Az; Douglas, AZ.

When an approved international traveler approaches the border in the SENTRI lane, the system automatically identifies the vehicle and the identity of the occupants of the vehicle. This is accomplished through:

The RFID cards contain a file number that is read upon arrival.

The file number triggers the participant's data to be brought up on the CBP Officer's screen.

The data is verified by the CBP Officer and the traveler is released or referred for additional inspections.

All of the applicant data is stored in the secure CBP database. It is not stored on the card, and it is not transmitted with the RFID (RFID technology has the potential to track an individual's movements, create a profile of an individual's habits, and allow for secondary uses of that information).

Simultaneously, license plate readers and computers perform queries of the vehicles and occupants against law enforcement databases that are continuously updated. A combination of electric gates, tire shredders, traffic control lights, fixed iron bollards, and pop-up pneumatic bollards ensure physical control of the border crosser and their vehicle.

Participants in the program wait for much shorter periods of time than those in regular lanes waiting to enter the United States, even at the busiest time of day. Critical information required in the inspection process is provided to the Officer in advance of the passenger's arrival thus reducing the inspection time from an average of 30-40 seconds down to an average of 10 seconds.

Applicants to the SENTRI Program may submit their application online using the Global Online Enrollment System (GOES). Once the application is certified as true and complete, it will be submitted to CBP for processing. Applicants can monitor the status of their application by logging back into GOES, and will be advised of "Conditional Approval", or "Denial" through the GOES account posting. A $25 application fee will be charged at the time of application submission.

Step 1: To complete a SENTRI application via the Internet, click on the GOES link to be transferred to the online application.

Step 2: Once notification of conditional approval is received, you will be directed to schedule your appointment online through your GOES account.

Applicants have 30 days from that date to schedule an interview. Otherwise, applicants will be denied further enrollment consideration for failure to schedule an interview, which is the final requirement in determining program membership. This denial will not prevent an applicant from submitting a new application in the future. However, a new payment fee will be required. At the

vehicle fee will be required. Applicants must bring the following original documents with them to the interview. Please ensure the exact documents you provided during the online application are those presented at the time of interview.

Originals of evidence of citizenship that you listed on your application

If not a U.S. citizen, originals of evidence of immigration admissibility to the U.S., that you listed on your application

Valid driver's license (or state identification) issued in state where applicant lives

Vehicle registration and evidence of US automobile insurance by a company authorized to write automobile insurance in the US.

If the vehicle is not registered in the name of the applicant, a notarized letter authorizing its use by the applicant is required. A company vehicle requires written authorization on company letterhead.

Evidence of employment or financial support. (For instance, most recent year's tax return, pay receipt, or direct deposit salary statement. Those self-employed must present a business license, current tax information and bank statement)

Evidence of residence, (Mortgage or rent payment receipts)

During the Interview, information provided on the application will be verified and upon acceptance, CBP will:

Take a photograph of applicant for identification card purposes

Take applicant's fingerprint

Provide terms and conditions of the program

Answer any questions the applicant may have

Issue an RFID enabled identification document

Free and Secure Trade for Commercial Vehicles (FAST)

The Free and Secure Trade program, or FAST, is a commercial clearance program for known low-risk shipments entering the U.S. from Canada and Mexico. Initiated after 9/11, this innovative trusted traveler/trusted shipper program allows expedited processing for commercial carriers who have completed background checks and fulfill certain eligibility requirements.

More than 78,000 commercial drivers are enrolled in the FAST program nationwide. FAST enrollment is open to truck drivers from the U.S., Canada, and Mexico.

FAST vehicle lanes process cargo at land border ports of entry that serve commercial cargo: 17 ports on the northern border and 17 on the southern border. The majority of dedicated FAST lanes are located in northern border ports in Michigan, New York and Washington State and at southern border ports from California to Texas. Participation in FAST requires that every link in the supply chain, from manufacturer to carrier to driver to importer, is certified under the Customs-Trade Partnership Against Terrorism program, or C-TPAT.

CBP routinely conducts on-site visits to domestic and foreign C-TPAT member facilities to evaluate and validate their supply-chain security measures. More than 10,000 companies world-wide are certified C-TPAT members.

Applications for FAST can be completed and submitted at the GOES website.

The cost to apply for FAST membership is $50 U.S. or Canadian for 5 years.

Among the key benefits of FAST enrollment are:

Access to dedicated lanes for greater speed and efficiency in processing transborder shipments;

Reduced number of inspections resulting in reduced delays at the border;

Priority, front-of-the-line processing for CBP inspections; and,

Enhanced supply chain security while promoting the economic prosperity of the U.S., Canada and Mexico.

Global Entry

Global Entry is a U.S. Customs and Border Protection (CBP) program that allows expedited clearance for pre-approved, low-risk travelers upon arrival in the United States. Though intended for frequent international travelers, there is no minimum number of trips necessary to qualify for the program. Participants may enter the United States by using automated kiosks located at select airports.

At airports, program participants proceed to Global Entry kiosks, present their machine-readable passport or U.S. permanent resident card, place their fingertips on the scanner for fingerprint verification, and make a customs declaration. The kiosk issues the traveler a transaction receipt and directs the traveler to baggage claim and the exit.

Travelers must be pre-approved for the Global Entry program. All applicants undergo a rigorous background check and interview before enrollment.

While Global Entry's goal is to speed travelers through the process, members may be selected for further examination when entering the United States. Any violation of the program's terms and conditions will result in appropriate enforcement action and revocation of the traveler's membership privileges.

6

United States Coast Guard (USCG)

The United States Coast Guard is one of the five armed forces of the United States and the only military organization within the Department of Homeland Security. The Coast Guard protects the maritime economy and the environment, defends our maritime borders, and saves those in peril.

Since 1790 the Coast Guard has safeguarded the Nation's maritime interests and environment around the world. The Coast Guard is an adaptable, responsive military force of maritime professionals whose broad legal authorities, capable assets, geographic diversity and expansive partnerships provide a persistent presence along our rivers, in the ports, littoral regions and on the high seas. Coast Guard presence and impact is local, regional, national and international. These attributes make the Coast Guard a unique instrument of maritime safety, security and environmental stewardship.

At a Glance

- Over 43,000 active duty members, over 8,000 reservists, over 8,800 civilian employees, and over 30,000 volunteer Auxiliarists
- Responded to 19,790 Search and Rescue cases in 2012, (latest figures available) saved 3,560 lives and more than $77 million in property
- Removed 107 metric tons of cocaine bound toward the U.S. via the Transit Zone
- Continued the deployment of six Patrol Boats and 400 personnel to protect Iraqi critical maritime oil infrastructure and train Iraqi naval forces

- Conducted 919 escorts and patrols to support 190 domestic U.S. military cargo out-loads
- Conducted 25,500 container inspections, 5,000 facility safety and marine pollution related inspections, and 1,195 cargo transfer monitors to ensure safety and environmental stewardship of the maritime domain
- Conducted 1,424 boardings of high interest vessels designated as posing a greater-than-normal risk to the United States
- Interdicted nearly 3,000 undocumented migrants attempting to illegally enter the United States
- Conducted over 3,700 safety and security exams on vessels operating on the U.S. Outer Continental Shelf
- Conducted over 11,600 annual inspections on U.S. flag vessels inspected and certificated in accordance with 46 Code of Federal Regulation (CFR) § 2.01-7
- Conducted 4,603 investigations for reportable marine casualties involving commercial vessels
- Conducted over 49,000 recreational vessel boardings, issued over 12,000 citations, and visited 1,150 recreational boat manufacturers in conjunction with state efforts to provide education and ensure compliance with federal regulations
- Conducted over 6,000 fisheries conservation boardings
- Expended the remaining $23 million of the $142 million appropriated under the American Recovery and Reinvestment Act
- Investigated and responded to over 3,300 pollution incidents
- Verified more than 70,000 Transportation Worker Identification Credentials
- Screened over 436,000 vessels, including over 117,000 commercial vessels and 29.5 million crewmembers and passengers prior to arrival in U.S. ports.

History

The Coast Guard's evolution parallels that of the United States, a coastal nation heavily dependent upon the surrounding seas for commerce, resources, and protection against external threats. The predecessor services of the Coast Guard were created to protect the Nation's vital interests. As the Nation grew and those interests evolved, so did these agencies' duties and their relationships with each other. The eventual result was consolidation, beginning in 1915 with the merging of the Revenue Cutter Service and Life-Saving Service, to form the U.S. Coast Guard. By 1946, the Coast Guard had assimilated the Lighthouse Service and the Bureau of Marine Inspection and Navigation (formed after the combination of the Bureau of Navigation and the Steamboat Inspection Service). Since then, the Service has been assigned additional statutory responsibilities. The result is that today's Coast Guard, which carries out civil and military duties touching every facet of the maritime environment, bears little resemblance to its collection of ancestor services. Yet the process of integrating these agencies, each with its own culture and characteristics, shaped the Coast Guard in lasting ways.

Understanding the evolutionary process that led to the modern Coast Guard provides insight into the unique nature of our Service, and the principles of Coast Guard operations that flow from it. Coast Guard history can be divided into seven distinct periods. Its ability to uphold and protect the Nation's enduring maritime interests expanded—though not always evenly—during each of these eras.

1790 to 1865: Revenue Protection and More

The founding of the Revenue Marine was motivated by the financial needs of a new nation. After the War for Independence, the United States was deep in debt, and its emerging industries were under tremendous pressure from British imports. The U.S. merchant marine, a mainstay of the colonial economy, had been weakened by losses in the war. To secure its political independence, the United States first had to secure its financial independence. To accomplish this imperative, Alexander Hamilton, the first Secretary of the Treasury, proposed a bold economic plan, relying heavily on income generated by customs duties and tonnage taxes that discriminated against foreign goods and ships. Hamilton understood that the new nation could collect customs duties and tonnage taxes only from ships that made it safely to port. Essential to that end were lighthouses, of which there were twelve in 1789, each erected and maintained by local interests.

Realizing that lighthouses were of national value, Hamilton proposed to Congress that responsibility for all aids to navigation be given to the central government. Congress agreed, and on August 7, 1789, the Treasury Department was given responsibility for constructing and maintaining all of the Nation's aids to navigation.

In just its Ninth Act, the First Congress thus accepted safety of life at sea as a public responsibility and "launched the national government upon its course of guarding the coast in the interest of safety and security afloat." Hamilton also understood that in order for his plan to succeed "the Treasury needed a strong right arm" to suppress smuggling and ensure duties and taxes were paid by preventing the landing of cargoes in places other than ports with collectors. Therefore, he sought authorization from Congress to build "so many boats or cutters, not exceeding ten, as may be employed for the protection of revenue." Enacted on August 4, 1790, the Act to Provide More Effectually for the Collection of the Duties Imposed by Law on Goods, Wares, and Merchandise Imported into the United States, and on the Tonnage of Ships or Vessels, authorized the building of ten cutters. The Act also authorized a corps of 80 men and 20 boys—the Revenue Marine—charged with a single purpose: assistance in the collection of customs duties and tonnage taxes.

For nearly seven years, Revenue Marine cutters were the only armed ships the United States possessed, the Navy having been disbanded after the Revolution. Consequently, when the Quasi-War with France loomed in 1797, the Revenue Marine was available for duty and Congress assigned the Service its first military tasks. In the same Act that established the United States Navy, Congress authorized the President to augment the Navy with revenue cutters when needed. Eight revenue cutters were subsequently deployed under Navy control along the U.S. southern coast and in the Caribbean from 1798 to 1799. These cutters performed national defense duties and preyed upon French shipping. At the conflict's conclusion, the Navy retained three cutters and returned five to the Revenue Marine.

For the most part, the Navy considered the cutters too small and slow for strictly naval duties. Nevertheless, the need for sufficient numbers and types of warships led to the Revenue Marine's participation in naval operations on many other occasions. With only six frigates in service, the Navy needed the services of more armed vessels as the Nation entered the War of 1812. Revenue cutters again augmented the Navy, and one promptly captured the first British prize of the war.

Shallow-draft revenue cutters proved useful in the conflicts that erupted along the North American coastline as the Nation expanded. From 1836 to 1839, cutters engaged in littoral and riverine operations during the Seminole War in Florida. Revenue Marine vessels also participated in amphibious landing operations during the Mexican War from 1846–1848.

Supporting Maritime Commerce

From its earliest days, the Revenue Marine's efforts were not focused solely on customs collections. Instead, the Service adopted a wider role of protecting and fostering—as well as regulating— marine transportation and trade. During the presidencies of George Washington and John Adams, the Revenue Marine began maintaining aids to navigation, assisting lighthouse personnel, and charting coastal waters. It also carried out various health and quarantine measures at major ports, and other law enforcement activities.

The Service also took on the major task of finding and rescuing distressed mariners, something it had done hitherto on an ad hoc basis. In 1831, Treasury Secretary Louis McLane ordered Revenue Marine cutters to begin limited cruising during the winter months to assist mariners in distress. This initiative was so successful that in 1837 Congress authorized the President "to cause any suitable number of public vessels...to cruise upon the coast, in the severe portion of the season...to afford such aid to distressed navigators as their circumstances and necessities may require." Thus began a tradition of assistance to life and property that today is one of the Coast Guard's most widely appreciated missions.

During this same period, steamboats were plying the Nation's rivers and beginning to venture out to sea, but their boilers were notoriously unreliable and dangerous. In 1832, explosions destroyed 14 percent of all steamers in operation, with the loss of a thousand or more lives. The situation drew cries for action, and in 1838 Congress enacted the first navigation law for "better securing the lives...on board vessels propelled in whole or in part by steam." This Act, which gave U.S. district judges authority to appoint steamboat

is considered the beginning of an organization that would evolve over the next several decades into the Steamboat Inspection Service within the Treasury Department. It also launched what has become "an enduring national policy of regulating private enterprise in the interest of safety afloat."

Almost ten years later, Congressman William Newell of New Jersey, who years earlier had personally witnessed the grounding of the bark Terasto and the death of the crew, set in motion a series of legislative moves that led to the formation of the U.S. Life-Saving Service, effectively federalizing the efforts of independent volunteer organizations, like the Massachusetts Humane Society, which had long protected life in their local communities. The Life-Saving Service and the Revenue Marine worked together closely—Revenue Marine personnel often were temporarily assigned to the Life- Saving Service, and cutters provided material support to lifeboat stations along the U.S. coast.

Law Enforcement in a Restive Nation

The Revenue Marine aided the federal government in enforcing its sovereignty over U.S. affairs, but its actions were not always popular in a country that was still searching for a balance between central and state power. Congress passed the Embargo and Non-Intercourse Acts in 1807 and 1809, respectively, in an attempt to keep the United States neutral during the Napoleonic Wars. Both the Revenue Marine and the Navy were called upon to prevent banned trade — an uncomfortable policy that hurt large numbers of traders, shipping companies, fishermen, and coastal communities.

In 1832, the Revenue Marine was thrust into the national limelight when South Carolina challenged federal authority by refusing to recognize U.S. tariff laws. President Andrew Jackson sent five cutters to Charleston "to take possession of any vessel arriving from a foreign port, and defend her against any attempts to dispossess the Customs Officers of her custody." Due to its link to ocean trade and the revenue that it brought the U.S. Treasury, the Revenue Marine again became part of the federal government's "long arm"—a role it would reprise 29 years later as the country headed Cutters in the Civil War As war loomed in December of 1860, the Revenue Marine faced the same dilemma as the Army and Navy. "Each man in federal uniform was forced to decide, and to decide quickly, whether his supreme allegiance lay with a state or with the nation-state." Men chose sides, and the Revenue Marine lost men and cutters as a result.

Some of those who remained were ordered by President Abraham Lincoln into combat service with the Navy. The cutter Harriet Lane, which took part in the abortive relief expedition to Fort Sumter in 1861, is credited with firing the first naval shots of the Civil War. Other cutters in service with the Navy performed blockade duty. Cutters not assigned to the Navy patrolled the shipping lanes to safeguard U.S. trade from Southern privateers and to assist distressed vessels at sea. Simultaneously, their usual duty of protecting the Nation's customs revenue took on an added urgency, since that income was critical to the Union war effort.

1866 to 1914:

In the aftermath of the Civil War, the Nation's continuing territorial growth and the ongoing expansion of its overseas commerce highlighted the need for a more coordinated approach to maritime safety, security, and stewardship. Reforms that began in the late 1860s improved the effectiveness and efficiency of the Revenue Marine and Life Saving Services, laying the groundwork for the formation of the modern Coast Guard.

In 1869, George Boutwell, Secretary of the Treasury under President Ulysses S. Grant, formed an interim Revenue Marine Bureau under the leadership of N. Broughton Devereux. Devereux, in turn, established boards designed to overhaul and reorganize the Revenue Cutter Service, as it was now known. The Revenue Marine Bureau became a permanent agency in 1871 under Treasury official Sumner I. Kimball.

Kimball immediately set out to increase the professionalism of the Revenue Cutter Service. Six months after taking office, he issued revised Revenue Cutter Service regulations that provided for economy of operations, centralized control of the Service at headquarters, and officer accessions and promotions based on merit rather than political influence or seniority. Meanwhile, Bureau Chief Devereux's personnel board, headed by Captain John Faunce, USRCS, reviewed the qualifications of every Revenue Cutter Service officer and removed those found incompetent or otherwise unfit for duty. Officers retained were given rank commensurate with their capabilities, and were thereafter promoted based on the results they achieved on the professional examinations mandated in Kimball's regulations. As a result, by 1872 Kimball could proclaim his junior officer corps the best the Revenue Cutter Service had ever possessed. To ensure a continuous supply of

persuaded Congress in 1876 to authorize establishment of a training school, thus laying the foundation for the U.S. Coast Guard Academy.

Kimball and his staff also implemented the recommendations of Devereux's other board, which had analyzed the structure of the cutter fleet. From 1872 to 1881 the fleet size increased by just one cutter, but Kimball reduced fleet tonnage by replacing large, aging cutters with smaller, speedier, and more efficient ones sized according to the needs of the ports where they were to be stationed. He also steadily replaced sailing ships with steamers. By 1881, 60 percent of the vessels had been built after 1869, and the ratio of steamers to sailing cutters had risen from 2.5:1 to nearly 8:1.27 Thanks to the reforms of Kimball, Devereux, and Faunce, the Revenue Cutter Service now boasted a highly professional corps manning modern cutters well-suited to their missions. Upon appointment as chief of the Revenue Cutter Service, Kimball also instituted a program of inspecting the lifesaving stations in appalling conditions. As a result of his findings, Congress placed the Life-Saving Service under the supervision of the Revenue Cutter Service and appropriated funds to build lifesaving stations in states along the coast without one, and to staff the stations with paid surfmen. Kimball reorganized the Revenue Cutter Service to accommodate the Life-Saving Service, and applied his considerable talents to systematically improving readiness, training, personnel, and equipment standards. During this period, the Life-Saving Service also expanded its reach to cover the Gulf of Mexico, Great Lakes, and Pacific coast of the United States.

Despite Kimball's effort to inculcate discipline and professionalism, the Life-Saving Service was plagued by claims that unqualified lifesavers were given their jobs solely for reasons of politics and patronage. Compounding the situation were several high profile tragedies, chief among them the losses of the USS Huron in November 1877, and the steamer Metropolis in January 1878, which produced a tremendous outcry against the Life-Saving Service. Recognizing the need to improve rescue operations, Congress passed legislation on June 18, 1878, authorizing the construction of a number of additional lifesaving stations, removing the Life-Saving Service from the Revenue Cutter Service, and appointing Sumner Kimball General Superintendent of the new Service. Kimball steadily eliminated the system of political patronage that had grown with the Life-Saving Service, replacing it

Service remained in force, since Revenue Cutter Service officers continued to serve as inspectors and auditors for the lifesavers.

Meanwhile, the United States purchased the territory of Alaska in 1867, giving the Revenue Cutter Service a new set of sovereignty and resource protection responsibilities. In addition to increased law obligations, the Revenue Cutter Service performed many civil and humanitarian duties, and mounted scientific expeditions. It was entrusted by the Bureau of Education to deliver teachers to the native communities. In fact, so instrumental was the Revenue Cutter Service in establishing the authority of the federal government in Alaska that one could say that for many years the Revenue Cutter Service was the government along Alaska's western coast.

With the growth of the U.S. merchant marine, the marine safety and waterways management work of the revenue cutters—supporting marine transportation and trade—also expanded. Although they acted without a clear statutory mandate, cutter crews had long performed many tasks related to the safety of harbors and cruising grounds. In 1889, Congress passed laws to regulate anchorages, giving the Revenue Cutter Service the duty of enforcing these new laws. In 1906, lawmakers authorized the Service to clear derelict hulks from harbors and their approaches. And in 1910, the Service gained authority over some aspects of pleasure boating. The mission of safety at sea became important internationally with the sinking of the Titanic in 1912, and the loss of more than 1,500 lives. This tragic event led the Revenue Cutter Service to assume ice patrol duties the following year when the Navy, which originally had assigned two cruisers to perform that mission, announced it needed the warships elsewhere. The assumption of this seemingly natural function in the North Atlantic reflected long-standing Revenue Cutter Service practice in the Bering Sea. Sea and air ice patrols have now protected northern shipping for more than a century without incident.

The last half of the nineteenth century also saw the Revenue Cutter Service expand its mission of protecting marine resources. Revenue Cutter Service personnel patrolled the Pribilof Islands off Alaska to prevent the ongoing slaughter of seals. The Service also worked with the Bureau of Fisheries to encourage proliferation of "food fishes" and regulated the harvesting and sale of sponges in the Gulf of Mexico.

Spanish-American War

For three years prior to the outbreak of war in 1898, the Revenue Cutter Service conducted neutrality patrols, seizing ships suspected of smuggling ammunition and other supplies to Cuban rebels. By 1898, both the Navy and the Revenue Cutter Service were more modern, professional organizations than they had been on the eve of the U.S. Civil War. Reflecting this state of affairs, transfer of the revenue cutters to Navy control during the Spanish-American War went relatively smoothly. Once again, the Revenue Cutter Service provided important support to the war effort, performing blockade duty off Cuba, serving with Commodore George Dewey's Asiatic Squadron at Manila Bay in the Philippines, and guarding the homeland against possible Spanish attack. At the request of President McKinley, Congress awarded specially minted medals to the officers and the crew of the cutter Hudson (including the War's only gold medal to the captain, Lieutenant Frank H. Newcomb), recognizing their bravery under fire.

Establishment of the U.S. Coast Guard

The formation of the U.S. Coast Guard actually began with an attempt to abolish the Revenue Cutter Service. In 1911, President Taft appointed Frederick A. Cleveland to lead a commission charged with recommending ways to increase the economy and efficiency of government. The Cleveland Commission concluded that unifunctional agencies were more efficient and economical than multifunctional ones. The commission thus recommended combining the Lighthouse Service and Life-Saving Service, with their similar "protection" function, and apportioning the duties and assets of the multifunctional Revenue Cutter Service among other government agencies and departments. In particular, larger cutters and their crews would be transferred to the Navy. The Treasury, Navy, and Commerce and Labor Departments were asked to comment on the report. Secretary of Commerce and Labor Charles Nagel presciently suggested combining the Revenue Cutter Service, the Life-Saving Service, and the Lighthouse Service. While not sure where this new combined service organization should reside within the government, Nagel was adamant that it should not be in the Navy Department. Secretary of the Navy George Meyer wanted the cutters, but did not relish absorbing Revenue Cutter Service personnel into the Navy.

Moreover, he wrote: It is true that the chief functions of the Revenue Cutter Service can be performed by the Navy, but this cannot be done as stated in the Cleveland report in the regular performance of their military duties. All duties which interfere with the training of personnel for war are irregular and in a degree detrimental to the efficiency of the fleet.

Secretary of the Treasury Franklin MacVeagh was defiant in defense of the Service. He noted that the close and successful working relationship between the Revenue Cutter Service and the Life-Saving Service would be severed by abolishing the Revenue Cutter Service. He disagreed with the Cleveland Commission's conclusion that spreading Revenue Cutter Service duties across the government would generate efficiencies. Finally, he echoed the Navy's argument concerning the nature of Revenue Cutter Service and Navy duties, stating: The [RCS's] work is alien to the work of the Navy, alien to the spirit of the Navy, and alien, I think, to its professional capacities and instincts—alien certainly to its training and tastes.

Nevertheless, in April 1912, President Taft recommended that Congress adopt the Cleveland Commission's findings. Meanwhile, Secretary MacVeagh ordered Revenue Cutter Service Captain-Commandant Ellsworth Price Bertholf and Sumner Kimball, head of the Life-Saving Service, to draft legislation that would join the Revenue Cutter Service and Life-Saving Service in a new organization. When Taft and MacVeagh left office after the 1912 election, President Woodrow Wilson and his Treasury Secretary, William Gibbs McAdoo, strongly supported the bill combining the two services. The Senate passed the bill in 1914 and the House passed it in early 1915. On January 28, 1915, President Wilson signed into law "the Act to Create the Coast Guard" that combined the Life-Saving Service and the Revenue Cutter Service. At that time, Captain Bertholf was named the first Commandant of the Coast Guard. He realized that joining two organizations with vastly different cultures into a single military service presented a delicate challenge. However, he was absolutely convinced that the military character of the Revenue Cutter Service had to prevail even though large numbers of the lifesavers had no desire to change their civilian status. Consequently, while the Life-Saving Service and Revenue Cutter Service were joined at the top in 1915, they operated as separate entities within the Coast Guard for more than 15 years. Events would soon accelerate the development of a twentieth-century maritime security

the development of a twentieth-century maritime security force formed by the union of these two older institutions.

Only two years after its formation, the Coast Guard was called into action as the U.S. was plunged into war. World War I was the first in a series of events that would shape the Service during the next several decades, and expand its maritime duties. Some of these events, such as Prohibition and World War II, significantly increased the size of the Coast Guard.

Beginning in the summer of 1917, six cutters escorted convoys between Gibraltar and the British Isles. In addition, some Coast Guard officers were assigned to command Navy warships and air stations. At home, one of the Coast Guard's major tasks was port security. Concern over the possibility of accidents in the aftermath of an October 1917 collision involving the French ammunition carrier SS Mont-Blanc; the resulting explosion killed more than 1,600 civilians, injured more than 9,000 persons, and leveled a large portion of Halifax, Nova Scotia. U.S. ports handled more wartime shipping than Halifax, making the issue of port security even more pressing. As a result, the Treasury Department, working closely with the Navy, established Coast Guard Captain of the Port offices in New York, Philadelphia, Norfolk, and Sault Ste. Marie. The New York office soon became the Coast Guard's largest command.

Thus, the Coast Guard's role of ensuring maritime mobility in U.S. ports and waterways expanded considerably. Along the remainder of the U.S. coast, lifesaving station personnel doubled as coast watchers, maintaining a lookout for potential infiltrators.

The National Prohibition (Volstead) Act of 1919 prohibited the manufacture, sale, and transportation of alcoholic beverages within the United States. With no other federal agency prepared to enforce the new law at sea, the bulk of the burden for enforcing the Volstead Act on U.S. waters fell to the Coast Guard. Over the next ten years, the Coast Guard budget increased dramatically and the Service grew accordingly. The enlisted force tripled in size, as did the fleet. The Service acquired and refurbished 31 Navy destroyers for use in picketing the foreign supply ships that lay offshore, outside U.S. territorial waters. A large force of specially designed Coast Guard patrol boats and harbor craft, plus a number of seized smuggling vessels, patrolled inshore waters and pursued the rumrunner contact boats. When even this proved insufficient, the Coast Guard began using aircraft to report suspicious vessels.

Coast Guard communications equipment, procedures, and intelligence methods were significantly improved. Tactics and techniques developed to combat the rumrunners would be used decades later to combat drug smugglers. Additionally, the Service developed international law expertise through its efforts to expand Prohibition enforcement authority over foreign-flagged vessels beyond the three nautical mile limit of the territorial sea.

After Prohibition, Admiral Russell R. Waesche, Sr., Coast Guard Commandant from 1936 to 1945, guided one of the greatest transitions in the Service's history. In many ways, his vision was responsible for today's Coast Guard. Waesche oversaw the addition of many responsibilities, the most sweeping of which was Congressional authorization for the Coast Guard to enforce all U.S. laws at sea and within territorial waters. Waesche also saw the need to regulate boating activity in the Nation's waters. Lacking the manpower to perform this function, in 1939, he created the civilian uniformed volunteer force now called the Coast Guard Auxiliary to meet this specific need. By 1940, the Auxiliary had 2,600 personnel and 2,300 boats that augmented the Coast Guard at a fraction of the cost of a full-time force.

Waesche's greatest force multiplier, however, was the military Coast Guard Reserve, created in 1941. This gave the Coast Guard the potential to perform many roles and missions that would otherwise be impossible for a small service. Also in 1939, as part of President Franklin Roosevelt's reorganization plans, the U.S. Lighthouse Service was placed under the Coast Guard adding nearly 50 percent more civilians to the Service.

With the outbreak of war in Europe in 1939, the Coast Guard—having had its civil responsibilities vastly increased since World War I—once again shifted focus to emphasize military preparedness. Coast Guard forces played a major role in asserting national sovereignty over U.S. waters and shipping. Coast Guard cutters and aircraft performed extensive convoy protection and antisubmarine duties in both the Atlantic and Pacific Oceans. Coast Guard craft rescued the survivors of torpedo attacks off the U.S. coast, while Coast Guard coast-watchers maintained beach patrols and guarded U.S. ports. Coast Guard personnel manned Navy warships as well as Navy and Army amphibious ships and craft, and took part in every major amphibious invasion of the war. During the war, a few farsighted officers doggedly pursued the copters, initially to perform antisubmarine surveillance but their role in search and rescue (SAR) was quickly recognized.

The Roosevelt Administration also decided it would be convenient and cost-effective to temporarily transfer the Bureau of Marine Inspection and Navigation to the Coast Guard. The roots of this agency stretched back to 1838, when the Steamboat Inspection Service was created. In 1932, this agency had merged with the Bureau of Navigation, which had been created in 1884. Now called the Bureau of Marine Inspection and Navigation, this civilian agency joined the Coast Guard permanently in 1946. As a result, Coast Guard missions now touched every facet of domestic maritime activity. The Service's duties expanded overseas as well, as the U.S. took the lead in shaping the post-war world.

After the war, the Coast Guard maintained a significant global peacetime presence as part of its efforts to safeguard transoceanic navigation. Coast Guard cutters continued to maintain a network of open ocean weather stations until 1977, by which time improvements in weather forecasting and aircraft navigation and safety made the service obsolete.

During the Vietnam War, the Coast Guard played a major role in "Operation Market Time," which involved the interdiction of trawlers used by North Vietnam for infiltration and re-supply activities. In all, five large cutters and twenty-six 82-foot patrol boats and their crews were assigned to the operation. By the end of the Operation, the Coast Guard had boarded nearly a quarter of a million sampans and junks and destroyed more than 1,800 of them.

The Coast Guard's civil duties continued to expand in the period following World War II. In 1958, the Service developed AMVER, a ship reporting system able to identify other ships in the area of a vessel in distress so that assistance could be vectored to the site. In 1965, the Service took responsibility for coordinating all SAR operations in U.S. waters, and that same year accepted responsibility for all of the Nation's icebreaking duties.

While the Coast Guard and most of its predecessors had been part of the Treasury Department since their founding, the traditional direct link between collecting revenue and the Service had faded. The result was President Lyndon Johnson's decision to incorporate the Coast Guard into the newly formed Department of Transportation in April 1967. The influx of illegal drugs also

on the primary maritime interdiction role, and eventually expanded its Caribbean presence to disrupt the illegal drug trade. The Coast Guard's environmental protection responsibilities grew as well. While the Revenue Marine had been tasked with protecting valuable natural resources as early as 1822 and defending the marine environment as a whole beginning with the Refuse Act of 1899, growing environmental awareness in the United States pushed the Coast Guard deeper into the pollution prevention realm. The Torrey Canyon and Amoco Cadiz tanker groundings led to the Federal Water Pollution Control Act of 1972, in which Congress set a no-discharge standard for oil in U.S. navigable waters which was enforced by the Coast Guard. They were also given responsibility for coordinating and administering oil spill cleanup in the maritime realm.

The Service played a role in post-Cold War military operations as well. Coast Guard Port Security Units were deployed to the Persian Gulf during Operations Desert Shield and Desert Storm in 1990–1991. At the same time, Captains of the Port ensured the safe transport of expeditionary troops and munitions. In recent years, the unified combatant commanders have requested—and been provided—assets and personnel to conduct maritime interception operations, peacetime military engagement, and other warfare supporting tasks for deployed Navy Fleets.

Coast Guard personnel were among the first responders to the World Trade Center tragedy and assisted in evacuating more than half a million people by water from lower Manhattan. The Coast Guard also mobilized more than 2,700 reservists in the largest homeland defense and port security operation since World War II. These reservists, and their active duty counterparts, provided the manpower and expertise for cleanup efforts in New York City. They heightened security in ports and increased vigilance along the Nation's 95,000 miles of coastline, including the Great Lakes and inland waterways. The Coast Guard's National Strike Force was also at the forefront of a multi-agency response to anthrax cases in Washington, DC, and Florida.

Several initiatives begun after September 11, 2001, have changed the Coast Guard in a variety of ways. The Homeland Security Act of 2002 transferred the Coast Guard to the Department of Homeland Security as the maritime element of the Nation's new security organization. The Coast Guard is now an official member of the interagency U.S. Intelligence Community. New national intelligence resources, including Maritime Intelligence Fusion Centers and field intelligence collectors located at Coast Guard Sectors across the country, were created. The Coast Guard also organized and expanded its deployable specialized forces. Existing National Strike Force, Tactical Law Enforcement Teams, and dive locker capabilities were upgraded while a highly trained Maritime Security Response Team and strategically located Maritime Safety and Security Units were created. With these teams, the Coast Guard is capable of responding to a broad spectrum of high threat scenarios ranging from non-compliant and opposed vessel boardings to actual or potential attacks involving weapons of mass effect.

Hurricane Katrina struck the Gulf States on August 29, 2005, causing devastation to a 90,000 square mile area from Grand Isle, Louisiana, to Mobile, Alabama and inland. It was one of the worst natural disasters in U.S. history. The response that followed became the largest domestic SAR operation in recent U.S. history. Over 5,600 Coast Guard men and women deployed from around the country and rescued more than 33,500 people. They also responded to thousands of oil and hazardous material spills totaling over nine million gallons, repaired navigational aids, and restored waterways in and around some of the country's most vital ports.

The modern Coast Guard has evolved into a highly adaptable service capable of addressing all threats and hazards related to the maritime domain. The Coast Guard's ability to quickly shift from one mission to the next using the same platform and crew is perhaps its most important strength. This multi-mission capability, an enduring Coast Guard quality, was achieved by consolidation, and in some cases federalization of the distinctive skill sets and assets of highly specialized predecessor agencies. It is enabled by highly versatile people with specialty skills employing adaptable assets within an agile command and control structure, and is supported by broad legislative authorities and its relationships with governmental, commercial, and academic entities throughout the world.

Missions

By law, the Coast Guard has 11 missions:

Ports, Waterways & Coastal Security (PWCS)

The Homeland Security Act of 2002 divided the Coast Guard's eleven statutory missions between homeland security and non-homeland security. Reflecting the Coast Guard's historical role in defending our nation, the Act delineated Ports, Waterways and Coastal Security (PWCS) as the first homeland security mission. The Commandant of the Coast Guard designated PWCS as the service's primary focus alongside search and rescue.

The PWCS mission entails the protection of the U.S. Maritime Domain and the U.S. Marine Transportation System (MTS) and those who live, work or recreate near them; the prevention and disruption of terrorist attacks, sabotage, espionage, or subversive acts; and response to and recovery from those that do occur.   Conducting PWCS deters terrorists from using or exploiting the MTS as a means for attacks on U.S. territory, population centers, vessels, critical infrastructure, and key resources.   PWCS includes the employment of awareness activities; counterterrorism, antiterrorism, preparedness and response operations; and the establishment and oversight of a maritime security regime.   PWCS also includes the national defense role of protecting military outload operations.

PWCS is a new name for the Coast Guard's mission previously called Port and Environmental Security (PES).   PES included port security, container inspection, and marine firefighting.

In 2003, the Coast Guard addressed its PWCS responsibilities and functions by initiating Operation Neptune Shield (ONS).   The Coast Guard supplemented ONS with tactical and strategic documents: the 2005 publication of Chapter 10 to the Maritime Law Enforcement Manual, the 2006 Coast Guard Strategic Plan for Combating Maritime Terrorism, and the 2008 Combating Maritime Terrorism Strategic and Performance Plan.

The July 2005 terrorist bombings in London highlighted the need to protect U.S. mass transit systems, including ferries.   Later, the effects of hurricanes Katrina and Rita highlighted the criticality of preparedness for recovery of the MTS following a large-scale disaster.   The 2008 terrorist attack via the maritime domain against Mumbai, India, highlighted the tie between border security and PWCS.   After each event, the Coast Guard reviewed its PWCS strategy and made adjustments where appropriate.

The Coast Guard's systematic, maritime governance model for PWCS employs a triad consisting of domain awareness, maritime security regimes, and maritime security and response operations carried out in a unified effort by international, governmental, and private stakeholders.

Maritime domain awareness means the effective understanding of anything associated with the maritime domain that could impact the security, safety, economy, or environment of the U.S. Attaining and sustaining an effective understanding and awareness of the maritime domain requires the collection, fusion, analysis, and dissemination of prioritized categories of data, information, and intelligence. These are collected during the conduct of all Coast Guard missions. Awareness inputs come from Field Intelligence Support Teams, Maritime Intelligence Fusion Centers, Nationwide Automatic Identification System and other vessel tracking systems, and public reporting of suspicious incidents through America's Waterway Watch.

Maritime security regimes comprise a system of rules that shape acceptable activities in the maritime domain. Regimes include domestic and international protocols and/or frameworks that coordinate partnerships, establish maritime security standards, collectively engage shared maritime security interests, and facilitate the sharing of information. Domestically, the Coast Guard-led Area Maritime Security Committees carry out much of the maritime security regimes effort. Abroad, the Coast Guard works with individual countries and through the International Maritime Organization, a specialized agency of the United Nations. Together, regimes and domain awareness inform decision makers and allow them to identify trends, anomalies, and activities that threaten or endanger U.S. interests.

Defeating terrorism requires integrated, comprehensive operations that maximize effectiveness without duplicating efforts. Security and response operations consist of counterterrorism and antiterrorism activities.

Counterterrorism activities are offensive in nature. The Maritime Security Response Team (MSRT) is a highly specialized resource with advanced counterterrorism skills and tactics. The MSRT is trained to be a first responder to potential terrorist situations; deny terrorist acts; perform security actions against non-compliant actors; perform tactical facility entry and enforcement; participate in port level counterterrorism exercises; and educate other forces on Coast Guard counterterrorism procedures.

Antiterrorism activities are defensive in nature. As a maritime security agency, the Coast Guard uses its unique authorities, competencies, capacities, operational capabilities and partnerships to board suspect vessels, escort ships deemed to present or be at significant risk, enforce fixed security zones at maritime critical infrastructure and key resources, and patrol the maritime approaches, coasts, ports, and rivers of America. Coast Guard cutters, boats, helicopters, and shoreside patrols are appropriately armed and trained. Many current and planned antiterrorism activities support the Department of Homeland Security Small Vessel Security Strategy. Twelve Maritime Safety and Security Teams (MSSTs) enforce security zones, conduct port state control boardings, protect military outloads, ensure maritime security during major marine events, augment shoreside security at waterfront facilities, detect Weapons of Mass Destruction, and participate in port level antiterrorism exercises in their homeports and other ports to which elements of an MSST may be assigned for operations.

Viewing maritime initiatives and policies as part of a larger system enables a better understanding of their relationships and effectiveness. A well designed system of regimes, awareness, and operational capabilities creates overlapping domestic and international safety nets, layers of security, and effective stewardship making it that much harder for terrorists to succeed.

Drug Interdiction

The Coast Guard is the lead federal agency for maritime drug interdiction and shares lead responsibility for air interdiction with the U.S. Customs Service. As such, it is a key player in combating the flow of illegal drugs to the United States. The Coast Guard's mission is to reduce the supply of drugs from the source by denying smugglers the use of air and maritime routes in the Transit Zone, a six million square mile area, including the Caribbean, Gulf of Mexico and Eastern Pacific. In meeting the challenge of patrolling this vast area, the Coast Guard coordinates closely with other federal agencies and countries within the region to disrupt and deter the flow of illegal drugs. In addition to deterrence, Coast Guard drug interdiction accounts for nearly 52% of all U.S. government seizures of cocaine each year. For Fiscal Year 2002 the rate of Coast Guard cocaine seizures alone had an estimated import value of approximately $3.9 billion.

In 1870, Chinese immigrants became the first known drug smugglers when they began smuggling opium in merchant ship cargoes and baggage. Since then, drug smuggling by maritime routes has grown in size, scope and sophistication as demand skyrocketed. For example, around the turn of the century, when cocaine use was first in vogue, a relatively limited amount of the population was directly affected by the problems of cocaine abuse. But in later years, as the drugs of choice shifted from cocaine to heroin and opium, then later to marijuana and back to cocaine, drug smugglers began utilizing maritime sea and air routes to transport larger shipments of drugs to the U.S. For nearly a century, the maritime drug smuggling business slowly evolved while the Coast Guard focused its attention on the major events of the day, including World War I, Prohibition, World War II, the Korean and Vietnam wars.

During the 1920's Congress tasked the Coast Guard with enforcing the 18th Amendment, necessitating a dramatic increase in resources and funding for the Coast Guard. The massive effort needed to curtail the substantial level of alcohol smuggling required the single largest appropriation for personnel and new ship construction in its history. In addition, the Navy transferred more than 20 WWI-era destroyers and minesweepers for conversion to the Coast Guard's battle with rum-runners, which ended with the 21st Amendment repealing Prohibition. The Coast Guard's unique expertise in countering smuggling operations also came into play during the Vietnam War, when the Navy asked for our expertise to support "Operation Market Time," an intensive multi-year campaign to stop the Communist flow of arms and supplies by sea. The Coast Guard utilized its expertise in stopping smuggling while facilitating legitimate commerce. Our patrol boats and cutters patrolled 1,200 miles of coastline and had to contend with more than 60,000 junks and sampans. The Coast Guard and Navy's success in "Operation Market Time," substantially reduced the amount of at- sea smuggling, forcing the Viet Cong to use the longer and more difficult land route of the infamous Ho Chi Minh Trail.

Shortly after the war in Vietnam ended, the Coast Guard found itself fighting another war--a war that is still going on today with a determined, well-financed opposition. In the early 1970's maritime drug smuggling became

seizures while engaged in other operations, like Search and Rescue and Fisheries Law Enforcement. 1973 saw a dramatic increase in smuggling attempts and the Coast Guard conducted its first Coast Guard-controlled seizure on March 8, 1973, when the USCGC Dauntless boarded a 38-foot sports fisherman, the Big L and arrested its master and crew, with more than a ton of marijuana on board. Since then, the Coast Guard has seized countless tons of marijuana and cocaine. Since Fiscal Year 1997 to present, the Coast Guard has seized 806,469 pounds of cocaine and 333,285 pounds of marijuana.

Aids to Navigation

The waters of the United States and its territories are marked to assist navigation by the U.S. Aids to Navigation System. This system employs a simple arrangement of colors, shapes, numbers and light characteristics to mark navigable channels, waterways and obstructions adjacent to these.

Aids to Navigation can provide a boater with the same type of information drivers get from street signs, stop signals, road barriers, detours and traffic lights. These aids may be anything ˆfrom lighthouses, to minor lights, daybeacons, range lights, and sound signals, to lighted or unlighted buoys. Each has a purpose and helps in determining location, getting from one place to another or staying out of danger. The goal of the U.S. Aids to navigation System is to promote safe navigation on the waterway.

The U.S. Aids to Navigation System is intended for use with Nautical Charts. Charts are one of the most important tools used by boaters for planning trips and safely navigating waterways. Charts show the nature and shape of the coast, buoys and beacons, depths of water, land features, directional information, marine hazards and other pertinent information. This valuable information cannot be obtained from other sources, such as a road map or atlas.

The primary components of the U.S. Aids to Navigation System are beacons and buoys.

Beacons are aids to navigation structures that are permanently fixed to the earth's surface. They range from lighthouses to small, single-pile structures and may be located on land or in the water. Lighted beacons are called lights; unlighted beacons are called daybeacons. Beacons exhibit a daymark to make them readily visible and easily identifiable against background conditions. Generally, the daymark conveys to the boater, during daylight hours, the same significance, as does the aid's light or reflector at night. Buoys are floating aids that come in many shapes and sizes. They are moored to the seabed by concrete sinkers with chain or synthetic rope moorings of various lengths connected to the buoy's body. They are intended to convey information to the boater by their shape or color, by the characteristics of a visible or audible signal, or a combination of two or more such features.

A Private Aid to Navigation is a buoy, light or daybeacon owned and maintained by any individual or organization other than the U.S. Coast Guard. These aids are designed to allow individuals or organizations to mark privately maintained channels, privately owned marine obstructions, or other similar hazards to navigation.

The SAR Mission

Search and Rescue (SAR) is one of the Coast Guard's oldest missions. Minimizing the loss of life, injury, property damage or loss by rendering aid to persons in distress and property in the maritime environment has always been a Coast Guard priority. Coast Guard SAR response involves multi-mission stations, cutters, aircraft and boats linked by communications networks. The National SAR Plan divides the U.S. area of SAR responsibility into internationally recognized inland and maritime SAR regions. The Coast Guard is the Maritime SAR Coordinator. To meet this responsibility, the Coast Guard maintains SAR facilities on the East, West and Gulf coasts; in Alaska, Hawaii, Guam, and Puerto Rico, as well as on the Great Lakes and inland U.S. waterways. The Coast Guard is recognized worldwide as a leader in the field of search and rescue.

Living Marine Resources

Protecting the U.S. EEZ and key areas of the high seas is an important mission for the Coast Guard. The Coast Guard enforces fisheries laws at sea, as tasked by the *Magnuson-Stevens Fisheries Conservation and Management Act (MSFCMA)*. Our fisheries priorities are, in order of importance:

1. *Protecting the U.S. Exclusive Economic Zone from foreign encroachment*: The MSFCMA of 1976 extended U.S. fisheries management authority out to the full 200 miles authorized by international law. The U.S. EEZ is the largest in the world, containing 3.4 million square miles of ocean and 90,000 miles of coastline. Foreign fishers operating illegally in this area are, effectively, stealing resources from the U.S., and our fisheries managers have no way of measuring or accounting for this loss.

2. *Enforcing domestic fisheries law*: U.S. Domestic Fisheries support a $24 billion dollar industry. Fisheries Management Plans (FMPs), to ensure the sustainability of these fisheries are developed by regional Fisheries Management Councils, each of which have a non-voting Coast Guard member. The Coast Guard is responsible for enforcing these FMPs at sea, in conjunction with NOAA Fisheries enforcement ashore. In addition to FMP enforcement, we enforce laws to protect marine mammals and endangered species.

3. *International fisheries agreements*: Realizing that fish do not recognize national boundaries, the Coast Guard works closely with the Department of State to develop and enforce international fisheries agreements. Most notably, the Coast Guard enforces the United Nations High Seas Driftnet Moratorium in the North Pacific, where illegal drift netters may catch U.S. origin salmon.

Marine Protected Species

The nation's waterways and their ecosystems are vital to the country's economy and health. If the United States is to enjoy a rich, diverse and sustainable ocean environment, then the Coast Guard must assist in halting the degradation of our ocean's natural resources associated with maritime activities. This includes ensuring the country's marine protected species are provided the protection necessary to help their populations recover to healthy, sustainable levels. Providing adequate protection will require the United States to enact and enforce a wide range of regulations to govern marine resource management and use.

U.S. protected species management responsibilities and authority are described in the Endangered Species Act (ESA), Marine Mammal Protection Act (MMPA), Marine Protection, Research, and Sanctuaries Act, and other

the Department of Commerce and the Department of the Interior with management of the nation's protected species. The Department of Commerce, Department of the Interior and the Department in which the Coast Guard is operating are tasked with enforcement responsibility under the various acts and legislation. The goal under the Fish and Wildlife Service (FWS) Strategic Plan is to ensure the sustainability of fish and wildlife populations by focusing on imperiled species and marine mammal management. The National Marine Fisheries Service (NMFS) goal is to recover protected species through take reduction and reduction of marine mammal conflicts with human activities.

Coast Guard marine protected species program efforts must be closely aligned with the NMFS and the FWS management goals. The goal of the Coast Guard's marine protected species program is to assist the NMFS and the FWS in the development and enforcement of those regulations necessary to help recover and maintain the country's marine protected species and their marine ecosystems. Further, as a leader in living marine resource stewardship, the Coast Guard must be a model of compliance and awareness in its internal actions. Coast Guard objectives include assisting in preventing the decline of marine protected species populations, promoting the recovery of marine protected species and their habitats, partnering with other agencies and organizations to enhance stewardship of marine ecosystems and ensuring internal compliance with appropriate legislation, regulations and management practices.

While the Coast Guard shares enforcement responsibility with the NMFS and the FWS, their agents primarily focus on investigations ashore. The Coast Guard is the foremost agency with the maritime infrastructure, capability and authority to project a federal law enforcement presence into the U.S. Exclusive Economic Zone (EEZ) and upon the high seas. The Coast Guard's strategic plan for marine protected species is called OCEAN STEWARD (updated 2014).

Marine Safety Program

The Coast Guard is in the midst of implementing the Marine Safety Enhancement Plan (MSEP). The MSEP is a multi-layered, several-year comprehensive program to enhance Marine Safety systems, knowledge, and

ronmentally sound maritime commerce. Specific tasks include bolstering inspector and investigator capacity, improving technical competencies, reinvigorating industry partnerships, improving mariner credentialing services, and expanding rulemaking capability to meet current and future needs of the maritime public and industry.

Actions to implement the MSEP have included reprogramming and adding over 400 positions to the Marine Safety workforce, broadening its experience base by increasing civilian marine inspection and investigations positions, designating Feeder Ports and building the infrastructure to train entry-level marine inspectors, establishing seven National Centers of Expertise (each focusing on specific maritime industry sectors), and increasing responsiveness (shortening cycle times) to merchant mariners, maritime industry, and the American public. The MSEP was developed in late 2007, based on the Coast Guard's Marine Safety statutory requirements at that time. Since then, the Coast Guard Authorization Act of 2010 was enacted, increasing Marine Safety requirements. The documents below describe the MSEP and its ongoing implementation.

Defense Readiness

For more than 210 years, the Coast Guard has served the nation as one of the five armed forces. Throughout its distinguished history, the Coast Guard has enjoyed a unique relationship with the Navy. This began with the Quasi-War with France in 1798, and continued through the Civil War, the World Wars, Vietnam, the Persian Gulf War, and the Global War on Terror. Under Title 14 U.S.C. § 1, the Coast Guard is "at all times an armed force of the United States." As part of the Joint Force, the Coast Guard maintains its readiness to carry out military operations in support of the policies and objectives of the U.S. government.

The Defense Readiness mission supports the National Military Strategy and Department of Defense (DoD) operations by ensuring Coast Guard assets are capable and equipped to deploy and conduct joint operations in support the most critical needs of the combatant commanders in the following major national-defense missions:

Maritime interception/interdiction operations

Military environmental response
Port operations, security, and defense
Theater security cooperation
Coastal sea control operations
Rotary-Wing Air Intercept (RWAI) operations
Combating terrorism operations
Maritime Operational Threat Response (MOTR) support

These support the unified combatant commanders and require the Coast Guard to execute essential military operations in peacetime, crisis, and war.

U.S. national security interests are no longer defined solely in terms of direct military threats to America and its allies. The terrorist attacks on September 11, 2001 demonstrated the emerging threat of unconventional warfare faced on the U.S. home front from sophisticated and covert adversaries. The Coast Guard has assumed one of the lead roles in responding to these unscrupulous attacks upon our nation by sustaining counterterrorism operations in the maritime domain in and around our nation's harbors, ports and coastlines. Commercial, tanker, passenger, and merchant vessels have all been subject to increased security measures enforced by the Coast Guard.

Abroad, the Coast Guard assists foreign naval and maritime forces through training and joint operations. Many of the world's maritime nations have forces that operate principally in the littoral seas and conduct missions similar to those of the Coast Guard. Because of the Coast Guard's long-time experience and multi-mission capability, the Coast Guard is a powerful role model to other nations that is in ever-increasing demand. The service's close working relations with these nations not only improve mutual cooperation as a joint force, but also support U.S. diplomatic efforts in general: promoting democracy, economic prosperity, and trust between nations.

Migrant Interdiction

As the primary maritime law enforcement agency, the Coast Guard is tasked with enforcing immigration law at sea. The Coast Guard conducts patrols and coordinates with other federal agencies and foreign countries to interdict undocumented migrants at sea, denying them entry via maritime routes to the U.S., its territories and possessions. Interdicting migrants at sea means they can be quickly returned to their countries of origin without the costly processes required if they successfully enter the United States. The Coast Guard supports the National Policy to promote safe, legal, and orderly migration.

Illegal immigration can costs U.S. taxpayers billions of dollars each year in social services. In addition to relieving this financial burden on our citizens, the Coast Guard's efforts help to support the use of legal migration systems. Primarily, the Coast Guard maintains its humanitarian responsibility to prevent the loss of life at sea, since the majority of migrant vessels are dangerously overloaded, unseaworthy or otherwise unsafe.

Protection from political persecution and torture are important concerns for the U.S. During the course of migrant interdictions, Coast Guard crews may encounter migrants requesting protection. The Department of State (Bureau of Population, Refugees, and Migration) and the Bureau of Citizenship and Immigration Services establish the policies in this area and handle all potential asylum cases on our cutters.

The Coast Guard's role in migrant interdiction has been a part of its history since the service's inception. The mission gained high visibility during the first mass migration emergency the United States faced between April 21 and September 28, 1980. Fidel Castro permitted any person who wanted to leave Cuba free access to depart from the port of Mariel, Cuba. Known as the Mariel Boatlift, approximately 124,000 undocumented Cuban migrants entered the United States by a flotilla of mostly U.S. vessels in violation of U.S. law. The Coast Guard interdicted vessels en route to Mariel Harbor, as well as provided search and rescue assistance to vessels bound for the United States. The Coast Guard also provided assistance to other federal agencies in the processing, investigation and prosecution of boat owners suspected of violating U.S. law.

The hazards of illegal maritime migration was highlighted in 1981, when the bodies of 30 Haitian migrants washed ashore on Hillsboro Beach, FL. In response to 1980 mass migration from Cuba and the increasing number of Haitian migrants landing in the U.S., on September 29, 1981, President Reagan issued <u>Presidential Proclamation 4865,</u> which suspended the entry of undocumented migrants to the U.S. from the high seas.

120,000 migrants from 23 countries were interdicted. Haitian migrants began increased departures after a 1991 coup in Haiti. These migrants were processed for asylum claims first on ships, then at Guantanamo Bay, Cuba (GTMO). Those that were identified as leaving for economic reasons were returned to Haiti. The camp eventually became a magnet for those departing seeking food, shelter, and a chance to get into the U.S. During this time, the camp at GTMO contained over 12,000 migrants.

In 1992, President Bush issued Executive Order 12807 directing the Coast Guard to enforce the suspension of the entry of undocumented migrants by interdicting them at sea, and return them to their country of origin or departure.

In 1993, Operation ABLE MANNER commenced. This operation concentrated Coast Guard patrols in the Windward Passage (the body of water between Haiti and Cuba) to interdict Haitian migrants. Operation ABLE MANNER continued until a new government was in place in Haiti in 1994. Today, Haitian migrants still leave Haiti attempting to reach the U.S. Many travel to the Bahamas and enter on smaller boats, while some attempt direct entry to the U.S. in large boat loads. There is a Coast Guard Liaison Officer at the U.S. Embassy in Port au Prince, Haiti, who handles various migration, counterdrug, and international engagement issues with Haiti.

In 1994, the Coast Guard was involved in its largest peacetime operation since the Vietnam War, responding to two mass migrations at the same time-first from Haiti, then from Cuba. Over 63,000 migrants were rescued and prevented from illegally entering the U.S. in Operations ABLE MANNER and ABLE VIGIL. At its height, Operation ABLE MANNER involved 17 U.S. Coast Guard vessels, patrolling the coast of Haiti while Operation ABLE VIGIL involved 38 Coast Guard cutters patrolling the Straits of Florida. Migration from Cuba continues. There has been a shift from migrants taking to sea in rafts to employing smugglers. The dangers of this are no less than rafting as illustrated by the deaths of numerous migrants in 1998-2000, when overloaded vessels capsized.

The Dominican Republic has historically been a major source country for undocumented migrants attempting to enter the U.S.. Crossing the Mona Passage (the body of water between the Dominican Republic and Puerto Rico) to enter Puerto Rico, thousands of people have taken to sea in a variety of

the most common is a homemade fishing vessel known as a Yola. Most of these migrants are smuggled by highly organized gangs. From April 1, 1995 through October 1, 1997, the Coast Guard conducted Operation ABLE RESPONSE, with enhanced operations dedicated to interdicting Dominican migrants. Over 9,500 migrants were interdicted or forced to turn back.

In addition to the migrant threat from these Caribbean countries, there has been an alarming increase in the number of migrants from Asia, most of whom are from the People's Republic of China. Very often Chinese migrants rely on well-organized, extremely violent, alien smugglers to gain entry into the United States. The living conditions on the vessels used to smuggle migrants are appalling, with overcrowded holds and unsafe sanitary conditions. In many cases, migrants are transferred to smaller pick up vessels offshore for the final ride to the U.S., or they're taken to Central American countries and smuggled across the U.S. land border. Beginning in 1998, more Chinese migrants began making trips from China attempting to enter Guam, which continues to be a significant problem. The International Information Programs has additional information on Chinese Alien Smuggling.

In 1999 and 2000, Coast Guard cutters on Counterdrug patrol in the Eastern Pacific have encountered increasing numbers of migrants being smuggled from Ecuador to points in Central America and Mexico. While this may not have a direct connection to the U.S., the Coast Guard acts for humanitarian reasons. Most of these vessels do not have the proper conditions to transport these migrants and lack the safety equipment in the event of an emergency. The Coast Guard works with the flag state of the vessels and other countries to escort the vessels to the closest safe port.

Undocumented migrants continue to pose a threat to the U.S. today. While the primary threat comes from Haiti, the Dominican Republic, the People's Republic of China, and Cuba, the Coast Guard has interdicted migrants of various nationalities throughout the world.

Marine Environmental Protection

The Marine Environmental Protection program develops and enforces regulations to avert the introduction of invasive species into the maritime environment, stop unauthorized ocean dumping, and prevent oil and chemical spills. This program is complemented by the Marine Safety program's pollution prevention activities.

In 2008, the Coast Guard refined its planning to support implementation of the National Response Framework, the national all hazards, incident management, and emergency response architecture. The Coast Guard also incorporated lessons learned from the motor vessel (M/V) COSCO BUSAN Incident Specific Preparedness Report into an improved policy that better aligns response planning at local, state, and Federal levels.

Ice Operations

The Coast Guard conducts icebreaking services to assist vessels and communities in emergency situations and facilitate essential commercial maritime activities in the Great Lakes and Northeast regions. In 2008, the Coast Guard, in concert with the Government of Canada and the commercial icebreaking industry, sustained navigable waterways for commercial traffic and assisted with 680 ice transits, representing the transport of over $2B (U.S.) of cargo.

Beyond domestic operations, the Coast Guard operates the only U.S.-flagged heavy icebreakers capable of providing year-round access to the Polar Regions. In 2008, the busiest iceberg season in a decade, the International Ice Patrol facilitated commerce by broadcasting position information on 1,029 icebergs crossing south of 48 degrees north latitude.

Other Law Enforcement

Preventing illegal foreign fishing vessel encroachment in the EEZ is a primary Coast Guard role vital to protecting the integrity of the Nation's maritime borders and ensuring the health of U.S. fisheries. The Coast Guard also enforces international agreements to suppress damaging illegal, unreported, and unregulated (IUU) fishing activity on the high seas.

In 2008, the Coast Guard detected 81 incursions by foreign fishing vessels into the U.S. EEZ. The Coast Guard also participated in the 2008 multi-national high seas drift net (HSDN) enforcement campaign, Operation North Pacific Watch. Through this campaign, the Coast Guard interdicted two

Aircraft, Boats and Cutters

The U.S. Coast Guard uses a variety of platforms to conduct its daily business. Cutters and boats are used on the water and fixed and rotary wing (helicopters) aircraft are used in the air.

There are a total of 211 aircraft in CG inventory. This figure fluctuates operationally due to maintenance schedules. Major Missions: Search/Rescue, Law Enforcement, Environmental Response, Ice Operations, and Air Interdiction. Fixed-wing aircraft (C-130 Hercules turboprops and HU-25 Falcon jets) operate from large and small Air Stations. Rotary wing aircraft (H-65 Dolphin and HH-60 Jayhawk helicopters) operate from flight-deck equipped Cutters, Air Stations and Air Facilities.

All vessels under 65 feet in length are classified as boats and usually operate near shore and on inland waterways. Craft include: Motor Lifeboats; Motor Surf Boats; Large Utility Boats; Surf Rescue Boats; Port Security Boats; Aids to Navigation Boats; and a variety of smaller, non-standard boats including Rigid Inflatable Boats. Sizes range from 64 feet in length down to 12 feet.

A "Cutter" is basically any CG vessel 65 feet in length or greater, having adequate accommodations for crew to live on board. Larger cutters (over 179 feet in length) are under control of Area Commands (Atlantic Area or Pacific Area). Cutters at or under 175 feet in length come under control of District Commands. Cutters, usually have a motor surf boat and/or a rigid hull inflatable boat on board. Polar Class icebreakers also carry an Arctic Survey Boat (ASB) and Landing Craft.

The Coast Guard is investing approximately $30 billion in major acquisition projects that purchase and modernize the service's ships, boats, aircraft, and command, control, communication, computers, intelligence, surveillance and reconnaissance (C4ISR) systems. This process of "recapitalizing" older and difficult-to-maintain assets is essential in order to carry out the Coast Guard's missions, which help ensure the nation's maritime security.

The Coast Guard's mission capabilities—saving lives, interdicting smugglers and illegal migrants, enforcing our nation's laws and treaties, and protecting the nation's ports and natural resources—derive from the readiness of its fleets of cutters, boats, aircraft, and the C4ISR systems that link them together.

its reliance on outdated assets and shore infrastructure. The cost of sustaining these assets continues to rise, while their reliability declines. The Coast Guard must replace these with state-of-the-market assets that will continue to deliver high-quality service to the American people.

7

United States Immigration and Customs Enforcement

United States Immigration and Customs Enforcement (ICE), promotes homeland security and public safety through the criminal and civil enforcement of federal laws governing border control, customs, trade, and immigration.

ICE is the principal investigative arm of the U.S. Department of Homeland Security (DHS). Created in 2003 through a merger of the investigative and interior enforcement elements of the U.S. Customs Service and the Immigration and Naturalization Service, ICE now has more than 20,000 employees in offices in all 50 states and 47 foreign countries.

ICE's primary mission is to promote homeland security and public safety through the criminal and civil enforcement of federal laws governing border control, customs, trade and immigration. This mission is executed through the enforcement of more than 400 federal statutes and focuses on smart immigration enforcement, preventing terrorism and combating the illegal movement of people and goods.

In 2014:

- ICE conducted 315,943 removals.
- ICE conducted 102,224 removals of individuals apprehended in the interior of the United States.
- 86,923 (85 percent) of all interior removals involved individuals previously convicted of a crime.

- ICE conducted 213,719 removals of individuals apprehended while attempting to unlawfully enter the United States.
- 56 percent of all ICE removals, or 177,960, involved individuals who were previously convicted of a crime.
- ICE apprehended and removed 86,923 criminals from the interior of the U.S.
- ICE removed 91,037 criminals apprehended while attempting to unlawfully enter the United States.
- 98 percent of all ICE FY 2014 removals, or 309,477, clearly met one or more of ICE's stated civil immigration enforcement priorities.
- Of the 137,983 individuals removed who had no criminal conviction, 89 percent, or 122,682, were apprehended at or near the border while attempting to unlawfully enter the country.
- The leading countries of origin for removals were Mexico, Guatemala, Honduras, and El Salvador.
- 2,802 individuals removed by ICE were classified as suspected or confirmed gang members.

Definitions of Key Terms

Border Removal: An individual removed by ICE who is apprehended while attempting to illicitly enter the United States at or between the ports of entry by a CBP officer or agent. These individuals are also referred to as recent border crossers.

Criminal Offender: An individual convicted in the United States for one or more criminal offenses. This does not include civil traffic offenses.

Immigration Fugitives: An individual who has failed to leave the United States based upon a final order of removal, deportation or exclusion, or who has failed to report to ICE after receiving notice to do so.

Interior Removal: An individual removed by ICE who is identified or apprehended in the United States by an ICE officer or agent. This category excludes those apprehended at the immediate border while attempting to unlawfully enter the United States.

Other Removable Alien: An individual who is not confirmed to be a convicted criminal, recent border crosser or fall under another ICE civil enforcement priority category. This category may include individuals removed on national security grounds or for general immigration violations.

Previously Removed Alien: An individual previously removed or returned who has re-entered the country illegally again.

Reinstatement of Final Removal Order: The removal of an alien based on the reinstatement of a prior removal order, where the alien departed the United States under an order of removal and illegally reentered the United States [INA § 241(a)(5)]. The alien may be removed without a hearing before an immigration court.

Removal: The compulsory and confirmed movement of an inadmissible or deportable alien out of the United States based on an order of removal. An individual who is removed may have administrative or criminal consequences placed on subsequent reentry owing to the fact of the removal.

Immigration Enforcement

Immigration enforcement is the largest single area of responsibility for ICE. While certain responsibilities and close cooperation with U.S. Customs and Border Protection, U.S. Citizenship and Immigration Services, and others require significant ICE assets near the border, the majority of immigration enforcement work for ICE takes place in the country's interior.

ICE special agents help businesses secure a lawful workforce and enforce immigration laws against those who encourage and rely on unauthorized workers, sometimes taking advantage of their situation to offer low pay and inadequate conditions.

Multiple programs help ICE focus and improve on stated priorities to find and remove illegal aliens who are criminals, fugitives or recent arrivals. Immigration enforcement entails cracking down on those who produce fraudulent documents to enable unlawful activity. Additionally, several robust efforts seek to continue improving the safe and humane detention and removal of persons subject to those actions.

The Criminal Alien Program (CAP) provides ICE-wide direction and support in the biometric and biographic identification, arrest, and removal of priority aliens who are incarcerated within federal, state, and local prisons and jails, as well as at-large criminal aliens that have circumvented identification. It is incumbent upon ICE to ensure that all efforts are made to investigate, arrest, and remove individuals from the United States that ICE deems priorities by processing the alien expeditiously and securing a final order of removal for an incarcerated alien before the alien is released to ICE custody. The identification and processing of incarcerated criminal aliens, before release from jails and prisons, decreases or eliminates the time spent in ICE custody and reduces the overall cost to the Federal Government.

Additionally, integral to the effective execution of this program is the aggressive prosecution of criminal offenders identified by Enforcement and Removal Operations (ERO) officers during the course of their duties. ERO, in conjunction with the Offices of the United States Attorneys, actively pursues criminal prosecutions upon the discovery of offenses of the nation's criminal code and immigration laws. This further enhances public safety and provides a significant deterrent to recidivism.

National Fugitive Operations Program (NFOP)

The primary mission of NFOP is to reduce the fugitive alien population in the United States. It identifies, locates, and arrests fugitive aliens, aliens that have been previously removed from the United States, removable aliens who have been convicted of crimes, as well as aliens who enter the United States illegally or otherwise defy the integrity of our immigration laws and border control efforts.

A fugitive alien is a person who has failed to leave the United States after he or she receives a final order of removal, deportation or exclusion, or who has failed to report to ICE after receiving notice to do so.

The NFOP's "Absconder Apprehension Initiative" uses data available from National Crime Information Center databases as a virtual force multiplier. As part of the Alien Absconder Initiative, ERO developed and coordinated the "ICE ERO Most Wanted" program. This program publicizes the names, faces and other identifying features of the 10 most wanted fugitive criminals by ERO.

The Law Enforcement Support Center is a national enforcement operations facility administered by U.S. Immigration and Customs Enforcement (ICE), the largest investigative agency in the Department of Homeland Security (DHS). The center is a single national point of contact that provides timely immigration status, identity information, and real-time assistance to local, state, and federal law enforcement agencies on aliens suspected, arrested, or convicted of criminal activity. The center protects and defends the United States by sharing timely and relevant ICE information with our law enforcement partners around the world.

Located in Williston, Vermont, the center operates 24 hours a day, 7 days a week, 365 days a year. The primary users of the center are state and local law enforcement officers seeking information regarding aliens encountered in the course of their daily enforcement activities. The center serves as a national enforcement operations center, responding to inquiries from federal, state, and local criminal justice agencies concerning aliens under investigation or arrested.

National Crime Information Center—The Law Enforcement Support Center administers and validates all ICE criminal and administrative records in this nationwide law enforcement consortium and criminal database. There are now more than 301,600 ICE records at the National Crime Information Center.

Communications Center—The Law Enforcement Support Center operates a communications center that provides the National Crime Information ter hit confirmations (within 10 minutes) to law enforcement agencies 24 hours a day, seven days a week. In addition, center officers and specialists place immigration detainers on aliens suspected of residing in the country unlawfully. The communications center also performs instant immigration status checks for ICE Officers and provides telephonic assistance to local law enforcement agencies performing immigration alien queries.

Special Response Tasks—The Law Enforcement Support Center is the central point of contact for a number of special information requests. For example, the center conducts "Brady checks" for the FBI's National Instant Criminal Background Check System, screening the immigration status of foreign-born, non-citizen firearm permit applicants before authorizing purchase or possession of a weapon. In fiscal year, 2013 the center assisted with 126,122 Brady checks for the FBI. It also provides daily assistance to the U.S. Secret Service by assisting in the screening of persons seeking to visit or work on the White House grounds. In fiscal year, 2013 the center helped the Secret Service screen 41,560 individuals. The center also investigates ICE detainee claims to U.S. citizenship and certain urgent requests for relief when removal is imminent.

Law Enforcement Training—The center offers an on-site training and outreach program that provides instruction on how to access Law Enforcement Support Center information and instruction on ICE's role and responsibilities.

Secure Communities

The highest priority of any law enforcement agency is to protect the communities it serves. When it comes to enforcing our nation's immigration laws, U.S. Immigration and Customs Enforcement (ICE) focuses its limited resources on those who have been arrested for breaking criminal laws. ICE prioritizes the removal of criminal aliens, those who pose a threat to public safety, and repeat immigration violators.

Secure Communities is a simple and common sense way to carry out ICE's priorities. It uses an already-existing federal information-sharing partnership between ICE and the Federal Bureau of Investigation (FBI) that helps to identify criminal aliens without imposing new or additional requirements on

fingerprints of individuals who are arrested or booked into custody with the FBI to see if they have a criminal record. Under Secure Communities, the FBI automatically sends the fingerprints to DHS to check against its immigration databases. If these checks reveal that an individual is unlawfully present in the United States or otherwise removable due to a criminal conviction, ICE takes enforcement action—prioritizing the removal of individuals who present the most significant threats to public safety as determined by the severity of their crime, their criminal history, and other factors—as well as those who have repeatedly violated immigration laws.

Only federal DHS officers make immigration enforcement decisions, and they do so only after an individual is arrested for a criminal violation of local, state, or federal law, separate and apart from any violations of immigration law.

More than 283,000 convicted criminal aliens have been removed as a result of Secure Communities interoperability, by which the FBI automatically sends fingerprints of anyone arrested or booked by police for a state or local criminal offense to DHS to check against its immigration and enforcement records so that ICE can determine whether that person is a criminal alien or falls under ICE's civil immigration enforcement priorities. Since its inception in 2008 with 14 jurisdictions, Secure Communities has expanded to all 3,181 jurisdictions within 50 states, the District of Columbia, and five (5) U.S. Territories. Full implementation was completed on January 22, 2013.

ICE receives annual appropriations from Congress sufficient to remove a limited number of the more than 10 million individuals estimated to be in the U.S. who lack lawful status or are removable because of a criminal conviction. Given this reality, ICE must set sensible priorities.

Under the Obama administration, ICE has set clear and common-sense priorities for immigration enforcement focused on identifying and removing those aliens with criminal convictions. In addition to criminal aliens, ICE focuses on recent illegal entrants, repeat violators who game the immigration system, those who fail to appear at immigration hearings, and fugitives who have already been ordered removed by an immigration judge.

These priorities have led to significant results. In fiscal year 2013, ICE's prioritized, targeted enforcement resulted in the removal of more than 368,000 aliens, of which 98 percent fell into one of ICE's stated civil immigration enforcement priorities.

DACA and DAPA

On November 20, 2014, Secretary of Homeland Security Jeh Johnson issued new policies which allow certain aliens who arrived in the United States on or before January 1, 2010 to apply for deferred action, a form of prosecutorial discretion under which aliens are not removed from the United States and that authorizes them to seek permission to work lawfully in the United States. The Secretary's policies, known as Deferred Action for Childhood Arrivals (DACA) and Deferred Action for Parents of Americans and Lawful Permanent Residents (DAPA) apply to certain individuals who came to the United States as children under the age of 16 of who are parents of U.S. citizens or lawful permanent resident children. This process is open to any individual who can demonstrate he or she meets the guidelines for consideration, including those who are in removal proceedings, with a final order, or with a voluntary departure order. All deferred action decisions will be made by USCIS.

Detention Management

ICE Enforcement and Removal Operations (ERO) manages and oversees the nation's civil immigration detention system. ICE detainees placed in ERO custody represent virtually every country in the world, various security classifications, both genders and medical conditions ranging from healthy to terminally ill. Non-U.S. citizens who are apprehended and determined to need custodial supervision are placed in detention facilities. Those who are released from secure custody constitute ERO's "nondetained" docket. Every case, whether "detained" or "non-detained," remains part of ERO's caseload and is actively managed until it is formally closed. ERO processes and monitors detained and non-detained cases as they move through immigration court proceedings to conclusion. At that point, ERO executes the judge's order.

ERO's Detention Standards Compliance Unit ensures that detainees in ICE custody reside in safe, secure and humane environments and under appropriate conditions of confinement. ICE now uses Performance-Based National Detention Standards (PBNDS) that focus on results or outcomes. Each detention center must meet specified standards. As part of the restructuring of the former INS, the Homeland Security Act of 2002

ties related to the care and custody of unaccompanied alien children to the Department of Health and Human Services, Office of Refugee Resettlement. To that end, ERO developed policy and procedures regarding the appropriate case management of unaccompanied alien children in Federal custody while they wait for immigration proceedings.

Health Service Corps

The more than 900 members of ICE's Health Service Corps oversee medical care for detainees at facilities nationwide. In many instances, the care that detainees receive while in ICE custody is the first professional medical care of their adult lives. ICE Health Service Corps provides direct care to approximately 15,000 detainees housed at 21 designated facilities throughout the nation. It oversees medical care provided to an additional 17,000 detainees housed at non-ICE Health Service Corps staffed detention facilities across the country. When necessary, it authorizes and pays for off-site specialty and emergency care, consultations and case management.

In order to continually upgrade the quality of medical services delivered, ICE Health Service Corps actively seeks accreditation by the National Commission on Correctional Health Care and the American Correctional Association. It also complies with the Performance Based National Detention Standards.

In many instances, the care that detainees receive while in ICE custody is the first professional medical care they have received, and it is common for detainee health screenings to identify chronic and serious health conditions that were previously undiagnosed.

ICE Health Service Corps also provides medical support during flight, tactical ground and sea operations through the Special Operations Unit. This unit consists of specially trained commissioned officers who, in addition to meeting the medical needs of detainees, serve as liaisons between law enforcement officials and other key stakeholders.

National Gang Unit

U.S. Immigration and Customs Enforcement (ICE) recognizes that transnational criminal street gangs represent a significant threat to public safety in communities throughout the United States. The National Gang Unit (NGU) is a critical part of ICE's mission to bring the fight to transnational criminal gangs. The NGU identifies and develops intelligence on gang membership, associations, activities and international movements. It also deters, disrupts gang operations by tracing and seizing cash, weapons and other assets derived from illicit activities.

In 2005, ICE initiated Operation Community Shield, an international law enforcement initiative that combines Homeland Security Investigations' (HSI) expansive statutory and civil enforcement authorities to combat the growth and proliferation of transnational criminal street gangs, prison gangs and outlaw motorcycle gangs throughout the United States. With assistance from state, local, tribal and foreign law enforcement partners, the initiative helps HSI locate, investigate, prosecute, and where applicable, immediately remove gang members from our neighborhoods and ultimately from the United States.

HSI is the investigative arm of the Department of Homeland Security, and has positioned itself as the leader in transnational criminal gang investigations. As such, HSI is committed to sharing gang intelligence gathered through investigations to aggressively pursue leads.

Worksite Enforcement

U.S. Immigration and Customs Enforcement (ICE) has developed a comprehensive worksite enforcement strategy that promotes national security, protects critical infrastructure and targets employers who violate employment laws or engage in abuse or exploitation of workers.

An effective worksite enforcement strategy must address both employers who knowingly hire illegal workers, as well as the workers themselves. In worksite cases, ICE investigators adhere to high investigative standards, including the following:

ICE looks for evidence of the mistreatment of workers, along with evidence of trafficking, smuggling, harboring, visa fraud, identification document fraud, money laundering and other such criminal conduct.

ICE obtains indictments, criminal arrests or search warrants, or a commitment from a U.S. Attorney's Office to prosecute the targeted employer before arresting employees for civil immigration violations at a worksite.

ICE prioritizes its criminal investigations on the most egregious violators and concentrates its worksite inspection efforts on employers conducting business in critical infrastructure and national security interest industries/sectors (e.g. chemical, commercial facilities, communications, critical manufacturing, dams, emergency services, government facilities, information technology, nuclear reactors materials and waste and transportation systems). In pursuing this strategy, ICE applies risk assessment principles to critical infrastructure and worksite enforcement cases in order to maximize the impact of investigations against the most significant threats and violators.

Worksite enforcement investigations often involve egregious violations of criminal statutes by employers and widespread abuses. Such cases often involve additional violations such as alien smuggling, alien harboring, document fraud, money laundering, and fraud or worker exploitation. ICE also investigates employers who employ force, threats or coercion (for example, threatening to have employees deported) in order to keep the unauthorized alien workers from reporting substandard wage or working conditions. By uncovering such violations, ICE can send a strong deterrent message to other employers who knowingly employ illegal aliens.

ICE also works with the private sector to educate employers about their responsibilities to hire only authorized workers and how to accurately verify employment eligibility.

Human Rights Violators & War Crimes Unit

ICE and Homeland Security Investigations (HSI) operates the Human Rights Violators and War Crimes Unit (HRVWCU) within the National Security Investigations Division (NSID). Preceded by the U.S. Immigration and Naturalization Service, HSI has more than 30 years of experience in

focused on human rights violations in an effort to prevent the United States from becoming a safe haven to those individuals who engage in the commission of war crimes, genocide, torture and other forms of serious human rights abuses from conflicts around the globe. When foreign war crimes suspects, persecutors and human rights abusers are identified within U.S. borders, the unit utilizes its powers and authorities to the fullest extent of the law to investigate, prosecute and, whenever possible, remove any such offenders from the United States.

Since fiscal year 2004, ICE has arrested more than 275 individuals for human rights-related violations under various criminal and/or immigration statutes. During that same period, ICE has denied more than 139 individuals from obtaining entry visas to the United States and created more than 66,000 subject records, which prevented identified human-rights violators from attempting to enter the United States. In addition, ICE successfully obtained deportation orders to physically remove more than 590 known or suspected human rights violators from the United States. Currently, ICE is pursuing more than 1,900 leads and removal cases that involve suspected human rights violators from nearly 96 different countries.

The Human Rights Violators and War Crimes Center (HRVWCC) began as a pilot project in April 2008 to further increase the efficiency of these complex investigative and litigation actions. The center leverages the knowledge and expertise of a select group of special agents, attorneys, intelligence specialists, criminal research specialists and historians who are collectively collocated. The center also brings together various DHS components and other departmental agencies, to include the FBI and the Department of Justice to work collaboratively on human rights violators and war crimes investigations. It was established as a permanent ICE entity in October 2009.

The No Safe Haven Initiative

The United States grants admission to more refugees and asylum seekers annually than any other nation. Individuals fleeing wars, genocide, ethnic cleansing and various other forms of persecution have often view the United States as a safe haven. Upon entry, the vast majority of these people choose to remain here permanently and, ultimately, gain citizenship through the naturalization process.

Unfortunately, individuals who have perpetrated significant abuses against others in their home countries seek entry to evade prosecution and punishment. Frequently, these individuals hide among those they once persecuted, falsely claiming to be victims of abuse. They may be former officials of regimes that are or were potentially hostile to our nation and its interests, making them not only human-rights violators, but also national security threats. HSI's No Safe Haven Initiative targets these individuals. Those accused of human rights violations cannot escape justice by hiding in the United States. HSI is committed to keeping the nation safe by ensuring the secure removal of aliens with known ties to human rights violations. The Center operates four Regional Support Teams (RST) to identify, locate, investigate, prosecute and assist in removing human rights violators, torturers and war criminals from the United States. These RST's are considered the backbone of the center and are geographically oriented covering Latin America, Africa, Europe/Balkans, and Asia/Middle East. Each team consists of program managers/special agents, analytical/historical personnel and legal advisors. RSTs provide programmatic oversight over the field where the actual human rights investigations take place by leveraging all relevant agency expertise to support investigation and litigation activities within the designated target region.

Repatriation

ICE Enforcement and Removal Operations (ERO) facilitates the processing of illegal aliens through the immigration court system and coordinates their departure from the U.S. ERO's robust removals program halts the number of illegal alien absconders in the U.S.

Repatriation involves planning and coordinating removals across the country and developing and implementing strategies to support the return of all removable aliens to their country of origin.

Repatriation comprises the following divisions and their respective components:

Travel Document Units East and West
Post Order Custody Review Unit
ICE Air Operations
Commercial Operations
Charter Operations

Investigating Illegal Movement of People and Goods

ICE special agents, officers and attorneys enforce provisions of approximately 400 federal statutes. This large and diverse body of laws is reflected in the wide array of offices, programs and projects that make up ICE. People are smuggled and trafficked, while children are sexually exploited at home and abroad.

Illegal trade, in a very general sense, predominately involve guns, money and drugs, but ICE's responsibilities extend much further into all kinds of illegal and counterfeit merchandise coming into the country. For instance, ICE's responsibilities include the repatriation of cultural treasures out of the country to original owners abroad, and combatting the trade of child pornography and much more.

Browse through the "Investigating Illegal Movement of People and Goods" category of the What We Do drop-down menu to learn more.

Border Enforcement Security Task Force (BEST)

Border related crime, and the violence that is often associated with it, pose significant risks to public safety and the national security of the United States. In response to these threats, the Department of Homeland Security, along with our federal, state, and local law enforcement partners, remain committed to our focus on disrupting border related criminal activity associated with narcotics smuggling; human trafficking and smuggling; money laundering; bulk cash smuggling; weapons trafficking and smuggling; and other such serious crimes.

ICE partners with more than 100 fellow law enforcement agencies in BEST teams across 16 states. Each team focuses on disrupting criminal smuggling and trafficking operations and on denying criminal organizations the opportunity to transport their illicit funds. Since its creation in 2005, BEST has initiated more than 9,000 cases. In 2005, in response to the significant increase in violence along the Southwest Border in Mexico, the U.S Immigration and Customs Enforcement, Homeland Security Investigations (HSI), in partnership with U.S. Customs and Border Protection, as well as other federal, state, local, and international law enforcement officials created the Border Enforcement Security Task Force (BEST) in Laredo, Texas.

On December 7, 2012, President Barack Obama signed into law the Jaime Zapata Border Enforcement Security Task Force (BEST) Act, Public Law 112-205. The law was named in memory of Jaime Zapata, an HSI special agent assigned to the BEST who died on February 15, 2011, after being shot while on duty in Mexico. This law amends the Homeland Security Act of 2002 and authorizes the Secretary of Homeland Security to:

Establish BEST units

Direct the assignment of federal personnel to the program

Take other actions to assist federal, state, local, and tribal law enforcement agencies to participate

Several international law enforcement agencies serve as key members of the team.

To date, a total of 35 BESTs have been initiated across 16 states and in Puerto Rico. These teams comprise over 1,000 members who represent over 100 law enforcement agencies who have jointly committed to investigate transnational criminal activity along the Southwest and Northern Borders and at our nation's major seaports. On our country's northern border, Canadian law enforcement agencies like the Canada Border Services Agency, the Royal Canadian Mounted Police, the Ontario Provincial Police, the Niagara Regional Police Service, the Toronto Metropolitan Police, the Windsor Police Service and the Amherstburg Police Service are active members. On the southwest border, the Mexican Secretariat of Public Safety or SSP, and the Colombian National Police have both been active partners in the past, with both the BEST San Diego and BEST San Juan units.

Cornerstone

Cornerstone detects and closes down weaknesses within U.S. financial, trade and transportation sectors that can be exploited by criminal networks. Law enforcement entities share criminal typologies and methods with businesses and industries that manage the very systems that terrorists and criminal organizations seek to exploit. This sharing of information allows the financial and trade community to take precautions to protect itself from exploitation. In return, ICE receives information to more thoroughly investigate these complex and sophisticated criminal schemes.

ICE uses financial investigations to beat criminals at their trade. By following the money trail, law enforcement can identify and dismantle international criminal networks, seizing the networks' proceeds and related assets. ICE, along with other Department of Homeland Security component agencies, is charged with protecting the nation's borders. One way ICE does this is by investigating the illicit flow of money in and out of the United States.

ICE is a participant in the International Mass-Marketing Fraud Working Group to combat international consumer fraud, such as email and telephone scams.

ICE Homeland Security Investigations (HSI) launched the SEARCH (Seizing Earnings and Assets from Retail Crime Heists) Initiative as an ongoing, national initiative to address the threat of transnational crime being committed by organized retail crime rings. The SEARCH Initiative searches for illicit proceeds, seizes hidden assets and shuts down organized retail crime rings.

Project STAMP attacks human smuggling and human trafficking organizations from an aggressive anti-money laundering stance. ICE's Office of Homeland Security Investigations (HSI) follows money trails to identify key members of criminal organizations involved in human smuggling/human trafficking activity. Seizure of these assets is crucial to shutting down these organizations.

C3 is made up of the Cyber Crimes Unit, the Child Exploitation Investigations Unit and the Computer Forensics Unit. This state-of-the-art center offers cyber-crime support and training to federal, state, local and international law enforcement agencies. C3 also operates a fully equipped computer forensics laboratory, which specializes in digital evidence recovery, and offers training in computer investigative and forensic skills.

Forensic Services

The HSI Forensic Laboratory (HSI-FL) **Latent Print** (LP) Section provides finger and palm print services and support across all investigative disciplines. These services include, but are not limited to, processing evidence for latent prints (e.g., drug packaging and paraphernalia, firearms, computers, currency, compact discs), latent print comparison, inked print comparison, searching automated fingerprint identification system databases, and providing crime scene assistance.

The LP Section conducts the following forensic examinations:

- Automated Fingerprint Identification System (AFIS) Search
- Inked Fingerprint Examination
- Latent Print Processing
- Latent Print Examination

The HSI Forensic Laboratory **Questioned Document** (QD) Section specializes in determining the authenticity of documents and identifying the presence of alterations within those documents. Specialized equipment may be used during the examination process that will not affect or damage the original document. While the QD Section specializes in a full range of travel and identity documents, including but not limited to, passports, visas, driver's licenses, identification cards and vital records (e.g., birth, death, marriage), any questioned document may be submitted to the HSI Forensic Laboratory for forensic examination.

The **Operations Section** comprises two sub-sections: the Document Training and Alerts Section and the Law Enforcement Support Section.

The **Document Training and Alerts Section** uses information developed in the course of the Laboratory's forensic examinations to enhance the abilities of field agents to recognize identity document fraud when they encounter it in the course of their duties. Intelligence analysis and the forensic disciplines are utilized by the **Law Enforcement Support Section** staff to assist HSI and other law enforcement agency investigations of illicit activity in the United States and throughout the world as facilitated by document fraud. Examples of the types of criminal activities include the following:

- Financial Crime
- Narcotics Smuggling
- Identity Theft
- Human Trafficking and Smuggling
- Fraudulent Identity Document Vending
- Immigration Benefit Fraud

In addition to providing law enforcement support for current investigations, leads developed from on-going analysis of transnational criminal organizations are forwarded to HSI field offices and attachés.

The HSI-FL **Polygraph Program** consists of HSI special agents trained in the detection of deception as well as various interview techniques. The section conducts polygraph examinations in support of a wide variety of HSI investigations including counter-proliferation, human smuggling and trafficking, internal and narcotics. Polygraph examinations can establish a subject's credibility and identify additional leads, suspects and assets. Polygraph examinations are also given to foreign law enforcement officers seeking to join HSI vetted law enforcement units.

The HSI-FL oversees the **Evidence Recovery Teams** (ERTs) Program. The ERTs are designed to provide a standardized, agency-wide method for collecting physical evidence to ensure proper handling and preservation for subsequent scientific evaluation.

Human Trafficking

Human trafficking is one of the most heinous crimes that ICE investigates. In its worst manifestation, human trafficking is akin to modern-day slavery. Victims pay to be illegally transported into the United States only to find themselves in the thrall of traffickers. They are forced into prostitution, involuntary labor and other forms of servitude to repay debts—often entry in

United States. In certain cases, the victims are mere children. They find themselves surrounded by an unfamiliar culture and language without identification documents, fearing for their lives and the lives of their families. ICE relies on tips from the public to dismantle these organizations.

Trafficking in Persons is defined as:

Sex trafficking in which a commercial sex act is induced by force, fraud or coercion, or in which the person induced to perform such act has not attained 18 years of age; or

The recruitment, harboring, transportation, provision or obtaining of a person for labor or services, through the use of force, fraud or coercion for the purpose of subjection to involuntary servitude, peonage, debt bondage or slavery.

Money Laundering

In recent decades, U.S. law enforcement has encountered an increasing number of major financial crimes, frequently resulting from the needs for drug trafficking organizations to launder large sums of criminal proceeds through legitimate financial institutions and investment vehicles.

Cornerstone (see above) is used to detect and close down weaknesses within U.S. financial, trade and transportation sectors that can be exploited by criminal networks. The **El Dorado Task Force** consists of more than 260 members from more than 55 law enforcement agencies in New York and New Jersey—including federal agents, state and local police investigators, intelligence analysts and federal prosecutors. The El Dorado Task Force is headquartered at the New York Special Agent in Charge Office and at other locations in the New York/New Jersey Metropolitan area. It targets financial crime at all levels. Task force agents educate the private financial sector to identify and eliminate vulnerabilities and promote anti-money laundering legislation through training and other outreach programs. Prosecutors use a full range of criminal and civil laws to prosecute targets and forfeit the proceeds of their illicit activity. The El Dorado Task Force uses a systems-based approach to investigating financial crimes by targeting vulnerabilities such as the Black Market Peso Exchange and commodity-based money laundering.

Many developing nations are plagued by corrupt foreign officials who plunder state coffers for personal gain and then attempt to place those funds in the U.S. financial system. ICE leads investigations against corrupt foreign public officials who have used U.S. financial institutions and other investment vehicles to facilitate criminal acts involving the laundering of proceeds emanating from foreign public corruption, bribery or embezzlement.

Trade-based money laundering is an alternative remittance system that allows illegal organizations the opportunity to earn, move and store proceeds disguised as legitimate trade. Value can be moved through this process by false-invoicing, over-invoicing and under-invoicing commodities that are imported or exported around the world. Criminal organizations frequently exploit global trade systems to move value around the world by employing complex and sometimes confusing documentation associated with legitimate trade transactions. ICE established the Trade Transparency Unit initiative to target trade-based money laundering worldwide.

Bulk Cash Smuggling Center

U.S. Immigration and Customs Enforcement's (ICE) Homeland Security Investigations (HSI) National Bulk Cash Smuggling Center identifies, investigates and disrupts bulk cash smuggling activities around the world. The center is located at the ICE Law Enforcement Support Center in Williston, Vt. It operates 24 hours a day. More stringent federal laws against money laundering, along with anti-money laundering measures adopted by traditional financial institutions, have forced criminal organizations to shift the movement of their illicit proceeds outside of the established financial industry. To avoid the scrutiny of law enforcement, these criminal organizations increasingly employ non-traditional methods to move funds, including the smuggling of bulk cash into, out of and through the United States.

The center assists federal, state, tribal, local and foreign law enforcement authorities in their efforts to restrict the flow of funding that supports criminal enterprises. It provides real-time tactical intelligence, investigative support and expertise in the transportation and smuggling of bulk cash. By contacting the National Bulk Cash Smuggling Center, law enforcement officers gain access to financial investigative expertise that will help them better follow the money trail, seize and forfeit criminal proceeds.

The PATRIOT Act, enacted in 2001, criminalized the international smuggling of bulk cash. Between fiscal years 2003 and 2013, ICE HSI bulk cash smuggling investigations led to the arrest of more than 2,300 individuals and seizures of more than $543 million.

The Cultural Property, Art and Antiquities Program

This program is unique to Homeland Security Investigation's (HSI) portfolio. Returning a nation's looted cultural heritage or stolen artwork, promotes goodwill with foreign governments and citizens, while significantly protecting the world's cultural heritage and knowledge of past civilizations.

The theft and trafficking of cultural heritage and art is a tradition as old as the cultures they represent. What has changed is the ability of cultural pirates to acquire, transport and sell valuable cultural property and art swiftly, easily and stealthily. These criminals operate on a global scale without regard for laws, borders, nationalities or the significance of the treasures they smuggle.

Federal importation laws give HSI the authority to take a leading role in investigating crimes involving the illicit importation and distribution of cultural property and art. Customs laws allow HSI to seize cultural property and art that are brought into the United States illegally, especially when objects have been reported lost or stolen.

Specially trained investigators assigned to domestic and international offices partner with federal, state and local agencies; private institutions; and foreign governments to conduct investigations. These entities share HSI's mission to protect these objects and preserve cultural heritage. Since 2007, HSI special agents have participated in a training program to learn the latest techniques and trends for conducting criminal investigations of cultural property. As part of this program, the Smithsonian Institution's Museum Conservation Institute provides HSI special agents with on-site training on how to handle, store, photograph and authenticate cultural property and works of art.

Firearms, Ammunition, and Explosives Smuggling

As the primary federal law enforcement agency responsible for investigating international smuggling operations and enforcing U.S. export laws, Homeland Security Investigations (HSI) is committed to combating illegal firearms, ammunition and explosives smuggling activities that fuel violence both domestically and abroad. HSI fulfills this commitment by relying on the agency's extensive legal authorities and unique expertise in conducting illegal export and contraband smuggling investigations.

HSI firearms, ammunition, and explosives smuggling investigations have resulted in unprecedented bi-lateral interdictions, investigations and information-sharing activities that identify, disrupt, and dismantle transnational criminal networks operating within the United States, Mexico, Canada, Central America, the Caribbean, and around the World.

HSI and its law enforcement partners target the illegal movement of U.S. origin firearms, ammunition, and explosive weapons with the ultimate goal of preventing the procurement of these items by drug cartels, terrorists, human rights violators, foreign adversaries, and other transnational criminal organizations and individuals that utilize these weapons to facilitate criminal activity and commit acts of violence. HSI's investigative strategy includes the identification and prosecution of criminal networks and individuals responsible for the acquisition and movement of firearms and other dangerous weapons from the United States, as well as the seizure and forfeiture of money and valuable property derived from or used to facilitate this criminal activity.

Law Enforcement Information Sharing Initiative

The Law Enforcement Information Sharing Service is a web-based data exchange platform, hosted by the Department of Homeland Security (DHS), that allows law enforcement agencies to rapidly share and access data related to criminal and national security investigations. The automated service offers a more efficient system for requesting and sharing investigative information, helping investigators to more quickly identify patterns, connections and

DHS law enforcement information is processed through the ICE Pattern Analysis and Information Collection System and includes information from subject records and closed cases concerning people, businesses, vehicles (including aircraft and seacraft), firearms and more. The Law Enforcement Information Sharing Service currently provides federal, state, local, tribal and international law enforcement agency partners with access to more than 2.6 million subject records related to persons of interest, including suspects in child pornography, drug smuggling, immigration fraud, alien smuggling and a wide range of other cases. The service is compliant with all existing privacy and security requirements for safeguarding personal information and user authentication and access.

Narcotics Enforcement

Smuggling methods include the use of high-speed vessels, cargo containers, aircraft, commercial trucking, commercial vessel and human carriers. The National Security Presidential Directive/NSPD-25 directs U.S. government agencies to attack the vulnerabilities of drug trafficking organizations by disrupting key business sectors and weakening the economic basis of the drug trade. The illegal drug market in the U.S. is based on illegal narcotics grown or manufactured in foreign countries and smuggled across our nation's borders. ICE agents enforce a wide range of criminal statutes including Title 18 and Title 19 of the U.S. Code. These statutes address general smuggling issues as well as customs violations. ICE also enforces Title 21, which covers the importation, distribution, manufacture and possession of illegal narcotics.

ICE agents have extensive knowledge of the border environment and techniques employed by smuggling organizations to transport contraband into the United States. This expertise has been gained through years of experience in conducting undercover operations, utilizing confidential informants, special enforcement operations and conducting contraband smuggling investigations.

The methods used by smuggling organizations are always changing and through continued training, the use of emerging technologies and dedication, ICE has maintained its expertise in disrupting and dismantling these criminal organizations.

Child Exploitation Investigations Unit

Each year, countless children around the world fall prey to sexual predators. These young victims are left with permanent psychological, physical, and emotional scars. When a recording of that sexual abuse is made or released onto the Internet, it lives on forever. As part of ICE's Cyber Crimes Center (C3), the CEIU uses cutting edge investigative techniques to bring justice to consumers, producers and distributors of child pornography, as well as to predators engaging in child sex tourism. The efforts of the CEIU, in addition to ICE's participation in national programs like Operation Predator and international partnerships like the Virtual Global Taskforce, have resulted in the rescue of thousands of children.

Seeking to end this criminal activity and protect children worldwide, HSI developed Operation Predator, an international initiative to identify, investigate and arrest child predators who:

- Possess, trade and produce child pornography
- Travel overseas for sex with minors; and
- Engage in the sex trafficking of children.

HSI is a worldwide leader in the fight against the sexual exploitation of children. Prior to the creation of the agency in 2003, legacy U.S. Customs special agents investigated the disbursement of illegal child pornography that was often sent by mail or purchased overseas. With the advent of the Internet, the sharing and trading of child pornography now primarily occurs online. In addition to the legacy expertise, HSI special agents also have the authority to investigate the illegal movement of people and goods across U.S. borders, and because the Internet is borderless, the sharing of contraband online is an international crime. An image on the Web of a child being sexually abused can be seen by anyone anywhere in the world. Operation Predator draws on the agency's unique investigative and enforcement authorities to safeguard children. And, with 200 U.S. offices and more than 70 offices overseas, HSI has the ability to follow a case—to rescue a victim or arrest a predator—wherever in the world it may lead.

Collaborating with law enforcement partners around the country and the world, Operation Predator brings together an array of resources to target these child predators. As part of the effort:

HSI participates on all 61 Internet Crimes Against Children (ICAC) Task Forces across the United States, which are led by state and local law enforcement agencies.

HSI established a National Victim Identification Program at its Cyber Crimes Center, combining the latest technology with traditional investigative techniques to rescue child victims of sexual exploitation.

HSI is the U.S. representative to the Interpol working group that locates new child sexual abuse material on the Internet and refers cases to the country that the abuse is believed to be occurring in for further investigation. Also, HSI special agents stationed internationally work with foreign governments, Interpol and others to enhance coordination and cooperation on crimes that cross borders.

HSI works in partnership with the National Center for Missing & Exploited Children and other federal agencies to help solve cases and rescue sexually exploited children.

HSI is a founding member and current chair of the Virtual Global Taskforce, joining law enforcement agencies, non-governmental organizations and private sector partners around the world to fight child exploitation information and images that travel over the Internet.

Customs Cross Designation

In order to be more effective in that mission, HSI works collaboratively with federal, state and local partners in a force multiplier approach to investigations. As part of that approach, HSI is authorized under Title 19, section 1401 of the U.S. Code to cross-designate other federal, state and local law enforcement officers to investigate and enforce customs laws.

Customs cross-designation authority can also be extended to foreign law enforcement partners for cases that cross international boundaries. This authority enhances HSI's ability to work more closely with these counterparts, fostering secure relationships and cooperation between the U.S. and other countries.

After receiving standardized training, each cross-designated customs officer has the authority to enforce U.S. customs laws and to perform the duties of

HSI special agents as granted by the respective special agent in charge. Those duties include:

Designated customs officers are authorized to execute and serve search or arrest warrants, subpoenas and summonses in compliance with customs laws. Designated customs officers are authorized to conduct customs searches at the border for merchandise being imported into or exported from the U.S. and to effect seizures and arrests of persons or articles in violation of U.S law.

Designated customs officers are authorized to carry firearms in compliance with the HSI's firearms policy. Designation status for all officers is valid for a period of two years, after which time they must receive recertification training. Designation can be revoked at any time by the special agent in charge.

Foreign Corruption Investigations

ICE pursues corrupt foreign officials who plunder state coffers for personal gain and then attempt to place those funds in the U.S. financial system. The agency's Foreign Corruption Investigations Group, part of ICE Homeland Security Investigations, is charged with spearheading investigations that hold these individuals accountable.

Large-scale corruption on the part of public officials in other nations, particularly developing nations, poses a significant threat to public trust and government infrastructure. In many cases, public corruption exists in unstable environments in which criminal and terrorist organizations flourish. The ICE Foreign Corruption Investigations Group was established in Miami in 2003. Miami was chosen as the group's location due to the number of requests assistance requests received by that office from Central and South American and Caribbean governments.

ICE participates in the overall U.S. government response to the issue of large-scale foreign public corruption as a member of an ad hoc anti-kleptocracy working group, which was initiated by the National Security Council. ICE plays an integral role in developing the government-wide anti-kleptocracy strategy due to the agency's expertise in investigating international money laundering and enforcing customs and immigration law. ICE's extensive international investigative assets allow the agency to pursue a

sive international investigative assets allow the agency to pursue a wide array of investigative leads related to kleptocracy.

Since the inception of the Foreign Corruption Investigations Group, ICE has initiated more than 394 investigations, made 216 criminal arrests, secured 277 indictments and seized more than $153.5 million associated with foreign corruption.

Recent Investigations

ICE's Foreign Corruption Investigations Group, in coordination with Romanian authorities, arrested the former director of Romania's National Railroad—Romania's number one fugitive at the time. He was accused of stealing $110 million in government funds while in office. ICE located numerous properties, bank accounts and several corporations associated with the former director.

Operation Persistence began as a narcotics investigation, but was later turned over to the Foreign Corruption Investigations Group. Drug smugglers used an undercover vessel to transport 300 kilograms of cocaine from Colombia to Miami. Twenty individuals were indicted, extradited from Colombia and convicted for trying to smuggle drugs into the United States. Evidence from the investigation linked the drug smuggling operation to a corrupt Colombian official.

Human Smuggling

Human smuggling is the importation of people into a country via the deliberate evasion of immigration laws. This includes bringing illegal aliens into a country, as well as the unlawful transportation and harboring of aliens already in a country illegally. Some smuggling situations may involve murder, rape and assault. ICE has an ambitious strategy to dismantle organized human smuggling networks:

First, ICE pursues intelligence-driven investigations to target large-scale smuggling organizations regardless of where they operate. Particular emphasis is placed on smuggling rings that pose a national security risk, jeopardize lives or engage in violence, abuse, hostage-taking or extortion.

Second, ICE coordinates with partners at U.S. Customs and Border Protection to ensure aggressive investigation and prosecution of smuggling cases along the border.

Third, ICE targets all links in the smuggling chain, beyond the immediate smugglers. For example, ICE seeks to target the overseas recruiters and organizers, the fraudulent document vendors, and the transportation and employment networks that benefit from alien smuggling within the United States.

Finally, ICE pursues legislation to increase penalties against organized smugglers and provide additional criminal offenses to better address spotters who assist criminals with smuggling aliens and contraband.

Mass-Marketing Fraud

Mass-marketing fraud has become more widespread in recent years, thanks in part to the spread of low-cost communication technology that makes it easier to defraud victims on a global scale. For example, telemarketing or identity theft scams are frequently coordinated from overseas locations. As part of its commitment to combat mass-marketing fraud, ICE is a participant in the multi-agency International Mass-Marketing Fraud Working Group, which was established in 2007. The working group brings together law enforcement, regulatory and consumer protection agencies from seven countries to:

Exchange information and intelligence on mass-marketing fraud;

Coordinate cross-border operations to detect and disrupt mass-marketing fraud operations and apprehend their perpetrators; and

Drive public awareness and public education measures concerning international mass-marketing fraud schemes.

Trade Transparency Unit

Trade-based money laundering is the process of disguising criminal proceeds through trade to legitimize their illicit origins. Trade-based money laundering, rather than being a single activity, refers to a variety of schemes used together to disguise criminal proceeds, which can involve moving illicit

Criminal and terrorist organizations frequently exploit global trade systems to move value around the world by employing complex and sometimes confusing documentation associated with legitimate trade transactions. It is estimated that annual trade-based money laundering is worth billions of dollars and is growing each year. ICE established the Trade Transparency Unit to conduct ongoing analysis of trade data provided through partnerships with other countries' trade transparency units. One of the most effective ways to identify instances and patterns of trade-based money laundering is through the exchange and subsequent analysis of trade data for anomalies that would only be apparent by examining both sides of a trade transaction.

The unit is formed when the United States and any of its trading partners agree to exchange trade data for the purpose of comparison and analysis. Using state-of-the-art software and proven investigative techniques, the unit can easily identify previously invisible trade-based alternative remittance systems and customs fraud.

To help analyze the data, the unit has developed a specialized ICE computer system called the Data Analysis & Research for Trade Transparency System. Containing both domestic and foreign trade data, the computer system allows users to see both sides of the trade transaction, making the transaction transparent. This investigative tool was specifically designed to identify international trade anomalies and financial irregularities indicative of trade-based money laundering, customs fraud, contraband smuggling, and even tax evasion.

ICE initiated the Trade Transparency Unit concept in Washington, D.C., in 2004 and subsequently established foreign Trade Transparency Units in Argentina, Brazil, Colombia, Paraguay, Mexico and Panama. Additionally, ICE also works with international organizations such as the Financial Action Task Force to bring awareness to this global issue. As the network of trade transparency units grows, so will the open exchange of trade data between all participating countries. This will play an increasingly important role in thwarting money laundering and transnational crime, including international organized crime.

Preventing Terrorism

Most ICE offices and programs have a role in preventing terrorism. Several are on the front lines of this effort, either identifying dangerous persons before they enter the U.S. or finding them as they violate immigration or customs laws. ICE also works to prevent the illegal export of U.S. technology that could be used or repurposed to do harm.

Counter-Proliferation Investigations Program

Illicit transactions involving our strategic technology not only jeopardize our economic and national security but also endanger the safety of our citizens and soldiers. In today's globalized society, enhanced communications technology and transportation means that rogue states, criminal organizations and terrorist groups have greater potential to acquire and trade nuclear, chemical and biological weapons than ever before. One of Immigration and Customs Enforcement's (ICE) highest priorities is to prevent illicit procurement networks, terrorist groups and hostile nations from illegally obtaining U.S. military products, sensitive dual-use technology, weapons of mass destruction (WMD), or chemical, biological, radiological and nuclear materials. ICE Homeland Security Investigation's (HSI) Counter-Proliferation Investigations (CPI) Program oversees a broad range of investigative activities related to such violations. The CPI Program enforces U.S. laws involving the export of military items, controlled dual-use goods, firearms and ammunition as well as exports to sanctioned or embargoed countries.

The CPI Program prevents sensitive U.S. technologies and weapons from reaching the hands of adversaries. The unit combats the trafficking and illegal export of the following commodities and services:

- Weapons of mass destruction and associated delivery systems;
- Military weaponry, equipment and technology;
- Controlled dual-use commodities and technology;
- Firearms and ammunition; and
- Financial and business transactions with sanctioned and embargoed countries and terrorist organizations.

Illicit Pathways Attack Strategy

Over the last two decades, transnational organized crime (TOC) has transformed in size, scope and impact—posing a significant threat to national and international security. TOC networks are proliferating, striking new and powerful alliances, and engaging in a range of illicit activities as never before. The result is a convergence of threats that have evolved to become more complex, volatile and destabilizing.

The TOC strategy seeks to build, balance, and integrate the tools of American power to combat TOC and related threats to our national security—and to urge our foreign partners to do the same.

It is organized around five strategic objectives:

- Protect Americans and our partners from the harm, violence, and exploitation of transnational criminal networks.
- Help partner countries strengthen governance and transparency, break the corruptive power of transnational criminal networks, and sever state-crime alliances.
- Break the economic power of transnational criminal networks and protect strategic markets and the U.S. financial system from TOC penetration and abuse.
- Defeat transnational criminal networks that pose the greatest threat to national security by targeting their infrastructures, depriving them of their enabling means, and preventing the criminal facilitation of terrorist activities.
- Build international consensus, multilateral cooperation, and public-private partnerships to defeat transnational organized crime.

The Illicit Pathways Attack Strategy (IPAS) is U.S. Immigration and Customs Enforcement's (ICE's) strategy to support the White House's TOC strategy.

Through IPAS, ICE will:

- Extend operating borders.
- Prioritize networks and pathways.
- Maintain robust interagency engagement.

- Coordinate with foreign partners in specific regions.
- Support efforts to combat crime through laws and policy.

ICE's IPAS efforts will initially focus on combating human trafficking and smuggling. Future phases of the strategy will focus on weapons trafficking, intellectual property theft, cybercrime, money laundering and counter-proliferation.

Project Shield America

Project Shield America is an industry and academic outreach program, the intent of which is to obtain the assistance and cooperation of those companies involved in the manufacture and export of U.S. origin strategic goods, technologies, and munitions items as well as academic researchers who study and research these and other strategic fields. The focus of Project Shield America is to prevent the proliferation of export-controlled technology and components, the acquisition of nuclear, chemical and biological weapons, and the unlawful exportation of weapon systems and classified or controlled technical data.

In seeking to both gather and provide information, Project Shield America was established to increase public awareness of the importance of export controls and to seek the cooperation of the technology manufacturing and academic research communities. Project Shield America liaisons are established between HSI special agents and manufacturers, exporters, and freight handlers. In this cooperative effort, private industry and the academic community can improve their export control measures while avoiding issues that might affect legitimate business or scholarship.

Project Shield America assists industry and academic research institutions to better understand current U.S. export laws and aids in the recognition, detection and resolution of illegal acquisition attempts of controlled and sensitive commodities, technology, and data by foreign governments, companies, or individuals. Only with the cooperation and diligence of the exporting and academic community can law enforcement succeed in preventing the proliferation of advanced conventional weapons and weapons of mass destruction. Through established contacts, private industry and the are encouraged to report all suspicious export inquiries to HSI. Cooperation will protect U.S. national security, secure the reputation of private industry, and protect research and development costs lost to illegal procurement.

Counterterrorism and Criminal Exploitation Unit

The Counterterrorism and Criminal Exploitation Unit is part of ICE's Homeland Security Investigations' (HSI) National Security Investigations Division. The unit prevents terrorists and other criminals from exploiting the nation's immigration system through fraud. It investigates non-immigrant visa holders who violate their immigration status and places a high priority on scrutinizing the activities of known or suspected terrorists and terrorist associations. It also combats criminal exploitation of the student visa system.

The unit comprises two sections:
- Terrorist Tracking and Pursuit Group, and
- SEVIS Exploitation Section

These sections work together and form an integrated national security force that draws upon government databases to gather and analyze leads on visitors to the United States. They also aim to identify potential security or criminal threats. The unit also coordinates with the National Counterterrorism Center to conduct criminal investigations of national security fraud.

The Terrorist Tracking and Pursuit Group leverages ICE expertise across partnering agencies dedicated to promoting national security. The group leads the DHS National Security Overstay Initiative in cooperation with U.S. Customs and Border Protection, Office of Biometric Identity Management, and the National Counterterrorism Center to identify non-immigrants that have overstayed the terms of their admission, which may pose a potential risk to the national security of the United States. This group also initiates high priority investigations based on recommendations from the Compliance Enforcement Advisory Panel, the DHS National Security Overstay Initiative and other Federal Agencies.

The **Student and Exchange Visitor Information System** (SEVIS) Exploitation Section (SES) proactively identifies, disrupts and dismantles organizational and individual exploitation of systemic SEVIS database

The SES identifies suspect groups, organizations, educational institutions and individuals through strategic analysis and refers leads to field offices for criminal investigation of terrorism-related activity, foreign intelligence operations, transnational organized crime or immigration fraud.

The SES also implements and manages **Project Campus Sentinel (PCS).** PCS is the Agent outreach program that partners with educational institutions to improve communications between designated school officials (DSO) and HSI agents by providing training to identify criminal activity and a mechanism to report SEVIS exploitation and fraud schemes that may compromise national security.

Joint Terrorism Task Force (JTTF)

The National Security Unit leads HSI's counterterrorism investigative efforts and provides collaboration and support to more than 100 Federal Bureau of Investigation JTTFs. It investigates, detects, interdicts, prosecutes and removes terrorists and dismantles terrorist organizations. ICE is involved in almost every foreign terrorism investigation related to cross-border crime. Foreign terrorists need to move money, weapons and people across international borders to conduct their operations, and ICE holds a unique set of law enforcement tools for disrupting these illicit activities.

In fiscal years 2009 and 2010, ICE special agents initiated 1,133 criminal investigations related to terrorism. During that same period, U.S. Immigration and Customs Enforcement (ICE) agents made 534 arrests and conducted thousands of seizures of money, arms, contraband and other assets related to illegal schemes. These efforts significantly contributed to preventing and disrupt national security threats against the United States. ICE is the largest federal contributor to the JTTF, through active participation in each of the 104 local JTTFs nationwide. The agency also plays a critical leadership role on the national JTTF.

The Export Enforcement Coordination Center serves as the primary forum within the federal government for executive departments and agencies to coordinate and enhance their export control enforcement efforts. The

maximizes information sharing, consistent with national security and applicable laws. This helps partner agencies detect, prevent, disrupt, investigate and prosecute violations of U.S. export control laws.

La w Enforcement Assistance Corner

The Law Enforcement Assistance Corner is an index of U.S. Immigration and Customs Enforcement (ICE) information for federal, state, local and tribal law enforcement agencies. This corner provides information on ICE's work in immigration and criminal law enforcement and the many ways they overlap. It pulls together links from the ICE.gov website to ensure that ICE's law enforcement partners can easily find relevant information in support of their mission and any current or future collaboration with ICE. In addition, the Law Enforcement Assistance Corner features two information sharing systems designed to allow the federal government to communicate sensitive information to state, local and tribal law enforcement agencies. This site has been designed as a tool to make exploring the work of ICE as easy as possible.

Visa Security Program

Homeland Security Investigations' (HSI) International Operations coordinates the Visa Security Program, which deploys HSI special agents with immigration law enforcement expertise to diplomatic posts worldwide to conduct visa security activities, such as:

- Examining visa applications for fraud,
- Initiating investigations,
- Coordinating with law enforcement partners, and
- Providing law enforcement training and advice to Department of State consulates.

The Visa Security Program interdicts criminals, terrorists and others who would exploit the legal visa process to enter the United States. The program serves as the agency's frontline in protecting the United States against terrorist and criminal organizations. While many security measures focus on screening names against lists of known terrorist or criminal suspects, the program relies on HSI special agents to identify potential terrorist or criminal suspects and stop them before they can reach the United States.

8

United States Secret Service

The United States Secret Service (USSS) safeguards the nation's financial infrastructure and payment systems to preserve the integrity of the economy, and protects national leaders, visiting heads of state and government, designated sites, and National Special Security Events.

The vision of the United States Secret Service is to uphold the tradition of excellence in its investigative and protective mission through a dedicated, highly-trained, diverse, partner-oriented workforce that employs progressive technology and promotes professionalism.

Its mission is to safeguard the nation's financial infrastructure and payment systems to preserve the integrity of the economy, and to protect national leaders, visiting heads of state and government, designated sites and National Special Security Events.

History

1865   The Secret Service Division was created on July 5, 1865 in Washington, D.C., to suppress counterfeit currency. Chief William P. Wood was sworn in by Secretary of the Treasury Hugh McCulloch.

1867   Secret Service responsibilities were broadened to include "detecting persons perpetrating frauds against the government." This appropriation resulted in investigations into the Ku Klux Klan, non-conforming distillers, smugglers, mail robbers, land frauds, and a number of other infractions against the federal laws.

1870   Secret Service headquarters relocated to New York City.

1874   Secret Service headquarters returned to Washington, D.C.

1875   The first commission book and a new badge were issued to operatives.

1877   Congress passed an Act prohibiting the counterfeiting of any coin, gold or silver bar.

1883   Secret Service was officially acknowledged as a distinct organization within the Treasury Department.

1894   The Secret Service began informal part-time protection of President Cleveland.

1895   Congress passed corrective legislation for the counterfeiting or possession of counterfeit stamps.

1901   Congress informally requested Secret Service Presidential protection following the assassination of President William McKinley.

1902   The Secret Service assumed full-time responsibility for protection of the President. Two operatives were assigned full time to the White House Detail.

1906   Congress passed Sundry Civil Expenses Act for 1907 that provided funds for Presidential protection by the Secret Service.

Secret Service operatives began to investigate the western land frauds. The Service's investigations returned millions of acres of land to the government.

1908   Secret Service began protecting the president-elect. Also, President Roosevelt transferred Secret Service agents to the Department of Justice. They formed the nucleus of what is now the Federal Bureau of Investigation (FBI).

1913   Congress authorized permanent protection of the president and the statutory authorization for president-elect protection.

1915   President Wilson directed the Secretary of the Treasury to have the Secret Service investigate espionage in the United States.

1917   Congress authorized permanent protection of the president's immediate family and made "threats" directed toward the president a federal violation.

1922   White House Police Force created on October 1, 1922, at the request of President Harding.

1930   White House Police Force was placed under the supervision of the Secret Service.

1951   Congress enacted legislation that permanently authorized Secret Service protection of the president, his immediate family, the president-elect, and the vice president, if he wishes. (Public Law—82-79).

1961   Congress authorized protection of former presidents for a reasonable period of time.

1962   Congress expanded coverage to include the vice president (or the next officer to succeed the president) and the vice president-elect. (Public Law 87-829).

1963   Congress passed legislation for protection of Mrs. John F. Kennedy and her minor children for two years. (Public Law 83-195).

1965   Congress authorized protection of former presidents and their spouses during their lifetime and minor children until age 16.

1968   As a result of Robert F. Kennedy's assassination, Congress authorized protection of major presidential and vice presidential candidates and nominees. (Public Law 90-331). Congress also authorized protection of widows of presidents until death, or remarriage, and their children until age 16.

1970   White House Police Force renamed the Executive Protective Service and increased its responsibilities to include the protection of diplomatic missions in the Washington, D.C., area. (Public Law 91-217).

1971   Congress authorized Secret Service protection for visiting heads of a foreign state or government, or other official guests, as directed.

1975   The duties of Executive Protective Service were expanded to include protection of foreign diplomatic missions located throughout the United States and its territories.

1977   The Executive Protective Service was officially renamed the Secret Service Uniformed Division on November 15, 1977.

1984   Congress enacted legislation making the fraudulent use of credit and debit cards a federal violation. The law also authorized the Secret Service to investigate violations relating to credit and debit card fraud, federal-interest computer fraud, and fraudulent identification documents.

1986   Treasury Police Force merged into the Secret Service Uniformed Division on October 5, 1986.

A Presidential directive authorized protection of the accompanying spouse of the head of a foreign state or government.

1990   The Secret Service received concurrent jurisdiction with Department of Justice law enforcement personnel to conduct any kind of investigation, civil or criminal, related to federally insured financial institutions.

1994   The passage of the 1994 Crime Bill Public Law 103-322, in part, revised Title 18 USC Section 470, providing that any person manufacturing, trafficking in, or possessing counterfeit U.S. currency abroad may be prosecuted as if the act occurred within the United States.

1997   Congress passed legislation in 1994 stating that Presidents elected to office after January 1, 1997, will receive Secret Service protection for 10 years after leaving office. Individuals elected to office prior to January 1, 1997, will continue to receive lifetime protection. (Public Law 103-329)

1998   Telemarketing Fraud Prevention Act (Public Law105-184) allowed for criminal forfeiture of fraud proceeds for convictions of 18 USC sections 1028, 1029, 1341, or 1344, or of a conspiracy to commit such an offense, if the offense involved telemarketing.

The Identity Theft and Assumption Deterrence Act (Public Law 105-318) amends 18 USC section 1028 to establish the offense of "Identity Theft." Penalties were established for anyone who knowingly transfers or uses, without authority, any means of identification of another person, with the intent to commit an unlawful activity that is a violation of the identity theft provisions of section 1028.

2000   Presidential Threat Protection Act (Public Law 106-544) was passed, which in part, authorized the Secret Service to participate in the planning, coordination, and implementation of security operations at special events of national significance ("National Special Security Event"), as determined by the President.

2001   The Patriot Act (Public Law 107-56) increased the Secret Service's role in investigating fraud and related activity in connections with computers. In addition it authorized the Director of the Secret Service to establish nationwide electronic crimes taskforces to assist the law enforcement, private sector and academia in detecting and suppressing computer-based crime; increased the statutory penalties for the manufacturing, possession, dealing and passing of counterfeit U.S. or foreign obligations; and allowed enforcement action to be taken to protect our financial payment systems while combating transnational financial crimes directed by terrorists or other

2002   The Department of Homeland Security was established with the passage of (Public Law 107-296) which in part, transferred the United States Secret Service from the Department of the Treasury, to the new department effective March 1, 2003.

2004   Barbara Riggs, a veteran agent of the Secret Service, became the first woman in the agency's history to be named Deputy Director.

2006   The network of Secret Service Electronic Crimes Task Forces expanded from 15 to 24 nationwide task forces dedicated to fighting high-tech, computer-based crimes through successful public-private partnerships.

2007   Protection began for presidential candidate Illinois Senator Barack Obama in May, the earliest initiation of Secret Service protection for any candidate in history. Presidential candidate New York Senator Hillary Clinton already received protection before she entered the race due to her status as former first lady.

2008   The Secret Service marked five years under the Department of Homeland Security. Since 2003, the Secret Service made nearly 29,000 criminal arrests for counterfeiting, cyber investigations and other financial crimes, 98% of which resulted in convictions, and seized more than $295 million in counterfeit currency. The Secret Service investigated and closed financial crimes cases where actual loss amounted to $3.7 billion and prevented a potential loss of more than $12 billion.

2009   The Secret Service expanded its fight on cyber-crime by creating the first European Electronic Crimes Task Force.

2014   The Secret Service underwent a major reshuffle following a series of high-profile security lapses that rocked the agency and saw Director Julia Pierson resigning and four other senior leaders ousted.

2015   Deputy Director Alvin Smith resigned under pressure. Smith was in charge of day to day operations at the Secret Service during this period. Incidents included reports that secret service agents were involved with a prostitution scandal in Colombia in 2012; a man armed with the knife jumping over the White House's perimeter fence and penetrating deep inside the building before being apprehended; and in February 2015 a drone crashed on the White House grounds forcing a security lockdown.

On March 1, 2015 Joseph Clancy, the new Director of the Secret Service, said he plans to regain the trust of the American people. His plan to make that happen is hire more people, improve training, and raise the fence around the White House. We've got to do a better job of mentoring, coaching, teaching, and training our people," he said.

Special Agents

Despite the incidents mentioned above, the United States Secret Service remains one of the most elite law enforcement organizations in the world. It has earned this reputation throughout more than 140 years of unparalleled service to the nation. As one of the oldest federal law enforcement agencies in the country, the Secret Service has dual missions that include investigations as well as protection. These are the unique characteristics that distinguish the Secret Service from other law enforcement organizations. During the course of their careers, special agents carry out assignments in both of these areas and must be available to be assigned to duty stations anywhere in the world.

Since its inception in 1865, the Secret Service has been involved in protecting the integrity of the nation's financial systems. Recent advances in technology have changed the nature of financial transactions throughout the world. Consequently, the Secret Service's investigative responsibilities have increased significantly. The Secret Service has jurisdiction in the United States for investigations involving the counterfeiting of U.S. and foreign obligations and securities. This authority has expanded to include the investigation of financial institution fraud, access device fraud, computer crimes, fraudulent government and commercial securities, fictitious financial instruments, telecommunications fraud, false identification and identity theft.

In the years since the Secret Service's protective mission was first mandated in 1901, the agency's jurisdiction has expanded over time and currently includes protection for the following:

- The president, the vice president, (or other individuals next in order of succession to the Office of the President), the president-elect and vice president-elect
- The immediate families of the above individuals
- Former presidents, their spouses for their lifetimes, except when the spouse remarries.

- Children of former presidents until age 16
- Visiting heads of foreign states or governments and their spouses traveling with them, other distinguished foreign visitors to the United States, and official representatives of the United States performing special missions abroad
- Major presidential and vice presidential candidates, and their spouses within 120 days of a general presidential election
- Other individuals as designated per Executive Order of the President
- National Special Security Events, when designated as such by the Secretary of the Department of Homeland Security

Uniformed Division

Established in 1922 as the White House Police Force, this organization was fully integrated into the Secret Service in 1930. With more than 1,300 officers today, the Uniformed Division is responsible for security at the White House Complex; the vice president's residence; the Department of the Treasury (as part of the White House Complex); and foreign diplomatic missions in the Washington, D.C., area. Uniformed Division officers carry out their protective responsibilities through a network of fixed security posts, foot, bicycle, vehicular and motorcycle patrols.

Officers are responsible for providing additional support to the Secret Service's protective mission through the following special support programs:

•The Countersniper Support Unit (CS): Created in 1971, the CS unit's purpose is to provide specialized protective support to defend against long-range threats to Secret Service protectees. Today CS is an operational element of the Presidential Protective Division.

•The Canine Explosives Detection Unit (K-9): Created in 1976, the mission of the K-9 unit is to provide skilled and specialized explosives detection support to protective efforts involving Secret Service protectees.

•The Emergency Response Team (ERT): Formed in 1992, ERT's primary mission is to provide tactical response to unlawful intrusions and other protective challenges related to the White House and its grounds. ERT receive specialized, advanced training and must maintain a high level of physical and operational proficiency.

•Magnetometers: The Secret Service began relying on magnetometer (metal detector) support by Uniformed Division officers to augment its protective efforts away from the White House following the attempted assassination of President Ronald Reagan. The Magnetometer Support Unit's mission is to ensure that all persons entering secure areas occupied by Secret Service protectees are unarmed.

Support Personnel

The men and women of the United States Secret Service come to the agency as the best of the best, from a variety of professional backgrounds. They undergo an intense selection process, and to make sure the Secret Service continues to hire the best candidates, the agency continually looks for exceptional men and women who desire a fast-paced, challenging and rewarding career. In addition to the agency's law enforcement positions, the Secret Service relies on the expertise of civilian personnel with diverse experience, including (but not limited to) forensic scientists, psychologists, law enforcement instructors, human resources specialists, budget analysts, firearms instructors, clerks, accountants, researchers, physical security and computer specialists, graphic designers, photographers, writers and attorneys.

James J. Rowley Training Center

Located just outside of Washington, D.C., the James J. Rowley Training Center (JJRTC) is comprised of almost 500 acres of land, six miles of roadway and 31 buildings. The protective, investigative, specialized tactical and executive/managerial training conducted at JJRTC is unique among federal law enforcement instructional entities.

The Secret Service provides a wide range of courses utilized by its personnel throughout their careers. The core curriculum provided by JJRTC is designed for special agents, Uniformed Division officers, special officers and physical security specialists. In a single year, hundreds of training recruits undergo extensive training in firearms marksmanship, use-of-force/control tactics, emergency medical techniques, financial crimes detection, physical/site/event protection and water survival training. At the other end of the professional spectrum, scores of veteran law enforcement, executive/managerial, administrative and technical personnel are offered comprehensive curriculum of specialized and technology-based training courses throughout their careers.

Advanced computer-driven methodologies enable JJRTC to reach beyond its Washington, D.C. metropolitan facilities to provide "on-site" educational experiences to personnel throughout the Secret Service's domestic and international field offices. The Secret Service supports its valued law enforcement partners from across the country by providing protective security, financial crimes, specialized tactical and weapons training to other federal, state and local law enforcement personnel.

Criminal Investigations

The United States Secret Service is responsible for maintaining the integrity of the nation's financial infrastructure and payment systems. As a part of this mission, the Secret Service constantly implements and evaluates prevention and response measures to guard against electronic crimes as well as other computer related fraud. The Secret Service derives its authority to investigate specified criminal violations from Title 18 of the United States Code, Section 3056.

Criminal investigations can be international in scope. These investigations include: counterfeiting of U.S. currency (to include coins); counterfeiting of foreign currency (occurring domestically); identity crimes such as access device fraud, identity theft, false identification fraud, bank fraud and check fraud; telemarketing fraud; telecommunications fraud (cellular and hard wire); computer fraud; fraud targeting automated payment systems and teller machines; direct deposit fraud; investigations of forgery, uttering, alterations, false impersonations or false claims involving U.S. Treasury Checks, U.S. Saving Bonds, U.S. Treasury Notes, Bonds and Bills; electronic funds transfer systems; Federal Deposit Insurance Corporation investigations; Farm Credit Administration violations; and fictitious or fraudulent commercial instruments and foreign securities.

Counterfeit Currency

The Secret Service has jurisdiction over violations involving the counterfeiting of United States obligations and securities. Some of the counterfeited United States obligations and securities commonly investigated by the Secret Service include U.S. currency (to include coins), U.S. Treasury checks, Department of Agriculture food coupons and U.S. postage stamps.

The Secret Service remains committed to the mission of combating counterfeiting by working closely with state and local law enforcement agencies, as well as foreign law enforcement counterparts, to aggressively pursue counterfeiters. The Secret Service maintains a working relationship with the Bureau of Engraving and Printing and the Federal Reserve System to ensure the integrity of the nation's currency.

History of Counterfeiting

The counterfeiting of money is one of the oldest crimes in history. At some periods in early history, it was considered treasonous and was punishable by death.

During the American Revolution, the British counterfeited U.S. currency in such large amounts that the Continental currency soon became worthless. "Not worth a Continental" became a popular expression of the era.

During the Civil War, one-third to one-half of the currency in circulation was counterfeit. At that time, approximately 1,600 state banks designed and printed their own bills. Each bill carried a different design, making it difficult to detect counterfeit bills from the 7,000 varieties of real bills.

While a national currency was adopted in 1862 to resolve the counterfeiting problem, it was soon counterfeited and circulated so extensively that it became necessary to take enforcement measures. As a result, on July 5, 1865, the United States Secret Service was established to suppress the widespread counterfeiting of the nation's currency.

Although the counterfeiting of money was suppressed substantially after the establishment of the Secret Service, this crime still represents a potential danger to the nation's economy.

Today, new forms of counterfeiting are on the rise. One reason for this is the ease and speed with which large quantities of counterfeit currency can be produced using modern photographic, printing and computer equipment.

You can help guard against this threat by being more familiar with your currency. Only with the public's cooperation and the aid of local law enforcement agencies can the Secret Service reduce and control this crime.

Financial Crimes

The Secret Service exercises broad investigative jurisdiction over a variety of financial crimes. As the original guardian of the nation's financial payment systems, the Secret Service has a long history of protecting American consumers and industries from financial fraud. In addition to its original mandate of combating the counterfeiting of U.S. currency, the passage of federal laws in 1982 and 1984 gave the Secret Service primary authority for the investigation of access device fraud, including credit and debit card fraud, and parallel authority with other federal law enforcement agencies in identity crime cases. The Secret Service also was given primary authority for the investigation of fraud as it relates to computers.

In the early 1990s, the Secret Service's investigative mission expanded to include concurrent jurisdiction with the United States Department of Justice regarding Financial Institution Fraud. Also during this time, the Internet and use of personal computers became commonplace and expanded worldwide. The combination of the information revolution and the effects of globalization caused the investigative mission of the Secret Service to expand dramatically. As a result, the Secret Service has evolved into an agency that is recognized worldwide for its investigative expertise and for its aggressive and innovative approach to the detection, investigation and prevention of financial crimes.

On October 26, 2001, President Bush signed into law H.R. 3162, the USA PATRIOT Act. The U.S. Secret Service was mandated by this legislation to establish a nationwide network of Electronic Crimes Task Forces (ECTFs). The concept of the ECTF network is to bring together not only federal, state and law enforcement, but also prosecutors, private industry and academia. The common purpose is the prevention, detection, mitigation and aggressive investigation of attacks on the nation's financial and critical infrastructures.

The following are primary offenses investigated by the Secret Service:

Identity Crimes—Identity crimes are defined as the misuse of personal or financial identifiers in order to gain something of value and/or facilitate other criminal activity. The Secret Service is the primary federal agency tasked with investigating identity theft/fraud and its related activities under Title 18, United States Code, Section 1028. Identity crimes are some of the fastest growing and most serious economic crimes in the United States for both financial institutions and persons whose identifying information has been illegally used. The Secret Service records criminal complaints, assists victims in contacting other relevant investigative and consumer protection agencies and works with other federal, state and local law enforcement and reporting agencies to identify perpetrators.

Identity crimes investigated by the Secret Service include, but are not limited to, the following:

- Credit Card/Access Device Fraud (Skimming)
- Check Fraud
- Bank Fraud
- False Identification Fraud
- Passport/Visa Fraud
- Identity Theft

Counterfeit and Fraudulent Identification—The Secret Service enforces laws involving counterfeit and fraudulent identification which means, where someone knowingly and without lawful authority produces, transfers or possesses a false identification document to defraud the U.S. Government. The use of desktop publishing software/hardware to counterfeit and produce different forms of identification used to obtain funds illegally remains one of the Secret Service's core violations.

Access Device Fraud—Financial industry sources estimate annual losses associated with credit card fraud to be in the billions of dollars. The Secret Service is the primary federal agency tasked with investigating access device fraud and its related activities under Title 18, United States Code, Section 1029. Although it is commonly called the credit card statute, this law also applies to other crimes involving access devices including debit cards, automated teller machine (ATM) cards, computer passwords, personal identification numbers, credit card or debit card account numbers, long-distance access codes, and the Subscriber Identity Module (SIM) contained within cellular telephones that assign billing.

Computer Fraud—Title 18 of the United States Code, Section 1030, authorizes the Secret Service to investigate computer crimes. Violations enforced under this statute include unauthorized access to protected computers, theft of data such as personal identification used to commit identity theft, denial of service attacks used for extortion or disruption of e-commerce and malware (malicious software) distribution to include viruses intended for financial gain.

The proliferation of the Internet has allowed the transition of traditional street crimes to flourish in the anonymity of cyberspace. The borders of a state or a country are no longer boundaries for cyber criminals to reach their victims. As a result of advancements in technology, the Secret Service established the Electronic Crimes Special Agent Program (ECSAP) and a network of Electronic Crimes Task Forces throughout the United States.

Agents assigned to ECSAP are computer investigative specialists, qualified to conduct examinations on many types of electronic evidence, including computers, personal data assistants, telecommunications devices, electronic organizers and other electronic media. ECSAP is the only program of its kind in the country with the level of expertise and culture of partnership-building with stakeholders across the spectrum of critical infrastructure.

The Secret Service's Crimes Task Force and Electronic Crimes Working Group Initiatives Electronic seek to prioritize investigative cases that involve some form of electronic crime. These initiatives provide needed support and resources with field investigations that have any one of the following criteria:

Significant economic or community impact

Participation of organized criminal groups involving multiple districts or transnational organizations

Use of schemes involving new technology

The task force/working group model brings together state and local law enforcement, prosecutors, private sector interests and academia in an effort to prevent cyber-crime and identity theft.

Forgery—Hundreds of millions of government checks and bonds are issued by the United States each year. This large number attracts criminals who specialize in stealing and forging checks or bonds from mail boxes in apartment complexes and private homes. During a fraudulent transaction, a check or bond thief usually forges the payee's signature and presents false identification.

Money Laundering—The Money Laundering Control Act makes it a crime to launder proceeds of certain criminal offenses, called "specified unlawful activities," which are defined in Title 18, United States Code, Sections 1956 & 1957; as well as Title 18, United States Code, Section 1961 (Racketeer Influenced and Corrupt Organizations Act). The Secret Service monitors money laundering activities through other financial crimes such as financial institution fraud, access device fraud, food stamp fraud and counterfeiting of U.S. currency.

Electronic Benefits Transfer Fraud—Congress enacted the Food Stamp Act of 1977 to provide nutritional food to low-income families. It further directed the Secret Service to aggressively pursue fraud in the food stamp program. The possession or use of food stamp coupons, "Authorization to Participate" cards or Electronic Benefit Transfer cards by unauthorized persons compromises the integrity of the Food Stamp Program and is a criminal violation of the Food Stamp Act.

Asset Forfeiture—The seizing and forfeiture of assets is a byproduct of the Secret Service's criminal investigations. As a result, the Secret Service, through its asset forfeiture program, provides assistance to investigative offices by supplying direction, expertise and temporary support personnel, as needed, in criminal investigations seizure and during the seizure and the forfeiture of assets.

Advance Fee Fraud- The perpetrators of advance fee fraud, known internationally as "4-1-9 fraud" (after the section of the Nigerian penal code which addresses these schemes), are often very creative and innovative. A large number of victims are enticed into believing they have been singled out from the masses to share in multi-million dollar windfall profits for no apparent reason.

If you have received an e-mail or fax from someone you do not know requesting your assistance in a financial transaction, such as the transfer of a

respond. These requests are typically sent through public servers via a generic "spammed" e-mail message. Usually, the sender does not yet know your personal e-mail address and is depending on you to respond. Once you reply, whether you intend to string them along or tell them you are not interested, they will often continue to e-mail you in an attempt to harass or intimidate you. If you receive an unsolicited e-mail of this nature, the best course is to simply delete the message.

Due to a number of aggravating circumstances -- the use of false names, addresses, stolen/cloned/prepaid cell phones and remote e-mail addresses -- verifying the location of and subsequent prosecution of these persons or groups is difficult. The act of sending an e-mail soliciting your assistance in a financial transaction is not a crime in itself. The installation of a credible spam filter and contacting your Internet Service Provider may help deter these unsolicited e-mails. However, there is currently no available program to completely block these types of messages.

If you have suffered a significant financial loss related to advance fee fraud, please contact your local Secret Service field office. Telephone numbers are available in your local telephone directory.

9

Science and Technology Directorate

The Science and Technology Directorate (S&T) is the primary research and development arm of the Department and provides federal, state and local officials with the technology and capabilities to protect the homeland.

It manages science and technology research, from development through transition, for the Department's operational components and first responders.

Established by Congress to provide innovative solutions to the nation's homeland security challenges, S&T is the core source of scientific and engineering expertise for the Department and uniquely postured to enhance our nation's security and resiliency.

Its mission is to strengthen America's security and resiliency by providing knowledge products and innovative technology solutions for the Homeland Security Enterprise (HSE).

It is operationally focused. S&T provides the Homeland Security Enterprise (HSE) with strategic and focused technology options and operational process enhancements. It is innovative and seeks innovative, system-based solutions to complex homeland security problems.

It also encourages partnerships and has the technical depth and reach to discover, adapt and leverage technology solutions developed by federal agencies and laboratories, state, local and tribal governments, universities, and the private sector—across the United States and internationally.

The S&T Directorate is organized into four groups that work together to ensure each aspect of S&T's work (operational analyses, requirements generation, test and evaluation, technology development, and acquisition support) is given the appropriate amount of emphasis.

First Responders Group (FRG)

The U.S. Department of Homeland Security Science and Technology Directorate's Support to the Homeland Security Enterprise and First Responders Group (FRG) strengthens the response community's abilities to protect the homeland and respond to disasters.

Through the engagement of, and partnership with, first responders and the emergency preparedness and response community at every stage, and at the local, state, tribal, and federal level, FRG pursues a better understanding of the response community's needs and requirements, provides technical assistance, and develops innovative solutions to the most pressing challenges faced during day-to-day and large-scale emergencies.

In close partnership with first responders at all levels, FRG identifies, validates, and facilitates the fulfillment of needs through the use of existing and emerging technologies, knowledge products, and standards. Prioritized areas of FRG focus and initiatives include:

- Making First Responders Safer.
- Helping First Responders Share Data and Critical Information.
- Helping First Responders Communicate Through Interoperability.
- Engaging, Communicating, and Partnering with First Responders.
- Three FRG divisions work together to carry out this mission:

National Urban Security Technology Laboratory (NUSTL): NUSTL tests, evaluates, and analyzes Homeland Security capabilities while serving as a technical authority to first responder, state and local entities in protecting our cities. NUSTL leads and provides independent Federal oversight for test programs, pilots, demonstrations, and other forms of evaluations of homeland security capabilities both in the field and in the laboratory.

Office for Interoperability and Compatibility (OIC): OIC provides local, tribal, state, and Federal stakeholders with the tools, technologies, methodologies, and guidance to enable improved communications interoperability at all levels of government. OIC manages a comprehensive research, development, testing, evaluation, and standards program to enhance emergency interoperable communications and improve alerts and warnings.

Technology Clearinghouse/R-Tech (TCR): TRC rapidly disseminates technology information on products and services to local, tribal, state, and agencies and private sector entities in order to encourage technological innovation and facilitate the mission of the DHS. R-Tech provides information, resources, and technology solutions that address mission capability gaps identified by the emergency response community.

The Homeland Security Advanced Research Projects Agency

HSARPA focuses on identifying, developing, and transitioning technologies and capabilities to counter chemical, biological, explosive, and cyber terrorist threats, as well as protecting our nation's borders and infrastructure. It supports cutting edge research to produce revolutionary changes in technologies and capabilities for homeland security.

Established through the Homeland Security Act of 2002, HSARPA uses innovation and modernization to push scientific limits and produce front line products that support organizations like the Secret Service, bomb squads, first responders, Transportation Security Administration, and officers along our borders.

HSARPA conducts analysis to understand these organizations' current missions, systems, and processes and ultimately identifies operational gaps where new technologies can have the most impact. Program managers lead teams of national experts to develop, test, and evaluate these new homeland security technologies and capabilities.

Select areas of HSARPA focus and their initiatives include:

•Borders and Maritime Security—Prevent contraband, criminals and terrorists from entering the U.S. while permitting the lawful flow of commerce and visitors.

The Borders and Maritime Security Division's mission is to enhance U.S. air, land, and maritime border security through the transition of scientific and technical knowledge and solutions to operational use, while maximizing the flow of commerce and travel. Our strategy involves three distinct activities:

•Understanding the technical dimensions of homeland security challenges
•Working collaboratively across the Homeland Security Enterprise
•Applying rigorous process and methodology

Its objectives are to provide technical solutions to DHS operating components in order to stop dangerous things and dangerous people from entering the country and to enable the protection of the public, the environment, and U.S. economic and security interests.

Borders consist of all air, land and maritime boundaries, including U.S. ports of entry, vast stretches of remote terrain, and inland waterways. The Division works closely with its operational partners (described below) to understand what technology they need to achieve their missions and to find technical solutions to fill those gaps in their existing capabilities.

The Borders and Maritime Security Division

This division consists of scientific and technical professionals responsible for funding, directing and managing the research, development, prototyping, test and evaluation of technical solutions for border, maritime, and cargo security. The Division's primary customers, its end-users, are the operating components within the Department of Homeland Security such as Customs and Border Protection, Immigration and Customs Enforcement, the U.S. Coast Guard, and the nation's First Responders. The Division's partners and performers include academia, national laboratories, private industry, and other members of the Homeland Security Enterprise.

The Chemical and Biological Defense Division (CBD)

CBD's mission is to detect, protect against, respond to, and recover from potential biological or chemical events. It focuses on saving lives and protecting the nation's infrastructure from chemical, biological, and agricultural threats and disasters.

It provides a comprehensive understanding and analyses of chemical and biological threats, develops pre-event assessment, discovery, and interdiction capabilities as well as capabilities for warning, notification, and analysis of incidents. The division optimizes recovery technology and processes, enhances the capability to inform attribution of attacks, and develops medical countermeasures against foreign animal diseases.

CBD carries out its activities through three technical areas of focus:

- Agricultural Defense
- Chemical and Biological Research and Development
- Threat Characterization and Attribution

In the execution of its program, the Division actively coordinates with interagency partners to refine requirements, maximize resources and minimize duplication. In spite of a broad and rich customer base and application space, CBD has applied its resources to deliver great value to the Homeland Security Enterprise (HSE) through the focus areas above. Examples of current projects are Foreign Animal Disease Vaccines and Diagnostics, Underground Transportation Restoration, Risk Assessment, and it's Forensics Program, described briefly below.

Foreign Animal Disease (FAD) Vaccines and Diagnostics

The outbreak of foot-and-mouth disease (FMD) in the U.K. in 2001 and South Korea in 2011 resulted in the slaughter of millions of animals and catastrophic economic losses for livestock and food industries. Fearing similar severe consequences if the highly contagious animal disease were to appear in the United States, federal scientists worked for years to develop and win approval of a unique new vaccine to protect America's cows, sheep and pigs. A multi-year collaboration between DHS S&T, United States Department of Agriculture (USDA), industry and academia resulted in a patent for the first successful FMD vaccine technology in more than 50 years and the first licensed FMD vaccine approved for manufacture in the United States.

The United States has been free from this serious animal disease since 1929 and has strict policies on the trade of livestock products with countries that have experienced problems. While the virus typically spreads naturally from infected animals, DHS officials do not rule out the possibility that it could be intentionally introduced into U.S. livestock herds by terrorists. An outbreak of a foreign animal disease among livestock could devastate the U.S. food industry, causing tens of billions of dollars in economic damage. During an outbreaks, our trading partners would halt the import of many agricultural products from the U.S., including meat and dairy, causing further economic damage.

In addition to the FAD vaccine project, DHS S&T's FMD related efforts include the development of additional assays to differentiate infected animals from those vaccinated, novel diagnostic tools and biotherapeutics to provide rapid protection.   The broader Agricultural Defense program includes enhancement of mitigation efforts for FMD and other high-priority FADs through the development of state-of-the-art countermeasures including novel screening tools, broad-spectrum therapeutics and vaccines, pre-outbreak surveillance, and other tools to minimize the impacts on business continuity in the face of an outbreak.

Underground Transportation Restoration (UTR)

Across the world, mass transit systems, including underground subway and passenger rail lines, have been targets of toxic chemical attacks or improvised explosive attacks by terrorists. The function of transit systems—to move large numbers of people quickly from point-to-point—makes it difficult to keep these systems off-line for long periods without major disruption to a city's transportation infrastructure. It is also difficult to screen passengers in underground transit systems due to the volume of people who regularly use them. These systems also offer other unique challenges for recovery due to the abundance of porous materials, dynamic air flow movement, and limited access points for remediation teams in protective gear. UTR was initiated by CBD to enhance the preparedness and resiliency of transportation systems to recover from biological events.

UTR identifies methods, tools, and protocols to meet requirements for rapid characterization, clean up, and clearance for re-use of physical structures (e.g., tunnels, stations) and trains. The project will identify system vulnerabilities and improve existing and emerging sampling, analysis, decontamination, and waste management technologies through targeted experiments, table-top exercises, and operational demonstrations. Guidance, decision frameworks, and support tools will be developed in collaboration with federal, state, and local partners. A primary UTR customer for the project's knowledge products is the New York City Metropolitan Transportation Authority. S&T is also engaging the BART (Bay Area Rapid Transit) system in San Francisco and working to secure participation of ton Metropolitan Area Transit Authority) in Washington, DC, MBTA (Massachusetts Bay Transportation Authority) in Boston, and CTA (Chicago Transit Authority) in Chicago.

Risk Assessment

Under Homeland Security Presidential Directives (HSPD) 10, 18, and 22, DHS is mandated to conduct the Biological, Chemical, Radiological and Nuclear, and Integrated Chemical, Biological, Radiological and Nuclear Terrorism Risk Assessments (BTRA, CTRA, RNTRA, and ITRA, respectively). These assessments are used to inform decisions about investments to improve the domestic defense posture and with the exception of the Radiological and Nuclear Terrorism Risk Assessment, are performed by DHS S&T on a periodic basis, along with tailored assessments and analyses conducted on an on-going basis to meet the needs of the HSE stakeholders. The assessments are designed to: 1) aid in identifying and prioritizing credible, high impact threats; 2) aid in identifying and prioritizing vulnerabilities and knowledge gaps; and 3) provide a HSE mechanism for optimizing resource allocation and product development to maximize the nation's chemical, biological, radiological and nuclear (CBRN) defensive posture.

In 2012, DHS published three BTRA-based "tailored assessments." The first report to HSE stakeholders provided a reference set of the extensive data collection efforts to date and allow other agencies to use the information in their own analysis, while increasing analytic transparency and data validation for the BTRA. The two additional reports added significant value to the risk modeling efforts across the HSE. In 2012, the CTRA published its third end-to-end assessment, analyzing 68 more chemicals than did the original 2008 publication. Several stakeholders leveraged the CTRA for tailored assessments and sensitivity studies as input to their operational strategies and guidance. The year 2013 was successful for the ITRA. DHS partnered with the Centers for Disease Control and Prevention (CDC), leveraging the ITRA to help inform decisions regarding the Strategic National Stockpile (SNS) investments, and optimize the contents of the SNS by evaluating the current risk mitigation capability and identifying opportunities to enhance its performance.

Forensics Program

In accordance with HSPD-10, Bioiodefense for the 21st Century, CBD conducts bioforensics research in support of criminal investigative cases and operation of the National BioForensics and Analysis Center (NBFAC™) with the ultimate goal of attribution, apprehension, and prosecution of the perpetrator to fulfill Biodefense for the 21st Century (HSPD-10). These activities provide facilities, analytical methods, and rigorous chain-of-custody controls needed to support the FBI and others in their investigation of potential biocrimes or acts of bioterrorism. Research and development projects in this program area work to develop improved methods for characterizing pathogens and their production methods through the use of advanced "omics" technologies.

Cyber Security Division

The DHS Science and Technology Directorate established the Cyber Security Division (CSD), within the Directorate's Homeland Security Advanced Research Projects Agency (HSARPA), in 2011 in response to the increasing importance of the cybersecurity mission.

CSD's mission is to contribute to enhancing the security and resilience of the Nation's critical information infrastructure and the Internet by (1) driving security improvements to address critical weaknesses, (2) discovering new solutions for emerging cybersecurity threats, and (3) delivering new, tested technologies to defend against cybersecurity threats.

The Cyber Security Division's objectives are to:

Develop and transition new technologies, tools, and techniques to protect and secure systems, networks, infrastructure, and users, improving the foundational elements of our nation's critical infrastructure and the world's information infrastructure; and,

Provide coordination and research and development (R&D) leadership across federal, state, and municipal government; international partners; the private sector; and academia to improve cybersecurity research infrastructure.

CSD's work serves a wide range of customers by coordinating and cooperating with partners within the Department and at other federal

in a wide range of industries; Internet security researchers around the world; and universities and national laboratories. CSD works to create partnerships between government and private industry, the venture capital community and the research community.

Explosives Division

The Explosives Division promotes the development of effective techniques to protect our citizens and our country's infrastructure against the devastating effects of explosives by seeking innovative approaches in detection, and in countermeasures. It provides the concepts, science, technologies and systems that increase protection from explosives and promotes the development of field equipment, technologies, and procedures to interdict person-borne bombs, and car and truck bombs.

It is working to develop:

• An automated high-speed, high-performance checked baggage explosives detection system with reduced false alarm rates, improved throughput, and reduced operation and maintenance cost for screening checked baggage.

• Next generation threat detection system for Transportation Security Administration passenger check points to screen evolving threats while improving passenger experience.

• An enhanced ability of screening systems and operators to detect explosives and improvised explosive device (IED) components within cargo parcels and pallets.

• Tools, techniques and knowledge to better understand, train and utilize the explosive detection canine.

• New or improved technical capabilities to detect person-borne IEDs at a standoff distance.

• Methods for detecting trace explosives on people and personal items at a standoff distance.

• Solutions to protect the nations surface transportation systems.

• Knowledge on homemade explosives detection thresholds and threat quantities for detection.

The Explosives Division is divided into four main strategic portfolios including:

• Aviation Security: Checked baggage, check point, air cargo and canine operations.

• Facilities Protection: Facility checkpoints and perimeters.

• Intermodal Security: Protection of commuters and infrastructure in subway, maritime (ferries), and surface (buses and heavy rail) transportation.

• Improvised Explosives: Understanding the homemade explosive threat to improve detection technology and develop detection requirements.

Resilient Systems Division

The Resilient Systems Division's (RSD) mission is to rapidly develop and deliver innovative solutions that enhance the resilience of individuals, communities, and systems by enabling the Whole Community to prevent and protect against threats, mitigate hazards, effectively respond to disasters, and expedite recovery.

RSD's vision is to strengthen our homeland resilience to all-hazards disasters through science and technology-based solutions.

Adaptive Risk Mitigation delivers innovative tools and processes that reduce the risk to people and infrastructure and can adapt to evolving threats, changing environments, and cascading consequences

Agile Disaster Management provides advanced situational awareness and real-time decision support tools for individuals, communities, and infrastructure to rapidly and effectively respond to disasters and reduce recovery time

Resilience Infrastructure develops resilient designs and design standards for services, structures, and systems that increase the resilience of critical infrastructure against all hazards.

Effective Training, Education, and Performance provides training and tools that enhance the contributions of individuals and teams to all aspects of resilience.

RSD's primary federal customers are the Department's Intelligence & Analysis (I&A), National Protection and Programs Directorate Office of Infrastructure Protection (NPPD/OIP), Office of Health Affairs (OHA), Federal

istration (TSA), U.S. Citizenship and Immigration Services (USCIS), U.S. Coast Guard (USCG), U.S. Customs and Border Patrol (CBP), U.S. Secret Service (USSS), and U.S. Immigration Customs Enforcement (ICE). RSD directly supports emergency responders; federal, state, and local emergency managers; and critical infrastructure owners and operators.

Acquisition Support and Operations Analysis (ASOA) Group

The group strengthens the Homeland Security Enterprise mission to secure the nation by providing analyses, engineering, and test expertise and products connecting Research, Development, and Acquisition to the operational end-user. ASOA is of the following:
- Chief Systems Engineer
- Federally Funded Research and Development Centers Program Management Office
- Operational Test and Evaluation
- Research and Development Analysis and Assessment
- Standards

ASOA expands the Science and Technology Directorate's (S&T) analytic and systems engineering competencies in support of the Homeland Security Enterprise as they acquire operationally focused, best value solutions that can be successfully transitioned to operational use. To accomplish this, ASOA provides coordinated policy, guidance, processes, products, and outreach in four critical areas: standards development; systems analysis; research and development testing and assessment; and operational testing and evaluation. Specifically, ASOA applies its expertise in the following ways:
- Assist component research and development and acquisition programs to apply a systems analysis approach to develop high-fidelity, testable operational and capability requirements on the "front end."
- Assist research and development and acquisition programs to apply a research and development test and assessment approach to support development, execution, and transition of technologies.
- Develop, promote, and facilitate a rigorous systems engineering process to institutionalize a "systems thinking" approach to programs and increase

ciency in transforming customer needs and requirements into operational capabilities.

• Through delegation by the Secretary act as the principal advisor on operational testing and evaluation and oversee Test and Evaluation (T&E) for DHS Major Acquisition Programs.

• Serve as the Executive Agent for the DHS' Federally Funded Research and Development Centers (FFRDCs), Systems Engineering and Development Institute (HSSEDI) and Studies and Analysis Institute (HSSAI).

• Serve as the Standards Executive for the development and use of standards that meet DHS enterprise needs with reliable, interoperable and effective technologies and processes.

• ASOA's Transportation Security Lab provide expertise, specialized facilities and test protocols necessary to develop and evaluate explosive screening and contraband detection technologies.

• ASOA's System Assessment and Validation for Emergency Responders (SAVER) Program assists emergency responders in making procurement decisions by conducting objective assessments and validations on commercial equipment and systems.

• Serves as the Component Acquisition Executive for the S&T Directorate.

The Research and Development Partnerships (RDP) group

RDP builds enduring partnerships that deliver technology solutions to the HSE resourcefully and swiftly. It's an urgent mission that demands close cooperation across the HSE and among the group's six offices:

• Homeland Security Science and Technology Advisory Committee
• Interagency Office
• International Cooperative Programs Office

Office of National Laboratories

• Chemical Security Analysis Center
• National Bio and Agro Defense Facility
• National Biodefense Analysis and Countermeasures Center
• Plum Island Animal Disease Center

Office of Public-Private Partnerships

• Commercialization Office
• Long Range Broad Agency Announcement Office
• Office of SAFETY Act Implementation
• Small Business Innovative Research Office
• Office of University Programs
• Special Projects Office

RDP also coordinates interactions with the White House through the Office of Science and Technology Policy.

Domestic Nuclear Detection Office (DNDO)

The Domestic Nuclear Detection Office works to enhance the nuclear detection efforts of federal, state, territorial, tribal, and local governments, and the private sector and to ensure a coordinated response to such threats.

The Domestic Nuclear Detection Office (DNDO) is a jointly staffed office within the Department of Homeland Security. DNDO is the primary entity in the U.S. government for implementing domestic nuclear detection efforts for a managed and coordinated response to radiological and nuclear threats, as well as integration of federal nuclear forensics programs. Additionally, DNDO is charged with coordinating the development of the global nuclear detection and reporting architecture, with partners from federal, state, local, and international governments and the private sector.

Strategic Objectives

• Develop the global nuclear detection and reporting architecture
• Develop, acquire, and support the domestic nuclear detection and reporting system
• Characterize detector system performance before deployment
• Facilitate situational awareness through information sharing and analysis
• Establish operational protocols to ensure detection leads to effective response
• Conduct a transformational research and development program
• Provide centralized planning, integration, and advancement of U.S. government nuclear forensics programs

Directorates

Architecture and Plans Directorate —Determines gaps and vulnerabilities in the existing global nuclear detection architecture, then formulates recommendations and plans to develop an enhanced architecture.

Product Acquisition & Deployment Directorate—Carries out the engineering development, production, developmental logistics, procurement and deployment of current and next-generation nuclear detection systems.

Transformational & Applied Research Directorate—Conducts, supports, coordinates, and encourages an aggressive, long-term research and development program to address significant architectural and technical challenges unresolved by R&D efforts on the near horizon.

Operations Support Directorate—Develops the information sharing and analytical tools necessary to create a fully integrated operating environment. Residing in the Operations Support Directorate is the Joint Analysis Center, which is an interagency coordination and reporting mechanism and central monitoring point for the GNDA.

Systems Engineering & Evaluation Directorate—Ensures that DNDO proposes sound technical solutions and thoroughly understands systems performance and potential vulnerabilities prior to deploying those technologies.

Red Team & Net Assessments—Independently assesses the operational performance of planned and deployed capabilities, including technologies, procedures, and protocols.

National Technical Nuclear Forensics Center—Provides national-level stewardship, centralized planning and integration for an enduring national technical nuclear forensics capability.

10

Department Administration and Programs

Management Directorate

The Management Directorate is responsible for Department budgets and appropriations, expenditure of funds, accounting and finance, procurement; human resources, information technology systems, facilities and equipment, and the identification and tracking of performance measurements. The Directorate for Management is responsible for:
- budget, appropriations, expenditure of funds, accounting and finance;
- procurement; human resources and personnel;
- information technology systems;
- facilities, property, equipment, and other material resources; and
- identification and tracking of performance measurements relating to the responsibilities of the Department.

Key to the success of the Department in bolstering national security is the effectiveness of its workforce. The Directorate for Management ensures that the Department's over 230,000 employees have well-defined responsibilities and that managers and their employees have efficient means of communicating with one another, with other governmental and nongovernmental bodies, and with the public they serve.

National Protection and Programs Directorate (NPPD)

The National Protection and Programs Directorate (NPPD) works to advance the Department's risk-reduction mission. Reducing risk requires an integrated approach that encompasses both physical and virtual threats and their associated human elements.

NPPD's vision is a safe, secure, and resilient infrastructure where the American way of life can thrive. NPPD leads the national effort to protect and enhance the resilience of the nation's physical and cyber infrastructure.

Divisions

The components of the National Protection and Programs Directorate include:

Federal Protective Service (FPS): FPS is a federal law enforcement agency that provides integrated security and law enforcement services to federally owned and leased buildings, facilities, properties and other assets.

The FPS mission is to render federal properties safe and secure for federal employees, officials and visitors in a professional and cost effective manner by deploying a highly trained and multi-disciplined police force. As the federal agency charged with protecting and delivering integrated law enforcement and security services to facilities owned or leased by the General Services Administration (GSA), FPS employs 1,225 federal staff (including 900 law enforcement security officers, criminal investigators, police officers, and support personnel) and 15,000 contract guard staff to secure over 9,000 buildings and safeguard their occupants. FPS provides comprehensive coverage for these facilities nationwide.

Protecting the critical infrastructure and key resources of the United States is essential to our nation's security, public health and safety, economic vitality and way of life. FPS protects one component of the nation's infrastructure by mitigating risk to federal facilities and their occupants.

FPS organizes its activities along three guiding principles: stakeholder service, technical expertise, and organizational excellence. Supporting these principles are immediate priorities that will allow FPS to meet its short-term goals and long-term strategic goals.

With nearly 40 years of law enforcement experience, FPS has established a physical security program to provide protection to GSA owned or leased eral facilities. From the installation of alarm systems, x-rays, magnetometers and entry control systems, to monitoring those systems 24 hours a day, 7 days a week, providing uniformed police response and investigative follow-up, FPS is organized to protect and serve. The provision of contract protective security officer services, crime prevention seminars tailored to individual agency and employee needs, facility security surveys, integrating intelligence gathering and sharing, and maintaining special operations capabilities all serve to make FPS a world-class security force. What FPS does every day embodies the spirit of the Department and contributes to the achievement of Department goals and organizational excellence.

Primary Protective Services
- Conducting Facility Security Assessments
- Designing countermeasures for tenant agencies
- Maintaining uniformed law enforcement presence
- Maintaining armed contract security guards
- Performing background suitability checks for contract employees
- Monitoring security alarms via centralized communication centers

Additional Protective Services
- Conducting criminal investigations
- Sharing intelligence among local/state/federal
- Protecting special events
- Working with FEMA to respond to natural disasters
- Offering special operations including K-9 explosive detection
- Training federal tenants in crime prevention and Occupant Emergency Planning

Office of Biometric Identity Management (OBIM)

OBIM provides biometric identity services to DHS and its mission partners that advance informed decision making by producing accurate, timely, and high fidelity biometric identity information while protecting individuals' privacy and civil liberties.

OBIM supports the Department of Homeland Security's responsibility to protect the nation by providing biometric identification services that help federal, state, and local government decision makers accurately identify the people they encounter and determine whether those people pose a risk to the United States. OBIM supplies the technology for collecting and storing biometric data, provides analysis, updates its watchlist, and ensures the integrity of the data.

OBIM was created in March, 2013, replacing the United States Visitor and Immigration Status Indicator Technology (US-VISIT) and streamlining operations.

Its Vision is a more secure nation through advanced biometric identification, information sharing, and analysis and its Guiding Principles are:

Enhance the security of our citizens and visitors

Facilitate legitimate travel and trade

Ensure the integrity of the immigration system

Protect the privacy of our visitors

Office of Cyber and Infrastructure Analysis (OCIA)

OCIA provides consolidated all-hazards consequence analysis ensuring there is an understanding and awareness of cyber and physical critical infrastructure interdependencies and the impact of a cyber threat or incident to the Nation's critical infrastructure.

OCIA's mission is to support efforts to protect the Nation's critical infrastructure through an integrated analytical approach evaluating the potential consequences of disruption from physical or cyber threats and incidents. The results of this analysis will inform decisions to strengthen infrastructure security and resilience, as well as response and recovery efforts during natural, man-made or cyber incidents.

Formerly the Infrastructure Analysis and Strategy Division (IASD) within the Office of Infrastructure Protection (IP), OCIA was established as an office of the National Protection and Programs Directorate (NPPD) in 2014. OCIA has

21, which calls for integrated analysis of critical infrastructure, and Executive Order 13636, identifying critical infrastructure where cyber incidents could have catastrophic impacts to public health and safety, the economy, and national security.

OCIA builds on the recent accomplishments of the Department's Homeland Infrastructure Threat and Risk Analysis Center (HITRAC) and manages the National Infrastructure Simulation and Analysis Center (NISAC) to advance understanding of emerging risks crossing the cyber-physical domain. OCIA represents an integration and enhancement of DHS's analytic capabilities, supporting stakeholders and interagency partners.

Informing Decisions through Integrated Analysis

OCIA uses all-hazards information from an array of partners to conduct consequence modeling, simulation, and analysis. OCIA's core functions include:

•Providing analytic support to DHS leadership, operational components, and field personnel during steady-state and crises on emerging threats and incidents impacting the Nation's critical infrastructure;

•Assessing and informing national infrastructure risk management strategies on the likelihood and consequence of emerging and future risks; and

•Developing and enhancing capabilities to support crisis action by identifying and prioritizing infrastructure through the use of analytic tools and modeling capabilities.

Office of Cybersecurity and Communications (CS&C)

CS&C has the mission of assuring the security, resiliency, and reliability of the nation's cyber and communications infrastructure.

The Office of Cybersecurity and Communications (CS&C), within the National Protection and Programs_Directorate, is responsible for enhancing the security, resilience, and reliability of the Nation's cyber and communications infrastructure.   CS&C works to prevent or minimize disruptions to critical information infrastructure in order to protect the public, the economy, and government services.   CS&C leads efforts to protect the

".com" domain—to increase the security of critical networks. In addition, the National Cybersecurity and Communications Integration Center (NCCIC) serves as a 24/7 cyber monitoring, incident response, and management center and as a national point of cyber and communications incident integration.

As the Sector-Specific Agency for the Communications and Information Technology (IT) sectors, CS&C coordinates national-level reporting that is consistent with the National Response Framework (NRF).

Congress created the Office of the Assistant Secretary for Cybersecurity and Communications in 2006. CS&C carries out its mission through its five divisions:

The Office of Emergency Communications

Established in 2007 in response to communications challenges faced during the attacks on September 11, 2001 and Hurricane Katrina, the Department of Homeland Security (DHS) Office of Emergency Communications (OEC) supports and promotes communications used by emergency responders and government officials to keep America safe, secure, and resilient. The office leads the Nation's operable and interoperable public safety and national security and emergency preparedness (NS/EP) communications efforts. OEC provides training, coordination, tools, and guidance to help its Federal, state, local, tribal, territorial and industry partners develop their emergency communications capabilities. OEC's programs and services coordinate emergency communications planning, preparation OEC supports emergency communications interoperability by offering training, tools, and workshops; regional support; and, providing guidance documents and templates. These services assist OEC's stakeholders in ensuring they have communications during steady state and emergency operations. OEC plays a key role in ensuring Federal, state, local, tribal and territorial agencies have the necessary plans, resources, and training needed to support operable and advanced interoperable emergency communications, and evaluation, to ensure safer, better-prepared communities nationwide.

OEC plays a key role in ensuring Federal, state, local, tribal and territorial agencies have the necessary plans, resources, and training needed to support operable and advanced interoperable emergency communications.

OEC plays a role in supporting response efforts by ensuring that its stakeholders have the tools needed to communicate during steady state and emergency operations. OEC manages priority telecommunications services programs that support emergency communications and restoration. Following response efforts, OEC works with its stakeholders and regional personnel to document best practices and lessons learned to promote improvements in emergency communications during future events.

The NCCIC

The Department of Homeland Security is responsible for protecting our Nation's critical infrastructure from physical and cyber threats. Information sharing is a key part of the Department's important mission to create shared situational awareness of malicious cyber activity. Cyberspace has united once distinct information structures, including our business and government operations, our emergency preparedness communications, and our critical digital and process control systems and infrastructures. Protection of these systems is essential to the resilience and reliability of the Nation's critical infrastructure and key resources; therefore, to our economic and national security.

The National Cybersecurity and Communications Integration Center (NCCIC) is a 24x7 cyber situational awareness, incident response, and management center that is a national nexus of cyber and communications integration for the Federal Government, intelligence community, and law enforcement.

The NCCIC shares information among the public and private sectors to provide greater understanding of cybersecurity and communications situation awareness of vulnerabilities, intrusions, incidents, mitigation, and recovery actions.

The NCCIC Vision is a secure and resilient cyber and communications infrastructure that supports homeland security, a vibrant economy, and the health and safety of the American people. In striving to achieve this vision, the NCCIC will:

Focus on proactively coordinating the prevention and mitigation of those cyber and telecommunications threats that pose the greatest risk to the Nation.

Pursue whole-of-nation operational integration by broadening and deepening engagement with its partners through information sharing to manage threats, vulnerabilities, and incidents.

Break down the technological and institutional barriers that impede collaborative information exchange, situational awareness, and understanding of threats and their impact.

Maintain a sustained readiness to respond immediately and effectively to all cyber and telecommunications incidents of national security.

Serve stakeholders as a national center of excellence and expertise for cyber and telecommunications security issues.

Protect the privacy and constitutional rights of the American people in the conduct of its mission.

The NCCIC mission is to reduce the likelihood and severity of incidents that may significantly compromise the security and resilience of the Nation's critical information technology and communications networks. This mission defines the NCCIC's specific contribution to achieving its vision. To execute its mission effectively, the NCCIC will focus on three core strategic priorities and associated operational objectives. The NCCIC will implement this strategy by expanding and attaining the capabilities, products, and services required to meet each of its strategic priorities over the next five years. Many of these activities will be coordinated, developed, and executed collaboratively with the NCCIC's operational partners to the benefit of the entire community of cyber and communications stakeholders.

SECIR

The Stakeholder Engagement and Cyber Infrastructure Resilience (SECIR) division is the DHS primary point of engagement and coordination for national security/emergency preparedness (NS/EP) communications and cybersecurity initiatives for both government and industry partners, and is the Executive Secretariat for the Joint Program Office for the NS/EP Communications Executive Committee. CS&C relies on SECIR to streamline coordination and engagement with external partners, while leveraging capabilities and significant subject matter expertise in order to meet stakeholder requirements.

Establishes and maintains the Nation's NS/EP communication and cybersecurity engagement initiatives by working with government and industry to promote and enhance the security and resilience of NS/EP communications and cyber infrastructure.

Maintains meaningful lines of communication and engagement among critical infrastructure owners and operators; federal interagency partners; divisions within DHS; and state, local, tribal and territorial government agencies for cyber and NS/EP communications security and resilience.

Leads the development of strategic risk assessments and the delivery of key mitigation capabilities to owners and operators that are designed to reduce risks to the Nation's critical cyber and NS/EP communications infrastructure.

Leads the development and implementation of education, outreach, and awareness, and cyber workforce and NS/EP communications development initiatives.

Maintains program management capabilities through requirements, development, and communications coordination with legal, intra-agency and interagency partners, and strategic planning.

Operates multiple coordination, threat, and technical information and analytical collaboration exchanges to sustain partnerships that facilitate sharing actionable and relevant threat and vulnerability mitigation data in a secure environment on shared vulnerabilities in the Communications and Information Technology Sectors.

Performs the communications infrastructure identification, prioritization, and protection functions pursuant to Homeland Security Presidential Directive 7, implemented through the National Infrastructure Protection Plan. Communications and Information Technology Sector Specific Agency responsibilities are executed by SECIR, along with coordination with appropriate Sector and Government Coordinating Councils within the Critical Infrastructure Partnership Advisory Council.

Supports the National Security Telecommunications Advisory Committee (NTSAC), which is a Presidential Advisory Committee on NS/EP communications policy. SECIR coordinates the NSTAC work plan with several DHS advisory bodies that address cybersecurity and NS/EP communications, including the Enduring Security Framework under the Critical Infrastructure Partnership Advisory Council.

Federal Network Resilience (FNR)

FNR address critical cybersecurity requirements. It consists of the following branches:

Requirements and Acquisition Support (RAS) supports the long-term strategic prevention of attacks against Federal Civilian Executive Branch (FCEB) networks.

Network and Infrastructure Security (NIS) optimizes an agency's network services into a common solution for the federal government.

Cybersecurity Assurance (CA) assesses the state of operational readiness and cybersecurity risk across FCEB.

Cybersecurity Performance Management (CPM) provides oversight and operational support for the FCEB departments and agencies in their compliance with the Federal Information Security Management Act (FISMA)

FNR also collaborates across the federal government to enhance the nation's cybersecurity posture by:

identifying common requirements across the federal government,

collaborating with components of the federal enterprise to identify solutions,

implementing policy and technical solutions, and

monitoring the effectiveness of implemented solutions.

Network Security Deployment

NSD provides development, acquisition, deployment, operational, and customer support to satisfy the Department's mission requirements under the Comprehensive National Cybersecurity Initiative (CNCI). Specifically, NSD's mission is to improve cybersecurity to federal departments, agencies, and partners by developing the technologies and establishing the services needed to fulfill CS&C's cybersecurity mission. To meet that mission need, NSD designs, develops, deploys, and sustains the National Cybersecurity Protection System (NCPS), which provides intrusion detection, advanced analytics, formation sharing, and intrusion prevention capabilities that combat and mitigate cyber threats to the Federal Executive Branch information and networks.

NSD is comprised of five branches that support the design, development, deployment and sustainment of the NCPS:

Investment & Contracts Management

The Investment and Contracts Management (I&CM) branch of NSD is responsible for planning for, executing, and managing the acquisition strategy for NCPS, including preparing statements of work, independent government cost estimates, and other related acquisition documentation. The I&CM branch also formulates and executes the NCPS program and project budgets, including all phases of the Planning, Programming, Budget, and Execution process. I&CM develops and manages the NCPS Life Cycle Cost Estimate. Finally, I&CM oversees the performance of contracts in support of NCPS and performs integrated program control activities to ensure the program and project management status information is effectively and efficiently portrayed in a timely manner through program reviews, performance metrics, and program compliance.

Systems Engineering & Acquisition Oversight

The Systems Engineering & Acquisition Oversight (SE&AO) Branch provides systems engineering support for the NCPS, to include serving as a liaison with the system user community (e.g., the National Cybersecurity and Communications Integration Center) throughout the system's development cycle. SE&AO is responsible for maintaining a close interaction with the system user to ensure that NSD understands the underlying functional requirements, which is critical to developing and delivering an effective capability. SE&AO also ensures successful mission integration through an extensive round of developmental, system, and operational test events and develops secure solutions to interoperability issues by ensuring compliance with data standards, security requirements, interface control documents, and other architecture products. Finally, SE&AO provides program management oversight of the NCPS to ensure capabilities are coordinated and delivered effectively and efficiently. Program management functions include strategic and technical planning, assessment functions, and documenting and tracking program cost, schedule, and risks.

System Sustainment & Operations

NSD's System Sustainment & Operations Branch is responsible for operating and maintaining NCPS. Operations and maintenance include providing 24x7x365 systems administration and customer support services, Operations Center and Network Operation Center support, configuration management support, logistics support, performing technical refreshes, and performing continuous monitoring on NCPS equipment. The SS&O Branch is also responsible for coordinating with the Capability Development Branch to ensure that the designs of new capabilities work within the existing NCPS architecture.

Capability Development

The Capability Development Branch provides intrusion detection, advanced analytics, information sharing, and intrusion prevention capabilities. Capability Development is responsible for designing, developing, and deploying NCPS system capabilities. Capability Development also interfaces with industry to research emerging technologies and to create capability roadmaps that introduce new technologies into the architecture within a given capability area. Finally, Capability Development ensures that a deployed capability is properly integrated into the program's core infrastructure and properly transitioned to the NCPS operations and maintenance staff.

Services Integration

The Services Integration Branch leads engagements with departments and agencies (D/As) on the implementation of major NCPS initiatives that directly affect the D/As and require their participation to implement (e.g., EINSTEIN 3 Accelerated and NCPS Information Sharing capabilities). Services Integration is responsible for developing strategic engagement strategies and coordinating those strategies with the National Security Staff (NSS) Cyber Policy Committee (IPC) and coordinating the signature of Memoranda of Agreement (MOAs), Service Level Agreements (SLAs), and Letters of Agency (LOAs) from the D/As that are required to govern service implementation. Services integration is also responsible for conducting Technical Exchange Meetings (TEMs) to resolve D/As questions and technical issues prior to implementation.

Building Success through Partnerships

Centers (ISACs), State, local, and tribal governments, and international organizations to become the cybersecurity service provider of choice for the Federal Government. Through its leadership and contributions to critical initiatives such as the EINSTEIN program, Enhanced Cybersecurity Services (ECS), CNCI, stewardship of the National Information Exchange Model (NIEM) cyber domain, and partnerships with industry, NSD is driving national-level efforts to improve the cybersecurity posture of the Federal Government and Critical Infrastructure.

In addition, CS&C operates the **Enterprise Performance Management Office**, which ensures that the Assistant Secretary's strategic goals and priorities are reflected across all CS&C programs; measures the effectiveness of initiatives, programs, and projects that support those goals and priorities; and facilitates cross-functional mission coordination and implementation between CS&C components, within DHS, and among the interagency.

Office of Infrastructure Protection (IP)

IP leads the coordinated national effort to reduce risk to our critical infrastructure posed by acts of terrorism. In doing so, the Department increases the nation's level of preparedness and the ability to respond and quickly recover in the event of an attack, natural disaster, or other emergency.

The National Protection and Programs Directorate, Office of Infrastructure Protection (IP) leads and coordinates national programs and policies on critical infrastructure issues and has established strong partnerships across government and the private sector. The office conducts and facilitates vulnerability and consequence assessments to help critical infrastructure owners and operators and State, local, tribal, and territorial partners understand and address risks. IP provides information on emerging threats and hazards so that appropriate actions can be taken. The office also offers tools and training to partners to help them manage the risks to their assets, systems, and networks.

The vision of the Office of Infrastructure Protection is secure and resilient critical infrastructure across the Nation achieved through sound risk management, collaboration, information sharing, innovation, effective

The mission is to lead the national effort to protect critical infrastructure from all hazards by managing risk and enhancing resilience through collaboration with the critical infrastructure community.

The Office of Infrastructure Protection Strategic Plan: 2012-2016 addresses the Department's responsibilities for safeguarding critical infrastructure, both physical and cyber, by reducing risk, sharing information, enhancing resilience, and promoting preparedness for all hazards.

Infrastructure Information Collection Division (IICD)

The National Protection and Programs Directorate/Office of Infrastructure Protection's Infrastructure Information Collection Division (IICD) leads the Department's efforts to gather and manage vital information regarding the nation's critical infrastructure. Accurate critical infrastructure data is essential to developing and executing infrastructure protection programs at all levels of government. IICD helps ensure that the necessary infrastructure data is available to homeland security partners by identifying information sources and developing applications to use and analyze the data.

IICD equips federal, state, and local governments with tools for the collection, management, and visualization of infrastructure data to support national preparedness, response, and recovery efforts.

Infrastructure Security Compliance Division (ISCD)

The Infrastructure Security Compliance Division is responsible for implementing the Chemical Facility Anti-Terrorism Standards (CFATS), the nation's program to regulate security at high-risk chemical facilities, and a proposed Ammonium Nitrate Security Program.

To further the Department's mission of enhancing security and resilience for the nation's critical infrastructure, ISCD leads the nation's effort to secure America's high-risk chemical facilities and prevent the use of certain chemicals in a terrorist act on the homeland through the systematic regulation, inspection, and enforcement of chemical infrastructure security

DHS leads national implementation of the CFATS. In October 2006, Congress passed Section 550 of the DHS Appropriations Act of 2007, Pub. L. 109-295, authorizing and requiring the Department of Homeland Security (DHS) to regulate security at chemical facilities that DHS determines, in its discretion, are high-risk. To implement this authority, DHS issued the CFATS in 2007. Under CFATS, facilities that have been finally determined by DHS to be high-risk are required to develop and implement Site Security Plans (SSPs) or Alternative Security Programs (ASPs) that meet applicable risk-based performance standards (RBPS).

National Infrastructure Coordinating Center (NICC)

The National Infrastructure Coordinating Center (NICC) is the information and coordination hub of a national network dedicated to protecting critical infrastructure essential to the nation's security, health and safety, and economic vitality.

The NICC is both an operational component of the National Protection and Programs Directorate— specifically the Office of Infrastructure Protection's Contingency Planning and Incident Management Division—and a watch operations element of the DHS National Operations Center.

The NICC maintains 24/7 situational awareness and crisis monitoring of critical infrastructure and shares threat information, in order to reduce risk, prevent damage, and enable rapid recovery of critical infrastructure assets from incidents caused by natural disasters, attacks, or other emergencies.

NICC functions include:

• Situational Awareness: Collects, maintains, and shares information about threats to infrastructure

• Information Sharing and Collaboration: Integrating and disseminating information throughout the critical infrastructure partnership network. More about information sharing.

• Assessment and Analysis: Evaluating infrastructure data for accuracy, importance, and implications.

• Decision Support: Providing recommendations to critical infrastructure partners and DHS leadership.

•Future Operations: Supporting decision making for actions required 24–72 hours before and after an incident or event.

The NICC is committed to ensuring that the nation's critical infrastructure is prepared in case of a significant event, and well-informed and supported during and after the event.

The Protective Security Coordination Division (PSCD)

PSCD is a division within the National Protection and Programs Directorate's Office of Infrastructure Protection that provides programs and initiatives to enhance the protection and resilience of the nation's critical infrastructure with respect to all-hazards incidents.

PSCD provides strategic coordination and field operations support to reduce risk to the nation's critical infrastructure from a terrorist attack or natural disaster. PSCD programs help critical infrastructure owners and operators and state and local responders:

•Assess vulnerabilities, interdependencies, capabilities, and incident consequences

•Develop, implement, and provide national coordination for protective programs

•Facilitate critical infrastructure response to and recovery from all hazards

This is accomplished through a combination of data collection, assessment, and analysis to give government officials and private sector owners and operators what they need for risk mitigation and to build resilience. The Division's activities also inform Department initiatives such as infrastructure protection grant programs and research and development requirements.

The Division's work covers the following areas:

•Field operations through Regional Directors and Protective Security Advisors

•The Department's Office for Bombing Prevention

•Critical Infrastructure Vulnerability Assessments

Field Operations — Regional Directors and Protective Security Advisors

Regional Directors and Protective Security Advisors (PSAs) are on-site critical infrastructure and vulnerability assessment specialists deployed in 50 states and Puerto Rico. They coordinate vulnerability assessments and training, support incident management, and provide a vital communication channel between state and local officials, private sector owners and operators, and the Department. PSAs also play a pivotal role in the Office of Infrastructure Protection's initiative to increase critical infrastructure protection and resilience on a regional level. Learn more.

PSAs also support development of the national risk picture by identifying, assessing, monitoring, and minimizing risk to critical infrastructure at the state, local, and regional level.

Office for Bombing Prevention

The Office for Bombing Prevention enhances the nation's ability to detect, deter, prevent, and respond to improvised explosive devices—the preferred method of attack for terrorists—by:
• Coordinating national and intergovernmental bombing prevention efforts
• Evaluating domestic terrorist bombing prevention requirements and analyzing capability gaps
• Sharing information about terrorist tactics, techniques, and procedures
• Conducting training, outreach, and awareness events
Office for Bombing Prevention programs include:
• IED Multi-Jurisdiction Security Plans
• National Capabilities Analysis Database (NCAD)
• Bomb-making Materials Awareness Program (BMAP)
• Technical Resource for Incident Prevention (TRIPwire) and TRIPwire Community Gateway
The Office for Bombing Prevention is also the Department lead for implementing Homeland Security Presidential Directive 19: Combating Terrorist Use of Explosives in the United States.
Critical Infrastructure Vulnerability Assessments
The Protective Security Coordination Division develops and deploys a scalable assessment methodology to identify critical infrastructure vulnerabilities, support collaborative security planning, and provide options for consideration to enhance protective measures and risk mitigation

Available critical infrastructure vulnerability assessment programs:
- Buffer Zone Protection Program
- Site Assistance Visits
- Computer-Based Assessment Tool
- Regional Resiliency Assessment Program
- Sector Outreach and Programs Division (SOPD

The Sector Outreach and Programs Division (SOPD)

SOPD builds stakeholder capacity and enhances critical infrastructure security and resilience through voluntary partnerships that provide key tools, resources, and partnerships. The division operates the council and stakeholder engagement mechanisms for the critical infrastructure security and resilience community. The division also serves as the sector-specific agency for 6 of the 16 critical infrastructure sectors and collaborates with the other 10.

Its mission is to build, align, and leverage national public-private stakeholder partnerships and partnership programs to enhance critical infrastructure security and resilience

Division's services for enhancing critical infrastructure security and resilience across the sectors include:
- Serving as the sector-specific agency for 6 of the critical infrastructure sectors
- Coordinating across all 16 critical infrastructure sectors
- Providing expertise in critical infrastructure security and resilience
- Enabling critical infrastructure security partnerships and managing the Critical Infrastructure Partnership Advisory Council
- Developing and delivering stakeholder education, training, and exercises
- Facilitating information-sharing and managing the critical infrastructure information sharing environment

Sector-Specific Agency Responsibilities

Sector-specific agencies are the primary federal entities responsible for coordinating critical infrastructure security and resilience efforts within individual sectors. DHS is the sector-specific agency for 10 of the 16 sectors; IP is responsible for 6:
- Chemical Sector
- Commercial Facilities Sector
- Critical Manufacturing Sector
- Dams Sector
- Emergency Services Sector
- Nuclear Reactors, Materials, and Waste Sector

Sector-specific agency activities:
- Facilitate the public-private partnership across critical infrastructure sectors
- Develop strategic goals to mitigate risk and improve resilience
- Provide and promote education, training, information sharing, and outreach support
- Shape sector-specific goals that address physical, human, and cybersecurity risks and drive security and resilience activities and programs
- Provide, support, and facilitate technical assistance and consultations to identify vulnerabilities and mitigate incidents
- Implement the NIPP 2013 framework and guidance tailored to respective sectors
- Develop sector-specific plans with public and private sector partners

11

Other Departments, Agencies, and Organizations

Federal Law Enforcement Training Center (FLETC)

The Federal Law Enforcement Training Center provides career-long training to law enforcement professionals to help them fulfill their responsibilities safely and proficiently.

Its mission is "We train those who protect our homeland." To carry out this mission, the FLETC serves as an interagency law enforcement training organization for 91 federal agencies or Partner Organizations. The FLETC also provides training to state, local, rural, tribal, territorial, and international law enforcement agencies. During FY 2012, almost 70,000 students received FLETC training. Since it was established in 1970, approximately 1,000,000 law enforcement officers and agents have been trained at FLETC. Although the FLETC trains officers and agents from all federal departments and all three branches of government, it is a component of the Department of Homeland Security.

As an interagency training organization, the FLETC has the finest professionals from diverse backgrounds serving as faculty and staff. Approximately one-third of the instructor staff are permanent FLETC employees. The remainder of the cadre is comprised of federal officers and investigators who are on short-term assignments from their parent organizations or who recently retired from the field. This mix of permanent, detailed, and recently retired staff provides an appropriate balance of training

staff provides an appropriate balance of training expertise, recent operational experience, and fresh insight from the field.

The FLETC is headquartered at Glynco, Ga., near the port city of Brunswick, halfway between Savannah, Ga., and Jacksonville, Fla. In addition to Glynco, the FLETC operates other residential training centers in Artesia, N.M., and Charleston, S.C. The FLETC also conducts training at a non-residential facility in Cheltenham, Md. The Cheltenham center is primarily intended for use by agencies with large concentrations of personnel in the Washington, D.C., area. The FLETC maintains an office in Orlando, Fla., which provides a gateway to the technology and training expertise within a nationally recognized hub for simulation and training.

Since 1995, the FLETC has participated in the International Law Enforcement Academy (ILEA) Program. Over the years, academies have been established in Hungary, Thailand, Botswana, and El Salvador. The FLETC contributes academic, program, and operational support to the ILEAs, including instructors for the ILEA's core and specialized programs, and the Director at ILEA Gaborone and the Deputy Director at ILEA Bangkok.

Office of Health Affairs (OHA)

The Office of Health Affairs coordinates all medical activities of the Department of Homeland Security to ensure appropriate preparation for and response to incidents having medical significance.

Its mission is to advise, promote, integrate, and enable a safe and secure workforce and nation in pursuit of national health security.

The Office of Health Affairs (OHA) serves as the Department of Homeland Security's principal authority for all medical and health issues. OHA provides medical, public health, and scientific expertise in support of the Department of Homeland Security mission to prepare for, respond to, and recover from all threats. OHA serves as the principal advisor to the Secretary and the Federal Emergency Management Agency (FEMA) Administrator on medical and public health issues. OHA leads the Department's workforce health protection and medical oversight activities. The office also leads and coordinates the Department's biological and chemical defense activities and provides medical and scientific expertise to support the Department's preparedness and response efforts

Office Goals
- Provide expert health and medical advice to Department leadership
- Build national resilience against health incidents
- Enhance national and Department medical first responder capabilities
- Protect the Department workforce against health threats

OHA comprises the following divisions:

The **Health Threats Resilience Division** strengthens national capabilities to prepare and secure the nation against the health impacts of CBRN incidents and other intentional and naturally occurring events.

The **Workforce Health and Medical Support Division** leads the Department's workforce health protection and medical oversight activities.

Office of Intelligence and Analysis (I&A)

The Office of Intelligence and Analysis (I&A) is responsible for using information and intelligence from multiple sources to identify and assess current and future threats to the United States.

The Intelligence and Analysis (I&A) mission is to equip the Homeland Security Enterprise with the intelligence and information it needs to keep the homeland safe, secure, and resilient.

I&A's mission is supported by four strategic goals:

Analysis

Its analysis is guided by a Program of Analysis (POA), an assessment of key analytic issues, framed as key intelligence questions (KIQ). These KIQs are shaped by customer needs, Administration and Departmental leadership priorities, and resources. KIQs are organized by time frame.

- Immediate and Ongoing Threat KIQs focus on short term or operational issues such as imminent terrorist threats to the homeland. Production that addresses these threats provides the Administration and DHS leadership with the intelligence analysis to better inform near-term operational decision to increase the nation's security.

• Strategic Context KIQs focus on providing context, trend, or pattern analysis. Production that addresses these KIQs helps our customers understand recent threats in a broader, global, or historical perspective and they shape strategies to combat the threats or address gaps in homeland security. These would include, for example, how the evolving cartel-related violence in Mexico compares to past cartel wars or how threats to our national infrastructure are changing.

• Opportunity KIQs focus on emerging issues or topics for which reporting streams are new or fragmentary; for example, these KIQs may describe the kinds of polices or activities that have been effective in combating newly emerging threats.

As might be expected of an intelligence element supporting a Cabinet-level Department, about half of KIQs in the POA focus on providing intelligence to respond to the strategic needs of our customers. This is followed by focusing on immediate and ongoing threats. About 10 percent of the focus is on identifying new topics and issues that could impact the Department and its customers.

Collection

Homeland Security Standing Information Needs (HSEC SINs) form the foundation for information collection activities within the Department and provide other Intelligence Community (IC) and Homeland Security Enterprise members the ability to focus their collection, analytic, and reporting assets in support of the homeland security mission. The HSEC SINs document the enduring all-threats and all-hazards information needs of the Homeland Security Enterprise. The HSEC SINs are updated and published annually to ensure the information needs of the Homeland Security Enterprise are continuously collected, identified, and documented. The institutionalized use of HSEC SINs within collection, production, and dissemination practices enhances the ability of Homeland Security Enterprise members to effectively identify and share information with their stakeholders and partners.

Information Sharing

The Office of Intelligence and Analysis (I&A) has a unique mandate within the Intelligence Community and is the federal government lead for sharing information and intelligence with state, local, tribal and territorial governments and the private sector. It is these non-federal partners who now

Homeland Security Enterprise in preventing and responding to evolving threats to the homeland. I&A serves as the information conduit and intelligence advocate for state, local, tribal, and territorial governments. I&A supports state and major urban area fusion centers with deployed personnel and systems, training, and collaboration. This National Network of Fusion Centers is the hub of much of the two-way intelligence and information flow between the federal government and our state, local, tribal and territorial partners. The fusion centers represent a shared commitment between the federal government and the state and local governments who own and operate them. Individually, each represents a vital resource for merging information from national and local sources to prevent and respond to all threats and hazards. Collectively, their collaboration with the federal government, one another (state-to-state and state-to-locality), and with the private sector represents the new paradigm through which homeland security is viewed. Fusion centers have contributed and will continue to contribute to improvements in information sharing and collaboration that will enhance the nation's overall preparedness.

I&A assumes the program management role for the Department's engagement with the Nationwide Suspicious Activity Reporting (SAR) Initiative (NSI) Program Management Office (PMO). As part of that role, I&A is a direct liaison with the NSI PMO and facilitates the efforts of DHS components and fusion centers in becoming active NSI participants. Additionally, I&A leverages SAR data to create analytical products that assist federal, state, local and tribal partners in their respective homeland security missions.

DHS Intelligence Enterprise

The DHS Intelligence Enterprise consists of diverse components with distinct mission sets: Customs and Border Protection, Immigration and Customs Enforcement, U.S. Citizenship and Immigration Services, U.S. Coast Guard, Transportation Security Administration, U.S. Secret Service, and the Federal Emergency Management Administration. The U/SIA serves as the Chief Intelligence Officer (CINT) for the DHS Intelligence Enterprise. I&A works

and collective missions, with I&A acting as a catalyst for promoting enterprise-wide solutions and projects that are designed to capitalize on the individual strengths of the Department and make them mutually reinforcing. I&A also seeks to leverage the capabilities of the IC in support of these important homeland security missions.

Most recently, I&A has initiated the Homeland Security Intelligence Priorities Framework and the Intelligence Enterprise Management Catalogue. The two activities are important tools that will allow DHS to strategically assess all Departmental intelligence and intelligence-related activities. The Intelligence Enterprise Management Catalogue will be a central database that serves as a repository of data on the intelligence functions, capabilities, activities and assets of the DHS Intelligence Enterprise.We are part of a larger Homeland Security Enterprise that includes Departmental leaders and components, state, local, tribal, territorial and private sector partners and other Intelligence Community (IC) members, all of whom require and generate homeland security intelligence and information. I&A is a member of the U.S. Intelligence Community. The Under Secretary for I&A (U/SIA) also serves as DHS' Chief Intelligence Officer and is responsible to both the Secretary of Homeland Security and the Director of National Intelligence. I&A's budget is 100 percent funded in the National Intelligence Program (NIP).

Office of Operations Coordination and Planning

The Office of Operations Coordination and Planning is responsible for monitoring the security of the United States on a daily basis and coordinating activities within the Department and with governors, Homeland Security Advisors, law enforcement partners, and critical infrastructure operators in all 50 states and more than 50 major urban areas nationwide.

The Office of Operations Coordination and Planning works to deter, detect, and prevent terrorist acts by coordinating the work of federal, state, territorial, tribal, local, and private sector partners and   by collecting and fusing information from a variety of sources.

Goals

- conducting joint operations across all organizational elements.
- coordinating activities related to incident management.
- employing all Department resources to translate intelligence and policy into action.
- overseeing the National Operations Center (NOC) which collects and fuses information from more than 35 Federal, State, territorial, tribal, local, and private sector agencies.

Information is shared and fused on a daily basis by the two halves of the Office that are referred to as the "Intelligence Side" and the "Law Enforcement Side." Each half is identical and functions in tandem with the other, but requires a different level of clearance to access information. The Intelligence Side focuses on pieces of highly classified intelligence and how the information contributes to the current threat picture for any given area. The Law Enforcement Side is dedicated to tracking the different enforcement activities across the country that may have a terrorist nexus. The two pieces fused together create a real-time snap shot of the nation's threat environment at any moment.

Through the National Operations Center, the Office provides real-time situational awareness and monitoring of the homeland, coordinates incidents and response activities, and, in conjunction with the Office of Intelligence and Analysis, issues advisories and bulletins concerning threats to homeland security, as well as specific protective measures. The NOC—which operates 24 hours a day, seven days a week, 365 days a year—coordinates information sharing to help deter, detect, and prevent terrorist acts and to manage domestic incidents. Information on domestic incident management is shared with Emergency Operations Centers at all levels through the Homeland Security Information Network (HSIN).

Office of Policy

The Office of Policy is the primary policy formulation and coordination component for the Department of Homeland Security. It provides a centralized, coordinated focus to the development of Department-wide, long-range planning to protect the United States.

It serves as a central resource to the Secretary and other Department leaders for strategic planning and analysis, and facilitation of decision-making on the full breadth of issues that may arise across the dynamic homeland security enterprise.

What it does.

•Lead the coordination, integration, and development of DHS-wide policies, programs, strategies, and plans

•Facilitate decision-making by providing timely advice and analysis to the Secretary and other Departmental leaders

•Represent the Department at White House interagency policy committee meetings

•Develop long-term strategic priorities to increase operational effectiveness and mission execution

•Coordinate and support Departmental international engagement

•Serve as the point of contact for academics, the private sector, and other external homeland security stakeholders

Component parts:

Office of Policy Implementation and Integration

The Office of Policy Integration and Implementation (PII) provides policy development and analysis across the Department's mission portfolios, including: counterterrorism; CBRN; transborder security; immigration; resilience; and screening.

PII Comprises:

Counterterrorism Policy

Counterterrorism Policy serves as the Departmental policy lead for interagency counterterrorism. Key issues include countering violent extremism, disrupting terrorist travel and finance, and preventing terrorists from acquiring and using weapons of mass destruction.

Screening Coordination

Screening Coordination strengthens homeland security by enhancing screening and credentialing processes, programs, and technologies to facilitate legitimate travel and trade, ensure individual privacy and redress opportunities, and deter, detect, and deny access to individuals who pose a threat to the United States.

Resilience Policy

The Office of Resilience Policy works on the following issue areas: resilience, critical infrastructure protection, emergency preparedness and response, interoperable communications, climate change, space (e.g. satellites, solar storms), grants, and cybersecurity.

Immigration Policy

Immigration Policy is responsible for the development, evaluation, integration, and advocacy of Department policies in all mission areas related to immigration and border security matters. Key activities include regulatory development reflecting a Department- and Government-wide position on immigration matters; advising on the creation of an effective visa process that secures America's borders while facilitating legitimate travel; and developing integrated policy on refugee and asylum issues.

Chemical/Biological/Radiological/Nuclear Policy

This office is responsible for developing, coordinating, facilitating, and evaluating the effectiveness of policies and programs related to countering chemical, biological, radiological, and nuclear threats.   The scope of the office's work ranges across the spectrums of awareness, prevention, protection, response, and recovery

Transborder Policy

Transborder Policy is responsible for developing, implementing, and coordinating policy related to the security of our national transportation systems (aviation, mass transit, passenger rail, freight rail, highway trucks, buses, pipelines and maritime), the global cargo supply chain, key resources, and critical infrastructure

Homeland Security Advisory Council

The Homeland Security Advisory Council (HSAC) provides advice and recommendations to the Secretary on matters related to homeland security. The Council comprises leaders from state and local government, first responder communities, the private sector, and academia.

In July 2012, Secretary Napolitano directed the HSAC to form the Task Force on CyberSkills in response to the increasing demand for the best and brightest in the cybersecurity field across industry, academia and government. The Task Force, co-chaired by Jeff Moss and Alan Paller, conducted extensive interviews with experts from government, the private sector, and academia in developing its recommendations to grow the advanced technical skills of the DHS cybersecurity workforce and expand the national pipeline of men and women with these cybersecurity skills. On October 1, the HSAC unanimously approved sending the Task Force recommendations to the Secretary.

The Office for State and Local Law Enforcement

On the recommendation of the 9/11 Commission, Congress created the Office for State and Local Law Enforcement (OSLLE) in 2007 for two key purposes:

1.Lead the coordination of DHS-wide policies related to state, local, tribal, and territorial law enforcement's role in preventing, preparing for, protecting against, and responding to natural disasters, acts of terrorism, and other man-made disaster within the United States; and

2.Serve as the primary liaison between DHS and non-Federal law enforcement agencies across the country.

Responsibilities

•Serve as the primary Department liaison to state, local, tribal, and territorial law enforcement;

•Advise the Secretary on the issues, concerns, and recommendations of state, local, tribal, and territorial law enforcement;

•Keep the law enforcement community up-to-date on Department-wide activities and initiatives such as "If You See Something, Say Something™", the

Blue Campaign, Nationwide Suspicious Activity Reporting (SAR) Initiative (NSI), and the Department's efforts in Countering Violent Extremism;
  •Identify and respond to law enforcement challenges that affect homeland security;
  •Coordinate with the Office of Intelligence and Analysis to ensure the timely coordination and distribution of intelligence and strategic information to state, local, tribal, and territorial law enforcement; and
  •Work with the Federal Emergency Management Agency to ensure that law enforcement and terrorism-focused grants to state, local, tribal, and territorial law enforcement agencies are appropriately focused on terrorism prevention activities.

Law Enforcement Resources

The OSLLE has assembled a list of resources that can assist state, local, tribal, and territorial law enforcement in their efforts to keep our communities safe, secure, and resilient. The DHS State and Local Law Enforcement Resource Catalog and other helpful tools can be found in the Law Enforcement Resources section.

OSLLE Publication Archives

The OSLLE regularly publishes articles in law enforcement periodicals to keep the law enforcement community up-to-date on DHS initiatives, activities, and training opportunities. Previously published articles can be found in our Publication Archives.

Office of Strategy, Planning, Analysis and Risk (SPAR)

The Office is tasked to:

- Develop analytically driven, high-impact products that improve DHS and homeland security enterprise strategic direction, integration, and decision-making.
- Design and refine DHS processes necessary for the strategic management of the Quadrennial Homeland Security Review (QHSR) missions and for DHS strategy, planning, and analysis to have the intended, beneficial impact on homeland security activities.

Each of SPAR's functions, processes, and methodologies exist to advance one or more of SPAR's core purposes:

1.Articulate Long-term Vision. Articulate the long-term vision of the Department and the homeland security enterprise, and help define strategic priorities based on sound analysis, in order to manage homeland security risk.

2.Drive Integration. Design and refine DHS modeling, analysis, and strategic planning processes necessary to enhance mission execution by advancing cross-departmental and cross-enterprise, analytically-based, risk-informed priorities and helping portfolios of programs work more efficiently and effectively.

3.Ensure Informed Decision-Making by Homeland Security Leadership. Ensure that risk-informed policy and strategy drive departmental and enterprise decisions, including with regard to planning, programming, budgeting, and major acquisition oversight.

Office of International Affairs

The Office of International Affairs, in the Office of Policy, plays a central role in developing the Department's strategy for pushing the Homeland Security mission overseas and actively engages foreign allies to improve international cooperation for immigration policy, visa security, aviation security, border security and training, law enforcement, and cargo security.

The Office of International Affairs:

The Office provides the Secretary and the Department with policy analysis and management of the international affairs and foreign policies that impact the Department. Homeland security policy is multifaceted and successful implementation requires that it extend beyond U.S. borders and into the international community.

It also engages foreign allies, particularly Canada, Mexico and the United Kingdom, in guiding security agreements that further support the mission of the Department and improve immigration policy, visa security, aviation security, border security and training, law enforcement, and cargo security.

Responsibilities

•Advises, informs, and assists the Secretary and Deputy Secretary of Homeland Security on strategies, foreign policy matters, and the Department programs and operations that impact U.S. international relations.

•Builds strong support for actions against the global terrorism among nations and international organizations.

•Manages international activities within the Department in coordination with other federal officials with responsibility for counter-terrorism matters.

•Assists in the promotion of information and education exchange with nations friendly to the United States in order to promote sharing of best practices and technologies relating to homeland security.

•Coordinates all aspects of Department international affairs including developing, coordinating, and executing department international policy, including reviewing departmental positions on international matters, negotiating agreements, developing policy and programs, interacting with foreign officials, and working with Department personnel abroad.

Private Sector Office

The Office:

- Engages individual businesses, trade associations and other non-governmental organizations to foster dialogue with the Department.
- Advises the Secretary on prospective policies and regulations and in many cases on their economic impact.
- Promotes public-private partnerships and best practices to improve the nation's homeland security.
- Promotes Department policies to the private sector.

Loaned Executive Program

The Loaned Executive Program provides executive-level experts an opportunity to volunteer with Homeland Security to fill special, discreet needs for a limited period of time. Through the Loaned Executive Program, Homeland Security is working with the private sector on innovative solutions to our homeland security challenges. The Department is looking to the nation's top executives and industry experts to partner with us as we strive to solve problems, improve processes, and fully realize our mission. By serving as a loaned executive, subject matter experts have an opportunity to make a meaningful difference by protecting our nation.

DHS For a Day

The DHS for a Day program provides private sector stakeholders a glimpse into how various Department of Homeland Security (DHS) Components make our Nation safer on a day-to-day basis. The program also builds and strengthens connections between DHS and the private sector, ensuring that its partners across the country can participate fully in the Homeland Security Enterprise.